Communications
in Computer and Information Science **842**

Commenced Publication in 2007
Founding and Former Series Editors:
Phoebe Chen, Alfredo Cuzzocrea, Xiaoyong Du, Orhun Kara, Ting Liu,
Krishna M. Sivalingam, Dominik Ślęzak, Takashi Washio, and Xiaokang Yang

Liming Chen · Boulbaba Ben Amor ·
Faouzi Ghorbel (Eds.)

Representations, Analysis and Recognition of Shape and Motion from Imaging Data

7th International Workshop, RFMI 2017
Savoie, France, December 17–20, 2017
Revised Selected Papers

 Springer

Editors
Liming Chen
Ecole Centrale de Lyon/LIRIS
Lyon, France

Faouzi Ghorbel
Ecole Nationale des Sciences de
l'Informatique de Tunisie/CRISTAL
Manouba, Tunisia

Boulbaba Ben Amor ⓘ
Cité Scientifique
IMT Lille Douai/CRIStAL
Villeneuve-d'Ascq Cedex, France

ISSN 1865-0929   ISSN 1865-0937 (electronic)
Communications in Computer and Information Science
ISBN 978-3-030-19815-2   ISBN 978-3-030-19816-9 (eBook)
https://doi.org/10.1007/978-3-030-19816-9

This Springer imprint is published by the registered company Springer Nature Switzerland AG
The registered company address is: Gewerbestrasse 11, 6330 Cham, Switzerland

Preface

The *shape* and the *motion* of an object are important cues in understanding imaged scenes. Their study is an important research area with a plethora of applications, *e.g.*, medical diagnosis, video surveillance, affective and behavioral computing, computer animation, HMI, robotics, and cultural heritage conservation, to cite a few. The external boundary of an object is available in various forms, they include – landmark configurations, an object's contours (closed curves), 3D surfaces, and dense point clouds. Their analysis requires adequate mathematical representations, rigorous methodologies to filter out undesirable transformations, and sophisticated computational solutions. The *motion* in turn, describes the *shape*'s evolution or animation over time. One can cite the examples of facial shape evolution with the person's age, the evolution of a cancer cell over weeks or months, or the evolution of the body's skeletal or silhouette data over time and their use to predict a person's activity. Despite the development of mathematically solid methodologies, the question is still open from both methodological and application perspectives. The challenges are even more acute with the soar of deep machine learning, which fosters breakthroughs in many computer vision issues and more and new fields of application such as human brain understanding, the body's kinematic data analysis for rehabilitation and physical therapy, esthetic and reparation surgery, and 3D/4D microscopy. In addition, the rapid development of sophisticated medical imaging devices, cost-effective depth (Kinect-like) cameras, and the new generations of microscopes push forth to develop suitable mathematical representations, design relevant geometric tools, and set up computational solutions for advanced modeling, analysis, and understanding. The International Workshop on Representations, Analysis and Recognition of Shape and Motion from Imaging Data (RFMI)[1] is one of the earliest events launched to study these questions. Its ultimate goal is to promote interactions among researchers from different disciplines: Differential and Riemannian geometry, statistics, topology of spaces, computer vision and pattern recognition, as well as medical imaging to share their scientific reflections and results. Thus, the workshop contributes toward strengthening the relationship between many research areas that meet in facing similar challenges and using common tools.

The current edition (seventh) of the workshop received the endorsement of the prestigious International Association of Pattern Recognition (IAPR) and the current volume was accepted for publication in the CCIS series of Springer. The Program Committee of the workshop received 23 papers, of which eight were accepted as regular papers (i.e., 34% of acceptance rate) and nine as short papers. The workshop's program included two tutorial-oriented invited talks. Worldwide leading researchers were invited to give talks – Dr. Sylvain Calinon (senior researcher at Idiap Research Institute and lecturer at EPFL, Switzerland) presented "Robot Learning from Few

---

[1] http://www.arts-pi.org.tn/rfmi2017/index.html

Demonstrations by Exploiting the Structure and Geometry of Data" and Dr. Boulbaba ben Amor (Professor, IMT Lille Douai/CRIStAL, France) presented "Rate-Invariant Analysis of Trajectories on Kendall's Shape Space and Applications." Around 40 researchers attended the workshop from different countries including, USA, Japan, France, Norway, UAE, Tunisia, France, Germany, and Belgium. The workshop was organized at the Centre Paul-Langevin of the CNRS, in the authentic village Aussois located in Savoie (France), during December 17–20, 2017. It was also a pleasant occasion for many of the participants to discover a breathbreaking landscape in the snowy Alp mountains and deepen their friendly discussion through snowshoeing.

February 2019

Liming Chen
Boulbaba Ben Amor
Faouzi Ghorbel

Organization

General Chair

L. Chen   LIRIS/Ecole Centrale de Lyon, France

Co-chairs

F. Ghorbel   CRISTAL/ENSI, Tunisia
B. Ben Amor   CRIStAL/IMT Lille Douai, France

Steering Committee

A. Srivastava   Florida State University, USA
A. Hillion   IMT Atlantique, France
B. Ben Amor   CRIStAL/IMT Lille Douai, France
B. Dorizzi   Telecom SudParis, France
B. Sankur   Bogazici University, Turkey
B. Solaiman   IMT Atlantique, France
S. MHIRI   ENSI/CRISTAL, Tunisia
F. Ghorbel   ENSI/CRISTAL, Tunisia
F. Chaieb   ENSI/CRISTAL, Tunisia
J. Dugelay   Eurecom, France
M. Bennamoun   UWA, Australia
M. Hammami   FSS, Tunisia
C. Roux   IMT, France
Y. Wang   Beihang University, China
I. Kakadiaris   University of Houston, USA
A. Zoubir   Technische Universität Darmstadt, Germany
J. P. Thiran   EPFL, Switzerland
I. R. Ferah   ISAM, Tunisia
H. Bedoui   FMM, Tunisia
J. P. Haton   Loria, France
M. F. Haton   Loria, France
N. Werghi   Khalifa University, UAE

Publicity Chairs

A. Srivastava, FL, USA
Di Huang, China
Mohamed Hammami, Tunisie

Program Committee

H. Wannous	University of Lille, France
M. Jribi	INSAT/CRISTAL, Tunisia
M. Amine Mezghich	ENSI, Tunisia
S. Berretti	UF, Italy
M. Hajji	ENSI, Tunisia
A. Ben Abdallah	FM Monastir, Tunisia
A. Ben Azza	Sup'Com, Tunisia
A. Fleury	Mines-Douai, France
A. Hadid	University of Oulu, Finland
A. Hillion	IMT Atlantique, France
A. Ouled Zaid	ISI, Tunisia
B. Dorizzi	Telecom SudParis, France
B. Gokberk	Bogazici University, Turkey
B. Marius	University of Lille, France
B. Xia	Trinity College of Dublin, Ireland
C. Ben Amar	ENIS, Tunisia
C. Hamitouche	IMT Atlantique, France
V. Burdin	IMT Atlantique, France
C. Samir	ISIT CNRS, France
D. Huang	Beihang University, China
D. Ziou	University of Sherbrooke, Canada
D. Gadia	University of Milan, Italy
D. Masmoudi	ENIS, Tunisia
E. Dellandrea	ECL, France
E. Fendri	FSS, Tunisia
E. Zagrouba	UVT-ISI, Tunisia
F. Dibos	Institut Galilee, University of Paris 13, France
F. Drira	ENIS, Tunisia
F. El Ayeb	ISAMM, Tunisia
G. Sundaramoorthi	KAUST, KSA
H. Drira	IMT Lille Douai, France
H. Laga	University of South Australia, Australia
H. Li	Xi'an Jiaotong University, China
H. Meng	Brunel University, UK
H. Tabia	ENSEA, France
J. Su	TTU, USA
J. De Guise	ETS, Canada
J. Martinet	University of Lille 1, France
J. Ph. Thiran	EPFL, Suisse
K. Bailly	Pierre et Marie Curie University, France
K. Zreik	University of Paris 8, France

L. Ballihi	Mohamed V University, Morocco
L. Cammoun	Swiss Institute of Bioinformatics Lausanne, Switzerland
M. Mitrea	ARTEMIS, France
M. Vermande	University of Lille, France
M. Ardabilian	ECL, France
M. Devanne	University of Lille, France
M. Preda	ARTEMIS, France
M. Zaied	ENIG/REGIM, Tunisia
N. Richard	University of Poitiers, France
N. Werghi	Khalifa University, UAE
O. Losson	CRIStAL/University of Lille 1, France
P. Pala	UF, Italy
P. Turaga	ASU, USA
R. Chaine	Claude Bernard University of Lyon 1, France
R. Guermazi	ISIMS, Tunisia
S. Derrode	Ecole Centrale de Lyon, France
S. Joshi	UCLA, USA
S. Kurtek	OSU, USA
S. Lefevre	University of Bretagne Sud, France
S. Lecoeuche	IMT Lille Douai, France
S. Li	NLPR, CAS, China
S. Zafeiriou	Imperial College London, UK
T. Zaharia	ARTEMIS, France
T. Alashkar	Northeastern University, USA
W. Barhoumi	Eni-Carthage, Tunisia
W. Miled	INSAT, Tunisia
Y. Wang	Beihang University, China
Z. Zhang	Duke University, USA
D. Huang	Beihang University, China
X. Pennec	Inria, France
J. Yang	Shanghai Jiaotong University, China
X. Zhao	Xi'an Jiaotong University, China

Local Committee

A. Ben Tanfous	CRIStAL/IMT Lille Douai, France
F. Zehua	Ecole Centrale de Lyon, France
H. Mliki	ENET'COM Sfax, Tunisia
L. Ying	Ecole Centrale de Lyon, France
M. Amine Mezghich	CRISTAL/ENSI, Tunisia
N. Hosni	CRIStAL/ENSI-CRIStAL/IMT Lille Douai, Tunisia/France

Website Chairs

Mohamed Amine Mezghich	ENSI, Tunisia
Mehdi Hajji	ENSI, Tunisia

Contents

On Analyzing Motion Data

A Comparison of Scene Flow Estimation Paradigms

Iraklis Tsekourakis$^{(\boxtimes)}$ and Philippos Mordohai

Stevens Institute of Technology, Hoboken, NJ 07030, USA
`itsekour@stevens.edu`

Abstract. This paper presents a comparison between two core paradigms for computing scene flow from multi-view videos of dynamic scenes. In both approaches, shape and motion estimation are decoupled, in accordance to a large segment of the relevant literature. The first approach is faster and considers only one optical flow field and the depth difference between pixels in consecutive frames to generate a dense scene flow estimate. The second approach is more robust to outliers by considering multiple optical flow fields to generate scene flow. Our goal is to compare the isolated fundamental scene flow estimation methods, without using any post-processing, or optimization. We assess the accuracy of the two methods performing two tests: an optical flow prediction, and a future image prediction, both on a novel view. This is the first quantitative evaluation of scene flow estimation on real imagery of dynamic scenes, in absence of ground truth data.

1 Introduction

Scene flow is the 3D motion field that generates the optical flow when projected onto the image plane of a camera. It is arguably the last frontier that remains unexplored in 3D computer vision, even though the problem was formulated a relatively long time ago [1,2] and there are exciting applications, such as free-viewpoint video, motion capture, augmented reality and autonomous driving/driver assistance. The primary reasons for this are the inherent difficulty of the problem and the lack of data with ground truth that would aid the development of algorithms.

For over a decade since the original publication that defined the field [1], the relevant literature consisted of a sparse set of papers [3–9] that seemed well-positioned to spark a breakthrough, which has not come yet. It took a breakthrough in sensing technology with the advent of consumer depth cameras (RGB-D cameras, such as the Microsoft Kinect) to enable reliable scene flow estimation from RGB-D monocular sequences [10–14]. RGB-D cameras, however, suffer from their own limitations, namely their inability to operate outdoors due to sunlight interference and their short range. Moreover, monocular inputs hinder free-viewpoint video applications since texture information is not available for even the slightest viewpoint changes, with a few exceptions [12,13]. Collet et al. [15]

© Springer Nature Switzerland AG 2019
L. Chen et al. (Eds.): RFMI 2017, CCIS 842, pp. 3–19, 2019.
https://doi.org/10.1007/978-3-030-19816-9_1

present outstanding results on free-viewpoint video using a dense set of RGB and IR sensors. It is desirable, therefore, to achieve high-quality scene flow estimation from two or more passive cameras, since such a configuration would not suffer from these limitations. Our inputs are multi-view videos acquired by synchronized, calibrated, stationary cameras [16,17]. The synchronized and calibrated requirements for the cameras can be relaxed, but this is currently out of scope.

In this paper, we focus on point-wise methods that estimate scene flow in a decoupled fashion, by alternating between depth and motion estimation. This choice is not necessarily an endorsement of this type of scene flow estimation. Other strategies have different strengths and weaknesses: joint estimation of both shape and motion leads to higher consistency at a significant computational cost; 3D shape tracking does not allow the shape to be modified based on temporal constraints; patch-based estimation allows more complex reasoning and regularization, but may impose too much rigidity. All these approaches have attractive features, but we believe that our analysis should start with the fundamental case of estimating the depth and scene flow of each pixel.

A pixel with depth and scene flow estimates can be linked to corresponding pixels in different views at the same time instant via depth, to the corresponding pixel in the same view at the next time instant via optical flow, derived from scene flow, and to corresponding pixels in different views at the next time instant via depth and scene flow. We evaluate two viewpoint-based paradigms for estimating scene flow from depth maps and optical flow fields:

- a more common approach, which we term Optical Flow and Depth Difference (*OF+D*), in which scene flow is decomposed in two components: one parallel and one orthogonal to the image plane,
- an approach, we term Multiple Optical Flows (*MOF*), which combines multiple optical flows at each reconstructed 3D point to derive its scene flow.

Throughout this effort, we ensure that the two paradigms are tested on identical inputs under identical conditions to the extent possible.

Besides the difficulty of the problem itself, the second challenge to our research is the lack of suitable data with ground truth for quantitative evaluations. This is due to the lack of a convenient technique for generating ground truth motion fields, in 2D or 3D [18,19]. This has forced most authors to evaluate their methods on synthetic or static data. To overcome this obstacle, we perform two types of quantitative evaluation using frames from a sequestered camera in lieu of ground truth. In the first evaluation, we attempt to predict the optical flow of the validation camera by projecting the estimated scene flow. In the second evaluation, we attempt to predict the RGB image at time $t+1$ given RGB images and estimated scene flow for the other cameras at time t. According to all criteria, *MOF* is superior to *OF+D*. Moreover, the difference between its image predictions and predictions using the actual data of the validation camera is small.

In summary, the contributions of this work are:

- the *MOF* algorithm, which is a robust extension of the work of Vedula et al. [1],

- a comprehensive comparison of two viewpoint-based scene flow estimation paradigms, and
- novel criteria for evaluating scene flow estimation in the absence of ground truth scene flow.

The conclusions that can be drawn from our experiments are: (i) it is important to not neglect optical flows from additional views besides the reference view, if they are available, since using them can lead to significant noise reduction; and (ii) novel view prediction using the *MOF* algorithm is very similar in quality to predicted frames using data from the validation camera itself. This is an indication that scene flow has been estimated well.

2   Related Work

In this section, we review the scene flow literature. We categorize prior work according to whether the shape and motion estimation is joint or decoupled, whether they operate on pixels or surfaces, and whether they consider the topology of the shape fixed throughout the sequence. We include methods operating on RGB-D inputs, but not methods that segment N rigid bodies, e.g., [20].

We begin with joint shape and motion estimation. In the paper that defined the term, Vedula et al. [1] formulate and analyze three algorithms depending on the degree to which scene geometry is known. In a separate paper, Vedula et al. [21] extend space carving [22] to the 6D space of all shapes and flows, resulting in a tight approximation to shape and scene flow. Other joint estimation approaches that consider optical flow fields or temporal derivatives in multiple images have represented spatio-temporal shape using subdivision surfaces [4], surfels [3], level sets [23], watertight meshes [24], probabilistic occupancy-motion grids [25], and spatiotemporal orientation distributions [26].

Viewpoint-based methods for joint scene flow estimation include variational methods [5,7,27–29]. Typically, the shape is initialized by stereo matching and then shape and motion are jointly estimated resulting in convergence to the nearest local minimum of an appropriate energy function. Other viewpoint-based methods explore the high dimensional search spaces using Markov Random Fields [30], winner-take-all or dynamic programming [6], or by growing correspondence seeds [31].

An alternative approach is to segment the reference image in a set of patches and estimate their 3D motion from frame to frame [32–34]. Unlike points that only allow a 3D displacement estimation, patches allow the rotational motion estimation and also provide a basis for regularization. A more recent approach by Vogel et al. [9] models occlusion and relationships among neighboring patches.

To reduce computational complexity, authors decouple shape and motion estimation [8,35–37]. Wedel et al. [8] take into account stereo image pairs from two consecutive times and compute both depth and 3D motion associated with each point in the image. This is equivalent to our *OF+D* paradigm. On the other hand, Li et al. [38] extract a watertight mesh from point clouds reconstructed by variational stereo and address scene flow as volumetric deformation using [1] to estimate scene flow at each vertex.

If the topology of the shape can be recovered in the first frame and remains fixed throughout the sequence, methods that can track the shape over time have been proposed. The primitives to be tracked can be meshes [15,39–41], patches [42,43], volumetric elements [44,45] or sparse features followed by motion propagation to the rest of the mesh [46–51].

Recently, the emergence of consumer depth cameras has lead to the development of decoupled depth and motion estimation methods leveraging the accurate depth provided by these sensors. Due to the availability of a single viewpoint, most of these methods fall under the *OF+D* paradigm [10,11,52–54] Methods that operate on patches [55], layers [14], meshes [12], local twist motions [56] and 6D volumetric motion fields [13] have also been reported, but in all cases a single flow field is available.

None of these publications includes quantitative evaluation on videos of dynamic scenes. Some show results on synthetic [5] or static scenes [57]. The KITTI benchmark [58], used by [9], depicts static scenery. The exception is the work of Sizintsev and Wildes [26,59] who present quantitative evaluation of scene flow using a motorized stage to generate ground truth. Ground truth is acquired using structured light sensors on stop motion sequences. While this study is unprecedented and valuable, the experimental setup is not ideal since the fiducial markers that are placed on each independently moving surface to aid motion estimation also aid the algorithms being evaluated.

3   Problem Statement

The objective of this work is to compare two methods that isolate the fundamental 3D scene flow estimation of dynamic scenes captured by multiple, calibrated, stationary, synchronized cameras without any form of post-processing or optimization. Throughout we use the term *view* to indicate a viewpoint, or a specific camera, and *frame* to denote an image taken at a specific time t. We implement two different methods. They both need 2D optical flows and depth estimates as inputs. In order to compute the depths, we generate the cost volume using plane-sweeping stereo [60] and we extract the final depth estimates using SGM [61] on the cost volume. We compute optical flows for all cameras using the software of Sun et al. [62].

The first method is *OF+D*. It is a straightforward implementation of decoupled 3D shape and motion estimation. Given an optical flow estimate for a pixel **u**, we can approximate the scene flow that corresponds to the 3D point that pixel **u** projects to, as the summation of the optical flow vector with the depth difference between pixel **u** at time t and pixel **u'** at time $t+1$. **u'** is the location of pixel **u** according to the optical flow. The details are presented in Sect. 4. Second, we propose the *MOF* method that estimates the 3D scene flow using multiple 2D optical flows and depth estimates. An optical flow estimate provides two linear constraints on the three unknowns in the scene flow (V_x, V_y, V_z of the

3D motion). If we have two or more views of the same part of the scene that are not coplanar, we can recover the scene flow. Assuming we have more than two cameras, we apply MSAC [63] to remove outlying optical flows. We then use the method of Vedula et al. [1,2] as a solver on the selected candidate optical flows in order to extract the scene flow. Implementation details are given in Sect. 5.

Due to lack of publicly available multi-view datasets with scene flow ground truth, we evaluate the accuracy of the estimated scene flows for both methods first by comparing the projected scene flow on a novel view, that was excluded by all steps of the scene flow estimation, with the optical flow estimated using the data of the novel view. Second, we measure the quality of predicted frames on the novel view at time $t+1$ generated from frames at time t using the projected scene flow. While novel view synthesis as an evaluation metric is forgiving in textureless areas, it has been shown to be an effective evaluation strategy in general [64–66] and specifically for free viewpoint video [67].

Inputs: The depth maps used as inputs for both methods, *OF+D* and *MOF*, for the *ballet* and *breakdance* datasets were provided by the creators of the videos [16]. For *Cheongsam* and *Redskirt* [17], depths are computed in a multi-view configuration (See Sect. 7 for details on the datasets used). The depth estimation combines the plane-sweeping algorithm with Semi-Global matching (SGM) optimization. In plane sweeping stereo, we define a family of planes parallel to the image plane of the *reference view*. For each pixel, depth hypotheses are formed by intersecting the corresponding ray with the set of planes. We then define a square window centered at that pixel in the reference view and warp it to the *target views* using the homographies from the reference view to the target views through the current plane. We compute the normalized cross-correlation (NCC) between the window on the reference view and each warped window on the target views, and store the average as the likelihood of assigning to the pixel the depth corresponding to the current plane. Target images in which the matching window falls out of bounds are excluded. The likelihood volume is converted to a cost volume by negating the NCC scores. SGM is used for extracting a depth map that approximately optimizes a global two-dimensional energy function by combining 1D minimization problems in 8 or 16 directions. We use eight paths for dynamic programming and 256 discretized depths per pixel. We use the rSGM implementation provided by Spangenberg et al. [68]. The second input used for the methods of this work are the optical flow estimates. They are computed using the software of Sun et al. [62], which is a modern implementation of the Horn and Schunck model [69].

4   Scene Flow Estimation Using Optical Flow and Depth Difference (OF+D)

In this section, we describe multi-view scene flow estimation, using the optical flow for a single camera, and the depth difference between two consecutive frames for the same camera. The 2D optical flow is the projection of the scene flow onto the images. Respectively, the back-projected 2D optical flow onto the 3D space at the depth of the 3D point, represents the scene flow that is parallel to the image. What is missing to complete the scene flow vector is the change of depth, which is perpendicular to the image plane.

We use as inputs the optical flow OF_t, and the depths D_t and D_{t+1} of the current and the next frame for the reference camera. For each pixel (u,v), we project the 2D optical flow vector onto the reconstructed 3D point $\mathbf{x}$ at the depth $D_t(u,v)$. The resulting vector $SF_p(\mathbf{x})$ represents the scene flow component parallel to the image. In order to compute the change of depth, we first need to estimate the depth of the same point in the second frame. (u,v) at time $t+1$ will be located at $(u+OF_t(u,v,1), v+OF_t(u,v,2))$. Given that the target image location does not have integer pixel coordinates, we estimate the depth by applying bilinear interpolation. The vector $SF_o(\mathbf{x})$, which is orthogonal to the camera plane has norm equal to the difference of the depths:

$$|SF_o(\mathbf{x})| = D_{t+1}(u + OF_t(u,v,1), v + OF_t(u,v,2))$$
$$- D_t(u,v) \tag{1}$$

Finally, the scene flow estimate for the 3D point $\mathbf{x}$ that corresponds to the initial pixel (u,v) at time t is computed as:

$$SF(\mathbf{x}) = SF_p(\mathbf{x}) + SF_o(\mathbf{x}) \tag{2}$$

5   Scene Flow Estimation Using Multiple Optical Flows (MOF)

This section describes the second scene flow estimation paradigm. The inputs to *MOF* are the optical flows of the reference and the neighboring cameras on the left and on the right of the reference camera and the depths of the reference cameras. These are computed as described in Sect. 3. Depending on the configuration of each of the multi-view datasets tested during this project, we use optical flows for 1 or 2 cameras on each side of the reference camera. The main idea is that since we have a number of 2D optical flows from different viewpoints, we can leverage them in order to estimate scene flow accurately.

Based on the work of Vedula et al. [1,2], the relationship of a 3D point $\mathbf{x}$ $= (x,y,z)^T$ and the 2D image coordinates $\mathbf{u_i} = (u_i, v_i)^T$ of its projection in a camera C_i is described by the following formulas:

$$u_i = \frac{[\mathbf{P}_i]_1(x,y,z,1)^T}{[\mathbf{P}_i]_3(x,y,z,1)^T}, \tag{3}$$

$$v_i = \frac{[\mathbf{P}_i]_2(x,y,z,1)^T}{[\mathbf{P}_i]_3(x,y,z,1)^T}, \tag{4}$$

where $[\mathbf{P}_i]$ is the jth row of the 3×4 projection matrix $\mathbf{P}_i$ of camera C_i. If we know the 3D geometry, at time t, the differential relationship between $\mathbf{x}$ and $\mathbf{u_i}$

is represented by a 2×3 Jacobian $\frac{\partial \mathbf{u_i}}{\partial \mathbf{x}}$. This Jacobian describes the relationship between a small change in the point on the surface and its image in camera i. Now, if $\mathbf{x} = \mathbf{x}(t)$ is the 3D path of a point in the world, its scene flow is $\frac{d\mathbf{x}}{dt}$. The image of this point in camera C_i is $\mathbf{u_i} = \mathbf{u_i}(t)$. The relationship between the optical flow and the scene flow is given by:

$$\frac{d\mathbf{u}_i}{dt} = \frac{\partial \mathbf{u_i}}{\mathbf{x}} \frac{d\mathbf{x}}{dt} \tag{5}$$

This equation shows how optical flow can be computed if the scene flow is known. On the other hand, an optical flow estimate provides two linear constraints on the three unknowns in the scene flow. Thus, if we have two or more non-parallel cameras viewing the same part of the scene, the scene flow can be recovered. We use all the available optical flows in order to get more accurate scene flow estimates. The method of Vedula et al. gives the solution that minimizes the sum of least squares of the error obtained by reprojecting the scene flow onto each of the optical flows.

Given $N \geq 2$ cameras observing the same surface of the scene, we can solve for $\frac{d\mathbf{x}}{dt}$ by setting up the system of equations $\mathbf{B}\frac{d\mathbf{x}}{dt} = \mathbf{U}$, where

$$B = \begin{bmatrix} \frac{\partial u_1}{\partial x} & \frac{\partial u_1}{\partial y} & \frac{\partial u_1}{\partial z} \\ \frac{\partial v_1}{\partial x} & \frac{\partial v_1}{\partial y} & \frac{\partial v_1}{\partial z} \\ \cdot & \cdot & \cdot \\ \cdot & \cdot & \cdot \\ \frac{\partial u_N}{\partial x} & \frac{\partial u_N}{\partial y} & \frac{\partial u_N}{\partial z} \\ \frac{\partial v_N}{\partial x} & \frac{\partial v_N}{\partial y} & \frac{\partial v_N}{\partial z} \end{bmatrix}, U = \begin{bmatrix} \frac{\partial u_1}{\partial t} \\ \frac{\partial v_1}{\partial t} \\ \cdot \\ \cdot \\ \frac{\partial u_N}{\partial t} \\ \frac{\partial v_N}{\partial t} \end{bmatrix}. \tag{6}$$

However, in our problem there are outliers that lead to high errors in the resulting scene flow. To prevent these outliers from corrupting the least squares estimate, we apply the m-estimator sample consensus (MSAC) algorithm [63] to find the set of inlying optical flows that minimize the maximum likelihood error, starting from minimal samples of two optical flows. The selected inliers are then used in the least squares method (Eq. 6) in order to extract the scene flow. The capability of MSAC to discriminate between strong and weak inliers, compared to RANSAC that does not discriminate, leads to significant improvement in the solutions.

6 Evaluation Methodology

In the absence of ground truth, we perform two tests to evaluate the different scene flow estimation techniques. As a first test, given depth, we project the estimated 3D scene flow onto a novel view and compute the errors of the projected optical flow compared to the optical flow estimated using the data of the novel view. For the second test, we use the color prediction error in a novel view. The novel view prediction error was initially proposed by Szeliski [64] and later by other authors [19,65–67]. In all cases, we use a completely separate *validation camera* for evaluation and completely exclude its frames from optical flow and depth estimation. We always choose an *extrapolating view* with regards to each reference camera and its neighboring cameras used for the computation of scene flow, for validation so that errors are more pronounced in it. According to Szeliski [64], synthesizing extrapolating views is more challenging due to increased sensitivity to depth and other errors.

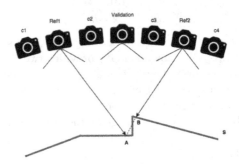

Fig. 1. An example of the multi-view setup used. S is the observed surface. For both sides of the validation camera we use a reference camera with two supporting cameras for the optical flow and depth estimation. Ref1 has c1 and c2 as supporting cameras, and Ref2 has c3 and c4. The importance of having this symmetric setup is illustrated by the fact that occlusions in one reference camera can be recovered by the symmetric reference camera. For example, point A is occluded in *Ref2*, but the correct flow at A in the validation camera can be projected from *Ref1*.

Yet, if we compute the scene flow of a reference camera on the one side of the validation camera, this creates an asymmetry in the noise of the projected optical flow on the opposite side of the validation camera. Thus, we compute the scene flow based on a second reference camera on the other side of the validation camera leading to more accurate and symmetric results. The configuration used can be seen in Fig. 1. It can be easily seen that occlusions could create noise in the estimation of the scene flow if only one reference camera is used. For example, in Fig. 1, $Ref1$ can see point A, that is what the validation camera sees as well, while A is occluded in $Ref2$. $Ref2$ sees point B instead. Figure 2 shows the importance of symmetry using data from the ballet sequences. All optical flows of the figure are shown in the validation camera. The left and right subfigures show the projected scene flows estimated for reference cameras on the left and right of the validation camera respectively. It is obvious that there are white parts (missing scene flow estimates) due to occlusions on each side of the dancer. Using both reference cameras lead to more accurate and dense scene flow estimates.

"Ground truth" Optical Flow: In order to have a comparison for both tests, we estimate the optical flow of the novel view using the data of this "excluded" validation camera. We name this "ground truth" optical flow or *OF*.

Fig. 2. Symmetric reference cameras on ballet data. Left to right: projected scene flow estimated from a reference camera to the left of validation camera, optical flow estimated for the validation camera using the software of Sun et al. [62], projected scene flow estimated from a reference to the right of validation camera, and Middlebury color coding [18]. (Color figure online)

6.1 Novel View Optical Flow Prediction Test

We project the 3D scene flow onto the validation camera in order to predict the optical flow for this excluded view. The resulting 2D optical flow is estimated without the use of the validation view data. We compare the projected optical flow from the *MOF* and *OF+D* estimated scene flows with the "ground truth" optical flow. The hypothesis here is that if the projected optical flow is similar to the"ground truth" optical flow, then the scene flow estimates are accurate and consistent between different views. When we project the scene flow to the validation view, it falls at non-integer pixel locations. In order to overcome this issue, we apply a bilateral filter, based on the implementation of Yoon and Kweon [70], to get a dense optical flow projection.

For each integer pixel location in the validation view, we find the k nearest 3D points that project close to the pixel. We then apply the bilateral filter, as the weighted summation of the neighbors based on color similarity and proximity, to compute optical flow at integer pixel coordinates. Let p and q be the target pixel and the neighbor pixel to be weighted respectively. We do not use data (colors) from the novel view in any step of this process. In order to represent the color of the target pixel, we find the 3D points that project close to the target pixel, and we use the color information of the nearest neighbor. Now p has been assigned a color and Δc_{pq} and Δg_{pq} represent the color difference and the spatial distance between pixels p and q. $f(\Delta c_{pq}, \Delta g_{pq})$ represents the strength of grouping by similarity and proximity. The color difference is computed as the Euclidean distance between two colors in RGB space.

$$\Delta c_{pq} = \sqrt{(R_p - R_q)^2 + (G_p - G_q)^2 + (B_p - B_q)^2} \tag{7}$$

The strength of grouping by color similarity is defined using the Laplacian kernel as

$$f_s = exp(-\frac{\Delta c_{pq}}{\gamma_c}) \tag{8}$$

where γ_c is determined empirically. Correspondingly, the strength of grouping by proximity is defined using the Laplacian kernel as

$$f_p = exp(-\frac{\Delta g_{pq}}{\gamma_p})$$ (9)

and γ_p is also determined empirically. According to (8) and (9), the weights can be written as

$$w(p, q) = k \cdot exp(-\frac{\Delta c_{pq}}{\gamma_c} - \frac{\Delta g_{pq}}{\gamma_p})$$ (10)

where k is a normalizing factor. Applying the bilateral filter described by the Eqs. (7–10) we obtain dense optical flow. In Sect. 7, we present quantitative results using the two of the most commonly used measures of flow accuracy, namely the endpoint (pixel distance) and angular errors, as defined in [18].

6.2 Novel View Future Image Prediction Test

For the second test, given a current frame of the validation camera, we use the projected optical flow, densified as above, to predict the RGB values of the image in the next frame. We need to apply a filter again to predict RGB values at integer pixel locations of the target frame at time $t + 1$. We once again find the nearest neighbors for each pixel and we average the optical flow of the neighbors with weights based on proximity. Equation (10) this time is modified to use proximity only as

$$w(p, q) = k \cdot exp(-\frac{\Delta g_{pq}}{\gamma_p})$$ (11)

Following this process, and given a current frame of the validation camera, we get a dense RGB prediction of the next frame. We then use the Manhattan distance in RGB over all pixels between the predicted image and the actual image of the next frame. Results are shown in Sect. 7.

7 Experimental Results

In this section, we present and evaluate the estimated scene flows computed by both the techniques described in this paper. We use four different multi-view video sequences made publicly available by their authors in widely different configurations. Cheongsam [17] is captured in a dome of diameter equal to 4.2 m by twenty cameras in a ring around the scene. It has 20 cameras and every video is 30 frames long, but one of them had to be dropped due to missing frames. Redskirt [17] is captured in the same dome, but the videos are 20 frames long. The ballet and breakdance data [16] are acquired by eight cameras forming a 30° arc, thus with much narrower baselines. The depth range in this scene is 7.6 m. Depth maps are provided for the ballet and breakdance videos.

Table 1. Average Endpoint and Angular errors of OF+D and MOF estimated scene flows, projected (resulting in optical flows) on novel views that were excluded from all estimation steps. In lieu of ground truth data, the errors are estimated based on the "ground truth" optical flows computed using the data of the novel views (OF). The average is taken over all pixels of all frames of a single evaluation camera. Angular errors are displayed in degrees.

	Endpoint		Angular	
	OF+D	MOF	OF+D	MOF
Cheongsam	8.61	0.64	29.79	5.73
Redskirt	4.95	0.75	25.21	7.45
Ballet	4.42	3.22	33.80	26.93
Breakdance	4.11	1.89	42.40	37.24

Table 2. Average RGB L1 distance of next frame prediction on novel views compared to actual images. The average is taken over all pixels of all frames of a single evaluation camera. The column labeled GT OF is the prediction using the "ground truth" optical flow.

	"GT" OF	OF+D	MOF
Cheongsam	4.57	7.23	4.95
Redskirt	5.69	7.81	6.56
Ballet	6.67	8.37	7.56
Breakdance	8.30	9.88	9.13

All experiments are performed using constant parameters for all parts of the methods tested, except the number of neighboring views in the computation of the scene flow using multiple candidate optical flows (Sect. 5). We use two neighboring views on each side of the reference camera for the ballet and breakdancer datasets, and one neighboring view on each side for the Cheongsam and Redskirt datasets, due to the wide angle between the neighboring views. The NCC window size for the plane-sweeping algorithm is 5×5 and 256 fronto-parallel planes with subpixel spacing are used for all datasets. For SGM, we use the rSGM implementation [68] with 8 paths, $P_1 = 11$, $\alpha = 0.5$, $\gamma = 35$ and $P_{2,min} = 17$. In the bilateral filter, we use $\gamma_c = 7$ and $\gamma_p = 4$.

For the Cheongsam and Redskirt data we create cost volumes for every frame using the plane-sweeping algorithm. Using these cost volumes and SGM, we extract the depth maps that were used as inputs to both scene flow estimation methods. The optical flows between consecutive frames needed as input to the methods described in this paper are estimated using the software of Sun et al. [62]. Then, we compute scene flow estimates for every frame in the videos tested using both methods as described in Sects. 4 and 5. We evaluate quantitatively the scene flows by projecting to 2D optical flows on a novel view according to Sect. 6.

Fig. 3. Novel view next frame prediction for cheongsam, redskirt, ballet and break-dance data. First column: Four instances of current frames of the validation camera. Second column: Next frames. Third column: next frame prediction based on "ground truth" optical flow estimation OF. Fourth column: next frame prediction based on estimated SF using $OF+D$. Fifth column: next frame prediction based on estimated SF using MOF. Data from the novel views were not used for $OF+D$ and MOF methods. Corresponding quantitative results shown in Table 2.

Tables 1 and 2 summarize the accuracy of all methods tested. Table 1 presents the optical flow prediction errors, while Table 2 shows the results on novel view synthesis as described in Sect. 6. These errors are averaged over all frames for all datasets. It has to be noted, that the angular errors between a flow vector (u, v) and the "ground truth" flow (u_{GT}, v_{GT}) were computed as defined in [18] according to the following formula

$$AE = cos^{-1} \left(\frac{1.0 + u \times u_{GT} + v \times v_{GT}}{\sqrt{1.0 + u^2 + v^2}\sqrt{1.0 + u_{GT}^2 + v_{GT}^2}} \right) \quad (12)$$

This metric aims to provide a *relative* measure of performance that avoids the "divide by zero" problem for zero flows. Errors in large flows are penalized less in AE than errors in small flows. Accuracy, in general is worse on the ballet and breakdance videos which have a lower frame rate than Cheongsam and Redksirt making motion estimation harder. The hypothesis for both tests, is that if accuracy using projected scene flows onto a novel view, whose data were not used to estimate the scene flows, is not degraded significantly compared to the one using the "ground truth" optical flows, then the scene flow estimation is considered successful. *MOF* presents significantly better and more robust performance than the *OF+D* method, and is always quite close to the *"illegal"* prediction using the "ground truth" optical flow.

Figure 3 shows instances of a current frame, the next frame, the estimated next frame using the scene flow computed by the two methods, and an estimation of the next frame using the "ground truth" optical flow computed of the software of Sun et al. for all datasets tested.

8   Conclusion

We have compared the two most prevalent core computations for scene flow estimation in multi-view videos. *OF+D*, which is also common in RGB-D scene flow estimation, may fail because it relies on a single optical flow field. *MOF* is more robust because it uses multiple measurements. Depending on data-specific factors, the average improvement of *MOF* compared to *OF+D* can be as high as 35%, as in the Cheongsam sequence. The increase of the error compared to the *OF* that actually uses the data from the novel view can be as low as 10%, as in the breakdance sequence, but it never gets higher than 15%. The data-specific factors include the mutli-view configuration of the cameras such as the angle between the neighboring cameras, and the baseline, as well as the frequency content of the images, and the speed of the objects in the scene.

The evaluation methodology using view and optical flow field synthesis proposed in this work, enables quantitative analysis of scene flow in cases where there are no ground truth data available. We claim that this analysis is more informative than tests on synthetic or static (stereo) data, e.g. from [57].

Acknowledgments. This research has been supported in part by the National Science Foundation award #1217797 and #1527294.

References

1. Vedula, S., Baker, S., Rander, P., Collins, R.T., Kanade, T.: Three-dimensional scene flow. In: ICCV, pp. 722–729 (1999)
2. Vedula, S., Baker, S., Rander, P., Collins, R.T., Kanade, T.: Three-dimensional scene flow. PAMI **27**(3), 475–480 (2005)
3. Carceroni, R.L., Kutulakos, K.N.: Multi-view scene capture by surfel sampling: from video streams to non-rigid 3D motion, shape and reflectance. IJCV **49**(2–3), 175–214 (2002)
4. Neumann, J., Aloimonos, Y.: Spatio-temporal stereo using multi-resolution subdivision surfaces. IJCV **47**(1–3), 181–193 (2002)
5. Huguet, F., Devernay, F.: A variational method for scene flow estimation from stereo sequences. In: ICCV (2007)
6. Gong, M.: Real-time joint disparity and disparity flow estimation on programmable graphics hardware. CVIU **113**(1), 90–100 (2009)
7. Basha, T., Moses, Y., Kiryati, N.: Multi-view scene flow estimation: a view centered variational approach. In: CVPR (2010)
8. Wedel, A., Brox, T., Vaudrey, T., Rabe, C., Franke, U., Cremers, D.: Stereoscopic scene flow computation for 3D motion understanding. IJCV **95**, 29–51 (2011)
9. Vogel, C., Schindler, K., Roth, S.: 3D scene flow estimation with a piecewise rigid scene model. IJCV **115**(1), 1–28 (2015)
10. Herbst, E., Ren, X., Fox, D.: RGB-D flow: dense 3-D motion estimation using color and depth. In: IEEE International Conference on Robotics and Automation (ICRA), pp. 2276–2282 (2013)
11. Jaimez, M., Souiai, M., Stuckler, J., Gonzalez-Jimenez, J., Cremers, D.: Motion cooperation: smooth piece-wise rigid scene flow from RGB-D images. In: 2015 International Conference on 3D Vision (3DV), pp. 64–72 (2015)
12. Dou, M., Taylor, J., Fuchs, H., Fitzgibbon, A., Izadi, S.: 3D scanning deformable objects with a single RGBD sensor. In: Proceedings of the IEEE Conference on Computer Vision and Pattern Recognition, pp. 493–501 (2015)
13. Newcombe, R.A., Fox, D., Seitz, S.M.: Dynamicfusion: reconstruction and tracking of non-rigid scenes in real-time. In: Proceedings of the IEEE Conference on Computer Vision and Pattern Recognition, pp. 343–352 (2015)
14. Sun, D., Sudderth, E.B., Pfister, H.: Layered RGBD scene flow estimation. In: Proceedings of the IEEE Conference on Computer Vision and Pattern Recognition, pp. 548–556 (2015)
15. Collet, A., et al.: High-quality streamable free-viewpoint video. ACM Trans. Graph. (TOG) **34**(4), 69 (2015)
16. Zitnick, C.L., Kang, S.B., Uyttendaele, M., Winder, S., Szeliski, R.S.: High-quality video view interpolation using a layered representation. ACM Trans. Graph. **23**(3), 600–608 (2004)
17. Liu, Y., Dai, Q., Xu, W.: A point cloud based multi-view stereo algorithm for free-viewpoint video. IEEE Trans. Visual. Comput. Graph. **16**(3), 407–441 (2010)
18. Baker, S., Scharstein, D., Lewis, J., Roth, S., Black, M., Szeliski, R.: A database and evaluation methodology for optical flow. IJCV **92**(1), 1–31 (2011)
19. Mordohai, P.: On the evaluation of scene flow estimation. In: Unsolved Problems in Optical Flow and Stereo Estimation Workshop (2012)
20. Menze, M., Geiger, A.: Object scene flow for autonomous vehicles. In: CVPR, pp. 3061–3070 (2015)

21. Vedula, S., Baker, S., Seitz, S.M., Kanade, T.: Shape and motion carving in 6D. In: CVPR, pp. 592–598 (2000)
22. Kutulakos, K.N., Seitz, S.M.: A theory of shape by space carving. IJCV **38**(3), 199–218 (2000)
23. Pons, J.P., Keriven, R., Faugeras, O.D.: Multi-view stereo reconstruction and scene flow estimation with a global image-based matching score. IJCV **72**(2), 179–193 (2007)
24. Kwatra, V., et al.: Fluid in video: augmenting real video with simulated fluids. Comput. Graph. Forum **27**(2), 487–496 (2008)
25. Guan, L., Franco, J.S., Boyer, E., Pollefeys, M.: Probabilistic 3D occupancy flow with latent silhouette cues. In: CVPR (2010)
26. Sizintsev, M., Wildes, R.: Spacetime stereo and 3D flow via binocular spatiotemporal orientation analysis. PAMI **36**(11), 2241–2254 (2014)
27. Liu, F., Philomin, V.: Disparity estimation in stereo sequences using scene flow. In: British Machine Vision Conference (2009)
28. Valgaerts, L., Bruhn, A., Zimmer, H., Weickert, J., Stoll, C., Theobalt, C.: Joint estimation of motion, structure and geometry from stereo sequences. In: Daniilidis, K., Maragos, P., Paragios, N. (eds.) ECCV 2010. LNCS, vol. 6314, pp. 568–581. Springer, Heidelberg (2010). https://doi.org/10.1007/978-3-642-15561-1_41
29. Vogel, C., Schindler, K., Roth, S.: 3D scene flow estimation with a rigid motion prior. In: ICCV (2011)
30. Isard, M., MacCormick, J.P.: Dense motion and disparity estimation via loopy belief propagation. In: Asian Conference on Computer Vision, vol. II, pp. 32–41 (2006)
31. Cech, J., Sanchez-Riera, J., Horaud, R.: Scene flow estimation by growing correspondence seeds. In: CVPR (2011)
32. Li, R., Sclaroff, S.: Multi-scale 3D scene flow from binocular stereo sequences. CVIU **110**(1), 75–90 (2008)
33. Tao, H., Sawhney, H.S., Kumar, R.: Dynamic depth recovery from multiple synchronized video streams. In: CVPR, pp. 118–124 (2001)
34. Zhang, Y., Kambhamettu, C.: On 3-D scene flow and structure recovery from multiview image sequences. PAMI **33**(4), 592–606 (2003)
35. Wedel, A., Rabe, C., Vaudrey, T., Brox, T., Franke, U., Cremers, D.: Efficient dense scene flow from sparse or dense stereo data. In: Forsyth, D., Torr, P., Zisserman, A. (eds.) ECCV 2008. LNCS, vol. 5302, pp. 739–751. Springer, Heidelberg (2008). https://doi.org/10.1007/978-3-540-88682-2_56
36. Rabe, C., Müller, T., Wedel, A., Franke, U.: Dense, robust, and accurate motion field estimation from stereo image sequences in real-time. In: Daniilidis, K., Maragos, P., Paragios, N. (eds.) ECCV 2010. LNCS, vol. 6314, pp. 582–595. Springer, Heidelberg (2010). https://doi.org/10.1007/978-3-642-15561-1_42
37. Müller, T., Rannacher, J., Rabe, C., Franke, U.: Feature- and depth-supported modified total variation optical flow for 3D motion field estimation in real scenes. In: CVPR (2011)
38. Li, K., Dai, Q., Xu, W.: Markerless shape and motion capture from multiview video sequences. IEEE Trans. Circuits Syst. Video Technol. **21**(3), 320–334 (2011)
39. Furukawa, Y., Ponce, J.: Dense 3D motion capture from synchronized video streams. In: CVPR (2008)
40. Furukawa, Y., Ponce, J.: Dense 3D motion capture for human faces. In: CVPR (2009)

41. Courchay, J., Pons, J.P., Monasse, P., Keriven, R.: Dense and accurate spatio-temporal multi-view stereovision. In: Asian Conference on Computer Vision, vol. II, pp. 11–22 (2009)
42. Cagniart, C., Boyer, E., Ilic, S.: Free-form mesh tracking: a patch-based approach. In: CVPR (2010)
43. Popham, T., Bhalerao, A., Wilson, R.: Multi-frame scene-flow estimation using a patch model and smooth motion prior. In: BMVC Workshop (2010)
44. Allain, B., Franco, J.S., Boyer, E.: An efficient volumetric framework for shape tracking. In: CVPR (2015)
45. Huang, C.H., Allain, B., Franco, J.S., Navab, N., Ilic, S., Boyer, E.: Volumetric 3D tracking by detection. In: The IEEE Conference on Computer Vision and Pattern Recognition (CVPR), June 2016
46. Starck, J., Hilton, A.: Correspondence labelling for wide-timeframe free-form surface matching. In: ICCV (2007)
47. Ahmed, N., Theobalt, C., Rossl, C., Thrun, S., Seidel, H.P.: Dense correspondence finding for parametrization-free animation reconstruction from video. In: CVPR (2008)
48. Varanasi, K., Zaharescu, A., Boyer, E., Horaud, R.: Temporal surface tracking using mesh evolution. In: Forsyth, D., Torr, P., Zisserman, A. (eds.) ECCV 2008. LNCS, vol. 5303, pp. 30–43. Springer, Heidelberg (2008). https://doi.org/10.1007/978-3-540-88688-4_3
49. Zeng, Y., Wang, C., Wang, Y., Gu, X., Samaras, D., Paragios, N.: Dense non-rigid surface registration using high-order graph matching. In: CVPR, pp. 382–389 (2010)
50. Budd, C., Huang, P., Hilton, A.: Hierarchical shape matching for temporally consistent 3D video. In: 3DIMPVT, pp. 172–179 (2011)
51. Huang, P., Hilton, A., Budd, C.: Global temporal registration of multiple non-rigid surface sequences. In: CVPR (2011)
52. Letouzey, A., Petit, B., Boyer, E., Team, M.: Scene flow from depth and color images. In: BMVC (2011)
53. Ferstl, D., Reinbacher, C., Riegler, G., Rüther, M., Bischof, H.: aTGV-SF: dense variational scene flow through projective warping and higher order regularization. In: 3DV (2014)
54. Hadfield, S., Bowden, R.: Scene particles: unregularized particle-based scene flow estimation. PAMI **36**(3), 564–576 (2014)
55. Hornacek, M., Fitzgibbon, A., Rother, C.: SphereFlow: 6 DoF scene flow from RGB-D pairs. In: CVPR (2014)
56. Quiroga, J., Brox, T., Devernay, F., Crowley, J.: Dense semi-rigid scene flow estimation from RGBD images. In: Fleet, D., Pajdla, T., Schiele, B., Tuytelaars, T. (eds.) ECCV 2014. LNCS, vol. 8695, pp. 567–582. Springer, Cham (2014). https://doi.org/10.1007/978-3-319-10584-0_37
57. Scharstein, D., Szeliski, R.S.: A taxonomy and evaluation of dense two-frame stereo correspondence algorithms. IJCV **47**(1–3), 7–42 (2002)
58. Geiger, A., Lenz, P., Stiller, C., Urtasun, R.: Vision meets robotics: the KITTI dataset. Int. J. Robot. Res. **32**(11), 1231–1237 (2013)
59. Sizintsev, M., Wildes, R.: Spatiotemporal stereo and scene flow via stequel matching. PAMI **34**(6), 1206–1219 (2012)
60. Gallup, D., Frahm, J.M., Mordohai, P., Yang, Q., Pollefeys, M.: Real-time plane-sweeping stereo with multiple sweeping directions. In: CVPR (2007)
61. Hirschmüller, H.: Stereo processing by semiglobal matching and mutual information. PAMI **30**(2), 328–341 (2008)

62. Sun, D., Roth, S., Black., M.: Secrets of optical flow estimation and their principles. In: CVPR (2010)
63. Torr, P.H., Zisserman, A.: MLESAC: a new robust estimator with application to estimating image geometry. CVIU **78**(1), 138–156 (2000)
64. Szeliski, R.: Prediction error as a quality metric for motion and stereo. In: ICCV, pp. 781–788 (1999)
65. Flynn, J., Neulander, I., Philbin, J., Snavely, N.: DeepStereo: learning to predict new views from the world's imagery. In: CVPR (2016)
66. Waechter, M., Beljan, M., Fuhrmann, S., Moehrle, N., Kopf, J., Goesele, M.: Virtual rephotography: novel view prediction error for 3D reconstruction. arXiv preprint arXiv:1601.06950 (2016)
67. Kilner, J., Starck, J., Guillemaut, J.Y., Hilton, A.: Objective quality assessment in free-viewpoint video production. Sig. Process. Image Commun. **24**(1–2), 3–16 (2009)
68. Spangenberg, R., Langner, T., Adfeldt, S., Rojas, R.: Large scale semi-global matching on the CPU. In: IEEE Intelligent Vehicles Symposium, pp. 195–201 (2014)
69. Horn, B.K.P., Schunck, B.G.: Determining optical flow. Artif. Intell. **17**(1–3), 185–203 (1981)
70. Yoon, K.J., Kweon, I.S.: Adaptive support-weight approach for correspondence search. PAMI **28**(4), 650–656 (2006)

On the Reliability of LSTM-MDL Models for Pedestrian Trajectory Prediction

Ronny Hug$^{(\boxtimes)}$, Stefan Becker, Wolfgang Hübner, and Michael Arens

Fraunhofer Institute of Optronics, System Technologies and Image Exploitation,
Gutleuthausstr. 1, 76275 Ettlingen, Germany
{ronny.hug,stefan.becker,wolfgang.huebner,
michael.arens}@iosb.fraunhofer.de

Abstract. Recurrent neural networks, like the LSTM model, have been applied to various sequence learning tasks with great success. Following this, it seems natural to use LSTM models for predicting future locations in object tracking tasks. In this paper, we evaluate an adaption of a LSTM-MDL model and investigate its reliability in the context of pedestrian trajectory prediction. Thereby, we demonstrate the fallacy of solely relying on prediction metrics for evaluating the model and how the models capabilities can lead to suboptimal prediction results. Towards this end, two experiments are provided. Firstly, the models prediction abilities are evaluated on publicly available surveillance datasets. Secondly, the capabilities of capturing motion patterns are examined. Further, we investigate failure cases and give explanations for observed phenomena, granting insight into the models reliability in tracking applications. Lastly, we give some hints how demonstrated shortcomings may be circumvented.

Keywords: Recurrent neural networks ·
Pedestrian trajectory prediction · Generative models

1 Introduction

One component of an object tracking system is the estimation and prediction of object motion based on observed measurements. Traditionally, this process is modeled using a Bayesian formulation [1] in approaches like the Kalman filter [2] or nonparametric methods, such as particle filters [3]. Alternatively, the inference problem can be construed as a sequence generation problem. This way, we can step in the direction of recurrent neural networks, like Long Short Term Memory (LSTM) networks [4], which are commonly used for sequence generation and processing. Due to the recent success of LSTM models in a variety of sequence processing tasks, like speech recognition [5,6] and caption generation [7,8], these models seem like a natural choice for the task of pedestrian trajectory prediction. In particular, we focus on the model introduced by Alex Graves [9], which was originally designed for the generation and prediction of handwriting. His proposed model (subsequently referred to as LSTM-MDL model),

© Springer Nature Switzerland AG 2019
L. Chen et al. (Eds.): RFMI 2017, CCIS 842, pp. 20–34, 2019.
https://doi.org/10.1007/978-3-030-19816-9_2

which consists of a LSTM network with a mixture density layer (MDL) [10] stacked on top, gained popularity in recent years and is applied in a wide range of applications, for example the prediction of basketball trajectories [11]. In the context of motion prediction in video surveillance data, the work of Alahi et al. [12,13] or Bartoli et al. [14] utilizes the aforementioned model to generate single trajectory predictions based on multiple correlated trajectories. Due to the capabilities of recurrent neural networks to model arbitrary functions and the results of the LSTM-MDL model in handwriting generation, we expect an adaptation of the model to be well suited for modeling complex trajectories in video surveillance data. Here, a trajectory with a significant number of state changes, which are mainly influenced by statistical long-term dependencies, is defined as complex. Since the domain of object tracking is particularly different to handwriting prediction in certain aspects, like position-dependent movement patterns, an adaptation of the model to use positional information is crucial.

The main contribution of this paper is an extensive evaluation of a slightly modified version of the LSTM-MDL model, combined with an investigation on the reliability of this model in the context of pedestrian trajectory prediction. Thereby, when it comes to evaluating the model, the fallacy of solely relying on prediction metrics, such as the final or average displacement error [12,15,16], is demonstrated. Further, it is shown how the overall capabilities of the model can lead to suboptimal prediction results. Here, such prediction metrics can lead up to false conclusions in evaluating the model as a whole, as these metrics are unable to describe the full range of the models capabilities to capture and represent motion in a scene. Towards this end, two-folded extensive experiments are provided. In a first step, the models abilities in predicting pedestrian trajectories is evaluated on several publicly available surveillance datasets. This evaluation shows that the model performs poorly, especially on datasets that consist mainly of complex trajectories, which is not obvious at a first glance. To ensure that this is not a cause of the models inability to capture complex, non-systematic motion from data, we examine the models modeling capabilities in our second series of experiments. As a last step, we further investigate failure cases of the model in the prediction task based on both of our experiments and give explanations for observed phenomena through synthetic toy examples. Furthermore, we demonstrate some problems and shortcomings that might occur when this model is applied to video surveillance tasks and give some hints on how these may be circumvented.

The remainder of this paper is structured as follows. Following this section, we introduce the variation of the LSTM-MDL model that we have used in this paper and discuss the adaptations made (Sect. 2). After that, we are investigating the reliability of this model for pedestrian trajectory prediction, going through the experimental Sect. 3. Finally, we showcase and discuss different problems and shortcomings with the model, that occur regarding prediction tasks (Sect. 4). Section 5 provides some final conclusions.

2   Preliminaries

For modeling human motion in a generative fashion, we are using a slight modification of the LSTM-MDL model described in [9]. Recurrent neural networks
are a natural choice for modeling sequence data, such as human motion represented as timely-ordered sequences of spatial positions. Additionally, regarding
the context of tracking pedestrians in a surveillance scenario, generative modeling provides advantages over discriminative training, as neither labeled training
data nor negative examples are required. Especially the latter is rather difficult
to obtain, as the concept of a negative example concerning pedestrian motion
is not well-defined. In its original form, the network was used to model hand-
written text, represented as a sequence of pen position offsets. Therefore, the
network learns an offset distribution conditioned on previous offsets. Consequently, sequence prediction, like endpoint prediction, is modeled implicitly by
this model.

While utilizing offsets helps stabilizing the learning process, presumably due
to the limitation of the input and output spaces, spatial information gets lost
(which does not harm handwriting generation). More specifically, spatial information only persists in an implicit fashion by performing path integration. Given
this fact, it is not ensured that the model captures spatial points of interest when
learning the model. In the context of handwriting generation, this particular feature is not necessary, as generated handwriting does not have to consider e.g.
obstacles in space. As a consequence, prediction in the original LSTM-MDL
model mostly relies on the previously observed sequence. This is where a major
difference between handwriting generation and pedestrian trajectory prediction
comes into play, where positions in a scene may lead to previous information
being disregarded in favor of immediate predictions given the current location,
e.g. for avoiding a static object. In this respect, the actual position of a person
in a scene is important when modeling future movement and must be used as
an input to the model. Following this, there are two possible ways to further
adapt the original model given the current position: either by trying to predict
the next *position* $\mathbf{x}^{t+1}$ (where will the person *be* next) or the next *offset* $\boldsymbol{\delta}^t$
(where will the person *go* next). During our experiments, we found that predict-
ing an offset distribution increases numerical stability while training, and also
improves results in general, as opposed to predicting a positional distribution.
Such changes were, for example, also made in [12], where the network is used
in that way to predict motion in crowded environments, generating a positional
distribution. In their work they stacked another neural network on top to model
crowd interactions, which may help in coping with instable positional predictions. Since their main focus was on predicting motion, a single Gaussian is used
instead of a multi-component Gaussian mixture, thus further reducing the problem complexity and modeling capabilities. In contrast, we examined the prediction and modeling capabilities of the model. Ultimately, we adapt the model by
changing the input layer to take positions instead of offsets. The adapted model
is depicted in Fig. 1. The output $\mathbf{y}$ of the model is a $6 \times K$ dimensional vector and consists of the parameters of a K component Gaussian mixture model:

$\mathbf{y} = (\mu_k, \sigma_k, \rho_k)_{k=1,...,K}$. This model generates a distribution with respect to the next offset $\boldsymbol{\delta}^t$. The next trajectory position can then be obtained by calculating $\mathbf{x}^t = \mathbf{x}^{t-1} + \boldsymbol{\delta}^{t-1}$ with $\boldsymbol{\delta}^{t-1} \sim \mathbf{y}^{t-1}$.

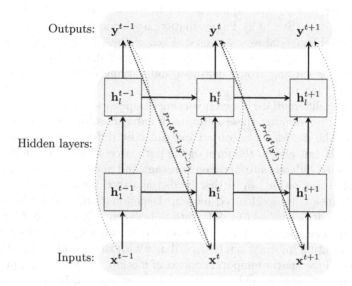

Fig. 1. Recurrent neural network prediction architecture with skip connections as described by Graves [9]. The model has been modified to take positions as input rather than offsets.

This model can be trained in a generative way, by maximizing the likelihood of the data given the output Gaussian mixture parameters. Therefore, the loss function $\mathcal{L}$ is defined as:

$$
\begin{aligned}
\mathcal{L}(\mathbf{x}) &= \sum_{t=1}^{T} - \log \left\{ \sum_k \pi_k^t \mathcal{N}(\boldsymbol{\delta}^{t+1} | \mu_k^t, \sigma_k^t, \rho_k^t) \right\} \\
&= \sum_{t=1}^{T} - \log \left\{ \sum_k \pi_k^t \frac{1}{2\pi\sigma_1\sigma_2\sqrt{1-\rho^2}} \exp \left\{ \frac{-Z}{2(1-\rho^2)} \right\} \right\}
\end{aligned}
\tag{1}
$$

with

$$
\boldsymbol{\delta}^{t+1} = \mathbf{x}^{t+1} - \mathbf{x}^t,
$$

$$
Z = \frac{(\delta_1 - \mu_1)^2}{\sigma_1^2} + \frac{(\delta_2 - \mu_2)^2}{\sigma_2^2} - \frac{2\rho(\delta_1 - \mu_1)(\delta_2 - \mu_2)}{\sigma_1\sigma_2}.
$$

It is important to note, that $\mu_k^t, \sigma_k^t, \rho_k^t$ themselves are dependent on the whole history of inputs $(\mathbf{x}^t, \mathbf{x}^{t-1}, ..., \mathbf{x}^0)$. Further, we opt to disregard the skip connections in the following, as gradient problems are less present during training in our rather small network. With this decision, we also follow other works (e.g. [12]) that do not use skip connections in their models.

3   Evaluation

In this section the effectiveness of the adapted LSTM-MDL model is evaluated
for the task of pedestrian trajectory prediction (Sect. 3.1). Additionally, we ran
an experiment to test the capabilities of the model to capture the statistics
present in the data (Sect. 3.2). For evaluation, a selection of widely-used, publicly
available surveillance datasets are used. Each of these datasets observes one or
multiple scenes from a bird eye view. The selected datasets cover real world
scenarios under varying crowd densities and varying complexity of trajectory
patterns.

In order to differentiate between varying complexities of trajectory patterns,
and thereby also ranking these datasets, a categorization of observed motion
is required. The motion of an object can not only differ in the way the object
follows a path, but also in the form of the path. According to the motion type,
it is possible to differentiate between constant and accelerated motion. In case
of accelerated motion, it can further be distinguished between uniformly accelerated and unequally accelerated motion. Depending on the form or shape of
the trajectory, it is common to differentiate between rectilinear and curvilinear
motion. Furthermore, the dynamics of an object can vary over time and also
depend on location information. In accordance with the introduced motion categorization and the spatio-temporal context of motion, we define a simple motion
as a constant, rectilinear, and temporally constant motion. In return, an object
performs a very complex motion when it is unequally accelerated, curvilinear,
and spatio-temporal varying.

Our entire evaluation was initially based on 3 datasets that together contain
5 scenes. Details of these datasets are summarized in Table 1.

Table 1. Details of pedestrian trajectories datasets.

Dataset details	UCY [17] students	UCY Zara	EWAP [16] ETH	EWAP hotel	SSD [18] Hyang
Video frame rate	25	25	25	25	29
Annotation rate	Non-equidistant	Non-equidistant	2.5	2.5	Non-equidistant
Interpolated	✓	✓	✗	✗	✓
Number of trajectories	967	489	360	390	219
Mean trajectory length	13.481	11.043	24.744	16.779	1581.087

For the purpose of this paper, we focus on the scenes *ETH*, taken from the
ETH Walking Pedestrians (EWAP) dataset [16], and *Hyang*, taken from the
Stanford Drone Dataset (SDD) [18]. We assume that these two scenes suffice
to show and discuss capabilities of the model, as these scenes represent the two
opposite ends of the covered range regarding the complexity of the underlying

data. Although in the chosen exemplary surveillance scenarios with an aerial view the complexity is limited compared to other scenarios like video network data or data captured on board a vehicle, it still allows for a variety in complexity of observed motion. This holds true for the scenes chosen for our evaluation. The trajectories from the *ETH* scene can be described as rather simple, where the amount of spatio-temporal variation is very limited and most trajectories can be adequately described with a constant velocity model following a straight line. However for *Hyang* the scene context strongly influences the person trajectories. For example, there are sidewalks with junctions leading to spatially depending changes in the curvature of the trajectories. With the occurring switches between rectilinear and curvilinear motion and an increased amount of walking paths this scenario can be rated as complex. To provide a better understanding of both scenes, example trajectories are depicted in Fig. 2.

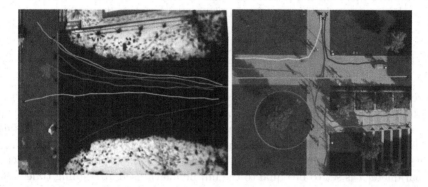

Fig. 2. Example trajectories taken from *ETH* (left) and *Hyang* (right) scenes.

For our experiments, we slightly modified the data of the *Hyang* scene[1]. First, the scene is recorded with a drone from different positions and split into 15 separate recordings containing different trajectories. Seven of these have a large overlap in the observed parts of the whole scenery. Because of that, we are able to project the trajectory data of these recordings into a single coordinate system, using a homography matrix for the transformation, to create a larger set of trajectories for training and evaluation. Secondly, the provided data provides manual annotation, roughly every 30 frames. Between these manual annotations, automatic annotations have been generated. We have replaced these automatic annotations with a linear interpolation to gain an equidistant annotation rate. Using a linear interpolation seemed to improve the results produced by a learned model. Lastly, we removed some trajectory association errors and annotation drift at the borders of the scene. In this paper we are using this version of the *Hyang* scene dataset.

---

[1] The modified ground truth will be provided upon request.

3.1   Applying the LSTM-MDL Model for Prediction

For evaluating the predictive capabilities of the model, we are measuring the performance on the task of predicting the endpoint of a pedestrian trajectory, given a portion of the respective trajectory. We trained 27 different model configurations for each scene in our evaluation, with a varying number of layers (1, 2, and 3), LSTM cell state size (128, 256, and 512 dimensional) and number of components (4, 8, and 16) in the Gaussian mixture model that is output by the model. Each configuration was trained 3 times on a different random subset of the respective dataset, using stochastic gradient descent with a learning rate of 0.005 and an exponential learning rate decay rate of 0.95. The unroll length is set to the lower percentile of the trajectory lengths in the given dataset. This provides a trade-off between the observation length and the number of training examples. In the evaluation, the results of these 3 iterations are averaged to cope with random effects in the trained models. No skip connections, as proposed by Graves [5], were used. The model is implemented in tensorflow [19].

To measure the endpoint prediction we are using the *final displacement error*

$$FDE = \frac{\sum_i \sqrt{(\hat{y}_i - y_i)^2}}{n} \tag{2}$$

where $\hat{y}_i$ and y_i are the predicted and real endpoints of all n trajectories T_i in the test dataset. These trajectories were not part of the training dataset and make up for 20% of the whole dataset. The predicted endpoint is determined by passing the first t trajectory points into the model and then generating the remaining l points by using a maximum likelihood estimate on the output mixtures. Here, the parameter t is set to be equal to the unroll length used at training time. The performance of the model is compared against a simple linear predictor that takes the last two of the t trajectory points to calculate a constant offset. This offset is added to the last given trajectory point l times to predict the trajectory endpoint. The prediction results for the *ETH* scene are depicted in Fig. 3.

In this simple scene, the model expectedly performs better than the linear predictor for nearly all trained configurations. This scene mostly features straight or slightly bent trajectories. For the latter, the linear predictor performs worse, as it doesn't capture curvature. The LSTM-MDL model on the other hand is capable of learning and representing more complex paths, meaning it can capture curved paths. Additionally, the linear predictor propagates a constant velocity in its prediction, whereas the LSTM-MDL model is, generally speaking, capable of modeling several velocity profiles and applying these according to given observations. Given these results, we expect the model to excel in more complex scenes, where curved paths are more common. Following this, we proceeded and scaled up the complexity of the data used. Figure 4 shows the results of the endpoint prediction for the *Hyang* scene.

This dataset contains a lot more major walking paths including two junctions, where the predictor has to choose from several continuations. Given the fact that the adapted LSTM-MDL model is capable of capturing a large variety of different paths and tendencies in choosing between different continuations at junction

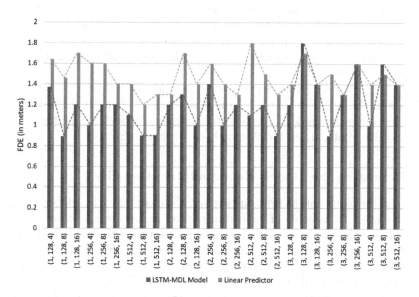

Fig. 3. Endpoint prediction results for *ETH* for the trained configurations (number of layers, LSTM cell state size, and number of gaussian components) of the LSTM-MDL model and the linear predictor.

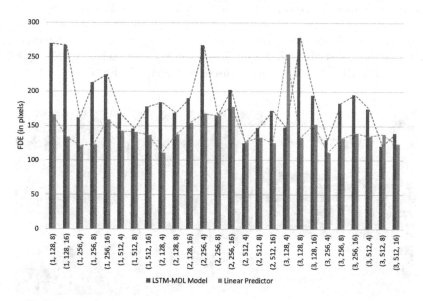

Fig. 4. Endpoint prediction results for *Hyang* for the trained configurations (number of layers, LSTM cell state size, and number of gaussian components) of the LSTM-MDL model and the linear predictor.

points, we expected the model to outperform the linear prediction by a large magnitude. Against the odds, the model fails to surpass the linear predictor. In fact, except in one case, the linear predictor outperforms the model. Furthermore, the results vary strongly depending on the trajectories used for testing, making the results supposedly random.

In order to give an explanation about why the adapted LSTM-MDL model outperforms the linear predictor for the first scene but fails on the second one, we first evaluate the models representation capacity in Sect. 3.2. Following this, we try to give explanations for observed phenomena in Sect. 4.

3.2   Evaluating the Models Representation Capacity

Looking at the results of the previous section, it appears that the adapted LSTM-MDL model is not capable of capturing motion in more complex scenes. This raises the question if the model is incapable of capturing more versatile motion or if the endpoint prediction is not well suited to measure the performance of this model. As a first step in answering this question, we ran another experiment to test the models capability to capture the statistics of the data. In terms of pedestrian motion these statistics include offsets, magnitudes, and the so called path coverage. The last term describes the number of paths from specified sources to sinks in the scene, and the distribution of trajectories with respect to these paths.

For calculating these measures, the models generative capabilities can be used to generate sample trajectories from different starting positions in the scene. In the context of this paper, we are again focusing on the two datasets *ETH* and *Hyang*. We provide sources and sinks for both scenes in the form of rectangles. The set of sources is equal to the set of sinks in each dataset. A rough representation of the paths present in the datasets is depicted in Fig. 5.

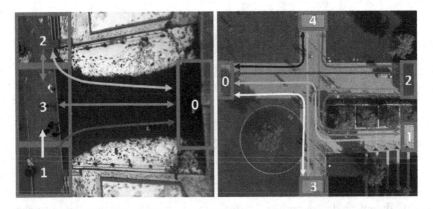

Fig. 5. Sources, sinks and main walking paths in the *ETH* (left) and the *Hyang* (right) scenes.

For generating sample trajectories from the model, we draw 100 positions from each source in the scene. Given these starting positions, we generate sample trajectories using the model by iterating the following steps:

1. Feed the current position into the model to generate a distribution for the next offset
2. Draw an offset from that distribution
3. Calculate the next trajectory point by adding the offset to the current position
4. Set the calculated point to be the next current position

We stop generating new positions when the trajectory enters one of the sinks (i.e. one of the other sources) in the scene or when we exceed a set limit of trajectory points. All sampled trajectories for one dataset are collected in a sample dataset $\mathcal{D}_S$, which will be compared to the training dataset $\mathcal{D}_T$.

For the comparison between $\mathcal{D}_S$ and $\mathcal{D}_T$ we calculate several statistics on both datasets:

1. Histogram of magnitudes
2. Histograms of x and y offsets
3. 2D Histogram of offsets
4. Path coverage

We compare the histograms by using the absolute Pearson correlation as a measure of similarity. These histograms will be referred to as the motion profile of the model. The path coverage is tested by checking which and how many of the paths in the original dataset are represented by the model. Additionally, the distribution of the samples over the paths is again compared by using the absolute Pearson correlation. As we have evaluated a total of 81 learned model checkpoints, Table 2 depicts an example for a *good* (subscripted with plus) and a *bad* (subscripted with minus) performing checkpoint. Here, the *good* and *bad* checkpoints perform accordingly in the measured dimensions. The given values are the mean of 3 runs of the same configuration with a different random selection of the training set.

Table 2. Statistics for a good (subscripted with plus) and a bad (subscripted with minus) checkpoint of the *ETH* and *Hyang* scenes.

Checkpoint	Motion profile			Path coverage		
	Magnitudes	Offsets (x, y)	Offsets	Paths	Distribution	Outlier ratio
ETH_	.318	.573, .934	.352	6/9	.827	18.7%
ETH+	.792	.818, .885	.422	5.67/9	.704	1.7%
Hyang_	.122	.870, .995	.844	7.33/20	.529	10.5%
Hyang+	.539	.964, .997	.929	10/20	.633	6.2%

Figure 6 shows samples generated from these checkpoints. The left column depicts samples from a *bad* and the right columns from a *good* model checkpoint.

The two rows show samples from models learned on the *ETH* and the *Hyang* dataset, respectively. It is visible, that the *bad* models produce much more random trajectories. Still, for *ETH* both models capture the major walking paths well. In contrast, for *Hyang*, the *bad* model captures less paths and both junctions are biased towards the left border of the scene, causing samples to deviate from the usual walking paths.

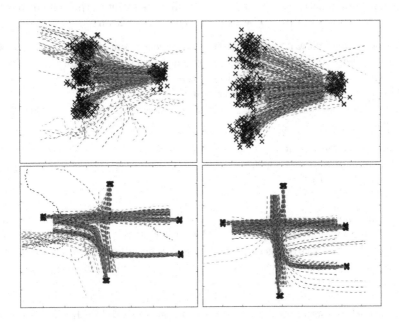

Fig. 6. Samples drawn from a good (right) and a bad (left) checkpoint learned on the *ETH* (first row) and *Hyang* (second row) scenes.

Concluding this evaluation of the data modeling capabilities of the adapted LSTM-MDL model, we figured that it is indeed capable of modeling complex motion in given trajectory data. On the other hand this also means, that our question, regarding the failure in the prediction task, is still unanswered and must be further investigated. Following this, we try to give reasons for this in Sect. 4.

4   On the Reliability of LSTM-MDL Models for Pedestrian Trajectory Prediction

Regarding the results shown in Sect. 3.2, the adapted LSTM-MDL model is capable of capturing the statistics in the data, thus still leaving our question concerning the poor prediction results unanswered. Thinking further, the reason why the endpoint prediction is not particularly good and somehow appears to become more random the better the model is, lies in the task and the common approach itself. Even if we have multiple hypotheses to choose from when predicting the endpoint of a given trajectory segment, we usually decide to go with the most probable path (maximum likelihood estimation), also if its probability is only slightly higher. That means, with an increasing number of paths, and especially junctions in those paths, the prediction will become more instable, the better the model is capable of representing the data. To clarify, this can be pictured using a small toy example. Take for example 3 synthetic datasets $\mathcal{D}_1$, $\mathcal{D}_2$, and $\mathcal{D}_3$ that contain trajectories that pass a 4-way junction. In $\mathcal{D}_1$, all trajectories start at the bottom and pass the junction to the left. Dataset $\mathcal{D}_2$ also contains trajectories starting at the bottom, but they pass the junction either to the left or to the right. The last dataset $\mathcal{D}_3$ adds the possibility of going straight over the junction. Now, if the model is large enough to cover all these paths, it may generate sample trajectories starting from the exact same position that end in very different positions. This is depicted in Fig. 7.

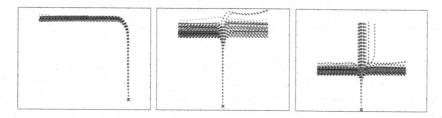

Fig. 7. Toy example datasets to showcase the problem with the modeling power of the adapted LSTM-MDL model for prediction tasks.

Concerning endpoint prediction, we have a chance of completely missing the true endpoint of 0, 50, and 66%. Depending on the absolute positioning of the trajectory itself, it may be biased more or less towards a specific endpoint region. This, in fact, still does not need to hold true for many trajectories in a real world dataset.

Another aspect to consider is the number t of observed points prior to the prediction. If there is at least one junction on a trajectory's path, the observed points *before* that junction do not necessarily provide useful information about the continuation of that particular trajectory. Different observation lengths could indeed lead to some bias towards a specific direction, but depending on the variation in the training data, this is more or less helpful. In general, this fact has to be taken into account, as trajectories generally vary in length, due to different walking speeds of pedestrians. This also holds true, even if two trajectories follow roughly the same path through the scene, when these are progressing at different velocities. Here, the model will eventually have richer information for predicting the continuation of the faster moving target, as for the slower moving target, when the number of observed trajectory points is fixed, because the former has progressed much further into the scene. The impact of the observation length is illustrated in Fig. 8. In this figure, a trajectory (blue) from $\mathcal{D}_3$ is chosen, which is heading towards the left side crossing the junction. The learned model should predict the most probable continuation of that trajectory (red), given trajectory points up to the junction, a few steps into the junction and mostly through the junction.

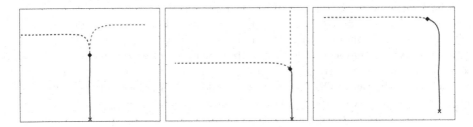

Fig. 8. Predicted continuation (red) of a partly observed trajectory (blue, starting at black cross) given 30 (right before the junction), 35 (few steps into the junction, already shows some tendencies), and 40 (almost through the junction, direction is now clear) trajectory points (up to the black diamond). (Color figure online)

It can be clearly seen how the choice of the observation length affects the predictions of the model. In this particular case, having only observed trajectory points just before entering the junction, the model does not even consider going to the left. Given some more points that provide some information about the continuation, the model switches to predicting a straight motion, which still is not as expected. This may happen because the model is robust to noise, at least to some extent. In the last case, it is clear how the trajectory should continue: to the left. The model also captures this and does an appropriate prediction.

In conclusion, the adapted LSTM-MDL models capability of capturing and representing a variety of complex paths is great for generating data, but somewhat obstructive for prediction tasks, such as endpoint prediction. Regarding this, another question arises that should be investigated further in future works: How can we possibly fix this? No matter what the exact solution will be, it will most probably involve a more sophisticated approach to generate predictions that do not solely rely on the most probable hypothesis. In fact, to exhaust all possibilities given by the LSTM-MDL, an approach that tracks and incorporates all hypotheses generated by the model should be preferred over the common approach. Also, another adaption of the model that incorporates the positions and offsets may provide the model with richer possibilities to model pedestrian motion. Besides that, when using this model as a predictor, the restrictions and problems discussed in this paper should be kept in mind.

5   Conclusions

In this paper, we explored how naïvely applying a LSTM-MDL model for predicting human trajectories can lead to unreliable results. While these excel in handwriting generation, model adaptations that consider explicit spatial information can unexpectedly collapse in prediction tasks. Especially in the context of surveillance data, common metrics like endpoint prediction result in the fallacy that the model cannot correctly represent the data. In order to demonstrate the capabilities of the model to capture the training data characteristics, an extensive comparison of different underlying data statistics was provided. As the model proves to be capable of capturing the data statistics, we further revealed the occurring reasons for the problems and shortcomings of the model on synthetic data. Finally, we provided research directions on how to overcome some limitations of the model.

References

1. Thrun, S., Burgard, W., Fox, D.: Probabilistic Robotics (Intelligent Robotics and Autonomous Agents). The MIT Press, Cambridge (2005)
2. Kalman, R.: A new approach to linear filtering and prediction problems. ASME J. Basic Eng. **82**, 35–45 (1960)
3. Arulampalam, M.S., Maskell, S., Gordon, N., Clapp, T.: A tutorial on particle filters for online nonlinear/non-gaussian bayesian tracking. IEEE Trans. Sig. Process. **50**(2), 174–188 (2002)
4. Hochreiter, S., Schmidhuber, J.: Long short-term memory. Neural Comput. **9**(8), 1735–1780 (1997)
5. Graves, A., Mohamed, A., Hinton, G.: Speech recognition with deep recurrent neural networks. In: International Conference on Acoustics, Speech and Signal Processing, pp. 6645–6649, May 2013
6. Chung, J., Kastner, K., Dinh, L., Goel, K., Courville, A., Bengio, Y.: A recurrent latent variable model for sequential data. In: Advances in Neural Information Processing Systems (NIPS) (2015)
7. Donahue, J., et al.: Long-term recurrent convolutional networks for visual recognition and description. In: Conference on Computer Vision and Pattern Recognition. IEEE (2015)
8. Xu, K., et al.: Show, attend and tell: neural image caption generation with visual attention. In: Bach, F., Blei, D. (eds.) Proceedings of the 32nd International Conference on Machine Learning, vol. 37, pp. 2048–2057. Proceedings of Machine Learning Research (PMLR), Lille (2015)
9. Graves, A.: Generating sequences with recurrent neural networks. arXiv:1308.0850 (2013)
10. Bishop, C.M.: Pattern Recognition and Machine Learning. Information Science and Statistics. Springer, Secaucus (2006)
11. Shah, R., Romijnders, R.: Applying deep learning to basketball trajectories. arXiv:1608.03793 (2016)
12. Alahi, A., Goel, K., Ramanathan, V., Robicquet, A., Fei-Fei, L., Savarese, S.: Social LSTM: human trajectory prediction in crowded spaces. In: Conference on Computer Vision and Pattern Recognition, pp. 961–971. IEEE (2016)
13. Alahi, A., et al.: Learning to predict human behaviour in crowded scenes. In: Group and Crowd Behavior for Computer Vision. Elsevier, Amsterdam (2017)
14. Bartoli, F., Lisanti, G., Ballan, L., Bimbo, A.D.: Context-aware trajectory prediction. arXiv:1705.02503 (2017)

15. Vemula, A., Muelling, K., Oh, J.: Modeling cooperative navigation in dense human crowds. In: 2017 IEEE International Conference on Robotics and Automation (ICRA), pp. 1685–1692, May 2017
16. Pellegrini, S., Ess, A., Schindler, K., van Gool, L.: You'll never walk alone: modeling social behavior for multi-target tracking. In: International Conference on Computer Vision, pp. 261–268 (2009)
17. Lerner, A., Chrysanthou, Y., Lischinski, D.: Crowds by example. Comput. Graph. Forum **26**(3), 655–664 (2007)
18. Robicquet, A., Sadeghian, A., Alahi, A., Savarese, S.: Learning social etiquette: human trajectory understanding in crowded scenes. In: Leibe, B., Matas, J., Sebe, N., Welling, M. (eds.) ECCV 2016. LNCS, vol. 9912, pp. 549–565. Springer, Cham (2016). https://doi.org/10.1007/978-3-319-46484-8_33
19. Abadi, M., et al.: TensorFlow: large-scale machine learning on heterogeneous systems (2015). Software: tensorflow.org

Pedestrian Tracking in the Compressed Domain Using Thermal Images

Ichraf Lahouli[1,2,3]([✉]), Robby Haelterman[1], Zied Chtourou[2],
Geert De Cubber[1], and Rabah Attia[3]

[1] Royal Military Academy, Brussels, Belgium
ichraf.lahouli@rma.ac.be
[2] VRIT Lab, Military Academy of Tunisia, Nabeul, Tunisia
[3] SERCOM Lab, Tunisia Polytechnic School, La Marsa, Tunisia

Abstract. The video surveillance of sensitive facilities or borders poses
many challenges like the high bandwidth requirements and the high computational cost. In this paper, we propose a framework for detecting and
tracking pedestrians in the compressed domain using thermal images.
Firstly, the detection process uses a conjunction between saliency maps
and contrast enhancement techniques followed by a global image content
descriptor based on Discrete Chebychev Moments (DCM) and a linear
Support Vector Machine (SVM) as a classifier. Secondly, the tracking
process exploits raw H.264 compressed video streams with limited computational overhead. In addition to two, well-known, public datasets,
we have generated our own dataset by carrying six different scenarios
of suspicious events using a thermal camera. The obtained results show
the effectiveness and the low computational requirements of the proposed
framework which make it suitable for real-time applications and onboard
implementation.

1 Introduction

For decades, many works have been done on pedestrian detection and tracking
using thermal imagery, especially for surveillance and driver's assistance applications. The reason is that such images allow working on day and night-time even
though the texture and the color information are missing. Nowadays, in parallel with the radar systems, the surveillance of borders, for example, is ensured
by new platforms like drones equipped with optical and/or thermal sensors and
transmission modules for a real-time video streaming to a central station in the
ground commonly named Ground Control Station (GCS). However, the amount
of information transmitted to the GCS is huge and full of redundancy and non-
pertinent information. Consequently, many problems of storage and analysis are
encountered in addition to the challenges caused by the high processing and the
high bandwidth requirements for the data streaming.

The motion-based segmentation is widely used to detect and track moving
objects like pedestrians. In this context, the majority of the works uses Optical
Flow (OF) and local feature descriptors such as SIFT and SURF. Wu et al. [1]

© Springer Nature Switzerland AG 2019
L. Chen et al. (Eds.): RFMI 2017, CCIS 842, pp. 35–44, 2019.
https://doi.org/10.1007/978-3-030-19816-9_3

used the OF to compute the dense particle trajectories of the objects and proposed an optimization method to filter the noisy trajectories due to the camera motion. Wang et al. [2] use dense OF and SURF descriptors to match the feature points. They also relied on a human detector to discard the inconsistent matches. Nevertheless, whether the OF is sparse or dense, is still computationally heavy and time-consuming which makes it not suitable for real-time applications. As an alternative, some studies focus on the possibility of exploiting the MVs in the MPEG compressed domain. Park et al. [3] estimated the camera motion using a generalized Hough transform and then tracked the centre of the ROI based on the spatial distribution of colours. Babu et al. [4] used motion vectors of compressed MPEG video for segmentation and a Hidden Markov Model (HMM) and motion history information for action recognition. Yeo et al. [5] used the MV information to capture the salient regions and to compute frame-to-frame motion similarity. Biswas et al. [6] used the orientation information of the MVs to classify the H.264 compressed videos. Käs and Nicolas [7] proposed an approach to estimate the trajectories of the moving objects in the compressed domain. Firstly, a Global Motion Estimation (GME) based on the MVs is performed to generate the masks which are the input of an object detection stage. Secondly, an object matching stage is used for the trajectories' estimation.

In 2014 and in the context of activity recognition, Kantorov et al. [8] used the MPEG MVs as local descriptors, Fisher Vector (FV) for coding and SVM for classification. They prove that, in comparison to the OF, the use of the MPEG MVs present a significant computational speedup ($\simeq 66\%$) while a small reduction of recognition accuracy is noticed ($\simeq 1\%$). Zhang et al. [9] proposed a real-time action recognition method in the compressed domain using the MPEG MVs. To improve the recognition accuracy, they proposed a sort of transferable learning by adapting the models of the OF Convolutional Neural Network (CNN) to the models of the MV CNN. In order to recognize activities of daily living, Poularakis et al. [10] proposed a motion estimation method based on the pre-computed MPEG MV instead of OF. In addition, they did not work on the whole frame but focused only on data in the Motion Boundary Activity Area (MBAA) [11] which also decreased the computational cost.

In this paper, we aim to present an efficient framework for pedestrians' detection and tracking in thermal images with low processing requirements. Concerning the detection process, the first step is to extract the Regions Of Interest (ROI)s using a conjunction between saliency maps and contrast enhancement techniques. Then, feature vectors are generated using the DCM [12]. Finally, a linear SVM is used to classify the ROIs into pedestrians and non-pedestrians. In order to validate the proposed ROI detector, two public, thermal pedestrian datasets are used: the OTCBVS benchmark -OSU Thermal Pedestrian Database [13] and the nine thermal videos taken from the LITIV2012 dataset [14]. A comparison is carried out between the proposed ROI detection process and the Maximally Stable Extremal Regions (MSER) detector in terms of calculation time and true positives and false positives rates. According to the obtained results, the proposed method is robust in terms of true positives rate and even beats MSER in terms of false positives rates and processing time. Concerning the tracking process, we proposed an approach which is based on the precomputed MPEG MVs of only the ROIs which are previously generated by the detection process. For the experiments, we generated our own dataset by carrying out six different scenarios of suspicious events and filmed the scene using a thermal sensor. The decoding of all the frames is not needed. Globally, the proposed method does not need a pixel by pixel or a frame by frame processing. It relies on some frames to detect the ROIs and on some MVs already computed (as an integral part of the MPEG4 AVC (H264 codec)) for tracking. This makes it adequate for real-time applications and for implementation on low-end computational platforms.

The paper is organized as follows: In Sect. 2, the proposed framework is presented in details by explaining the two processes of ROI detection and tracking using MPEG MVs. The Sect. 3 is allocated to the experiments and the results, including the comparison between the proposed detector and MSER, the choice of the re-direction rate and the performance of the tracking process. Finally, Sect. 4 summaries the present paper and exposes some perspectives of future works.

2   Proposed Methodology

In this section, we will try to explain the proposed framework in details. Actually, it relies on two main processes: the ROI detection process and the ROI tracking process. The first one extracts the ROIs which correspond to the pedestrians. The second one tracks these ROIs by using its MVs drawn directly from the MPEG compressed video. We will present the two processes consecutively.

2.1   Proposed ROI Detection Process

Our main purpose is to ensure the surveillance of borders and sensitive facilities using thermal images taken from an airborne platform. As we are in an outdoor environment, we assume that the pedestrians are brighter than their background. This means that our method is part of the 'Hot Spot' Methods. ROIs are detected according to certain restrictions regarding their brightness and their size. The proposed ROI detection process can be divided into three steps:

1. ROI extraction: A conjunction between a wavelet-based contrast enhancement technique [15] and a saliency map (produced on the basis of Lab colour space) [16],
2. Shape description: DCMs (up to order 4 * 4) are used as a global region content descriptor [12],
3. Classification: a linear SVM is used to classify the ROIs into humans and non-humans according to their DCM feature vectors.

Firstly, the saliency map and the contrast-enhanced image are computed and fused together using their geometric mean. Then, a brightness threshold is applied to generate a binary image which conserves only the hot spot areas. Finally, a size threshold allows discarding very small/big ROIs.

2.2 Proposed Tracking Process Using MPEG Motion Vectors

Since the videos transmitted between the remote platforms (drones/cameras) are usually streamed to the central station in a compressed form, we should propose an object tracking approach which avoids the decompression of each frame. In order to save the processing resources and reduce the computational cost, the tracking should be done in the compressed domain. Indeed, the tracking process is based on the motion information and not the visual features such as the shape like in the detection process. After the segmentation of the input image and the extraction of the ROIs, these regions are tracked in the compressed domain based on their motion vectors.

The H.264 video compression standard generates motion vectors that contain motion information between regions in different frames. It is not a pixel level processing. It starts by splitting each frame into macroblocks (usual squares of $8 * 8$ or $16 * 16$ pixels). Then, it estimates the displacements between these areas through time and stored it's as orientation and magnitude information. In our work, we will not extract the MPEG MVs of all the macroblocks. Actually, the algorithm starts by finding the macroblocks that cover each ROI. Then, it keeps tracking these macroblocks through time by computing the intermediate estimated positions based on its relative MPEG MVs. Although these MPEG MVs are useful, we cannot rely exclusively on its due to the noise and the errors generated by the motion compensation step. We propose to compensate these errors by launching the aforementioned ROI detection process at a re-detection rate namely **N**. The recall of the human detector will adjust the intermediate estimated positions of the ROIs. The choice of this frequency **N** is not fixed but depends on different parameters such as the frame rate and the resolution of the video sequence. An analysis in Sect. 3.3 shows how **N** is chosen.

3 Experiments and Results

3.1 Presentation of the Different Datasets

In order to validate the ROI detection process, two different public, thermal pedestrian datasets were used:

- *OSU Thermal Pedestrian Database* [13]: acquired by the Raytheon 300D thermal sensor. It is composed of 10 test collections with a total of 284 frames taken within one minute but not temporally uniformly sampled. The OSU thermal dataset covers a panoply of environmental conditions such as sunny, rainy and cloudy days.
- *LITIV2012 dataset* [14]: specifically the nine thermal sequences. Indeed, the dataset is composed of nine pairs of visualthermal sequences.

In order to validate the tracking process, we can not test on the two public datasets previously used to validate the proposed detection process. The reason is that both datasets do not provide H.264 encoding data so we needed to generate our own dataset. Since our main application is the video surveillance of borders and sensitive facilities, we carried out different scenarios of suspicious events in an outdoor environment and filmed the scene using a thermal sensor. Indeed, we recorded thermal videos of pedestrians taken from a stationary camera with an image resolution of 576 * 704 pixels and a frame rate of 25 frames per second (fps). Table 1 gives an overview of the six scenarios of suspicious events.

3.2 Validation of the Proposed Detection Process

Firstly, the proposed ROI extractor (first stage of the detector before the description and the classification stages) is compared to the MSER detector [17] which is a fast, widely used and simple region based detector. MSER was introduced in 2004 but is still up to date and widely used a region-based local extractor like recently in [18–23]. The popularity of MSER is due to its efficiency and its low complexity which makes it adequate for real-time applications. The implementation is done on Matlab. Thus, the DetectMSERFeatures function, available in the Computer Vision System Toolbox, is used. The experiments were run under the same set of parameters like size thresholds. Table 2 shows the robustness of the proposed detection process in terms of true detection with approximately 96% for the OSU Thermal Pedestrian Database and 95% for the LITIV2012 dataset. Furthermore, it beats MSER in terms of reducing the false alarms' rate which is a great criterion for surveillance purposes. Concerning the CPU time, the proposed detection process also beats MSER by running about two to three times faster. Regarding the desired application of the proposed framework, these two improvements are pertinent and make the proposed framework suitable for a real-time implementation on a drone for instance, in order to select and then send only true alarms to the GCS.

3.3 Validation of the Proposed Tracking Process

Re-detection Rate
In order to compensate the estimation errors caused by the extracted MPEG MVs, the proposed detection process is recalled at a re-detection rate. Choosing this parameter is a trade-off between keeping low computational requirements and guaranteeing good tracking accuracy. In other words, we have to avoid the re-launch of the ROI detector process and at the same time, we have to ensure the robustness of the whole framework. Indeed, the recall of the proposed detection process means the decompression of the frame and the application of image processing techniques that are more computationally costly than the simple extraction of the precomputed MPEG MVs. To set up the re-detection rate, we first applied the proposed detection process on a reference image **frame #i** to generate the ROIs. Then, the positions of these ROIs are estimated based exclusively on their MPEG MVs. To measure the estimation performance of the tracking using only the MPEG MVs, we computed the overlap between the real and the estimated positions of the ROIs. We consider an estimation as good if it satisfies the condition below:

$$\frac{A_{Detected} \cap A_{Estimated}}{\min(A_{Detected}, A_{Estimated})} \geq 70\% \tag{1}$$

Table 1. Suspicious Events' scenarios

Scenario	Description	Frame example
Brutal turn back	2 people move in one direction (policemen) + 1 single suspicious person walks in the opposite direction. Once he sees them he will rapidly turn back.	
Convergence/divergence	3 suspicious people converge, quickly exchange an object and then diverge and quit the scene.	
Velocity changes	1 single suspicious person who walks then runs then slows down again + non suspicious people.	
Occlusion/Non Occlusion	1 single suspicious person tries to hide behind a car + non suspicious people.	
Circular trajectory	1 single suspicious person moves around a car while focusing on it (robbery intention) + non suspicious people.	
Rapid dump of a suspicious object	1 single suspicious person walks carrying a backpack then puts it down near a vehicle + non suspicious people.	

Table 2. Proposed ROI detector vs MSER

Criterion	Proposed ROI extractor	MSER
OSU Thermal		
True detection rate	95.55%	**97.83%**
False alarms rate	**29.22%**	51.63%
CPU-time per image	**0.17 s**	0.46 s
LITIV2012		
True detection rate	**95.13%**	85.28%
False alarms rate	**26.25%**	39.76%
CPU-time per image	**0.098 s**	0.151 s

Where $A_{Detected}$ denotes the area of the detected ROI (at **Frame #(i)**) and $A_{Estimated}$ is the area of the estimated ROI (at **Frame #(i +N)**). We choose the same criterion as in [24].

We tested the estimation performance on the video sequences of our own dataset (frame rate = 25 fps) on a thermal video sequence composed of 676 frames in total. We started by detecting the ROIs at **frame #1** and then kept tracking these ROIs based exclusively on its MPEG MVs. At each frame, the overlap between the real positions (given by the ROI detector) and the estimated positions is computed. We found out that the estimation performance decreases disproportionally to the re-detection rate. In order to satisfy the condition in Eq. 1, N should be <28. In other words, to ensure the robustness of the proposed tracking process, the frequency to recall the detection process should be not more than 28 frames. As the frame rate is equal to 25 fps, choosing N equal to 25 means a recall of the detection process each 1 s. For the rest of the experiments, N = 25.

Tracking Example

At this stage, we will present an example that illustrates how the proposed approach works well. Figure 1 shows the effectiveness of the proposed framework to predict the trajectories of three different people in the convergence scenario. Figure 1(a) presents the initial **Frame #8** and the outputs of the proposed detection process in Blue. These bounding boxes correspond the initial ROI positions. Figure 1(b) presents the **Frame #(8+25)** and the target ROI positions in green. Figure 1(c) shows the estimated trajectories of the ROIs between the two frames. For each ROI, a trajectory is computed based on the MPEG MVs of the macroblocks that cover it. The example shows how the proposed framework was able to properly estimate the trajectories of the three pedestrians.

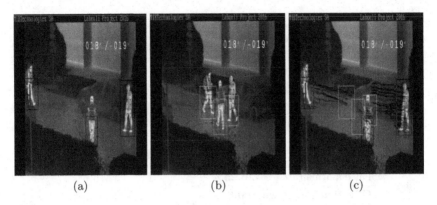

(a)   (b)   (c)

Fig. 1. Example of trajectories' estimations of three ROIs (convergence's scenario). (a): Initial **Frame #8** Initial ROI positions, (b): Target **Frame #(8+25)** Target ROI positions. (c): Estimated trajectories between **Frame #(8)** and **Frame #(8+25)**.

4   Conclusion and Future Works

This paper proposed an efficient approach for pedestrian detection and tracking in thermal images with low computational requirements. The proposed framework is not a frame neither a pixel level processing and it relies on the MPEG MVs which makes it suitable for real-time applications. The results show its effectiveness to detect and track pedestrians in thermal images even though there is no color or texture information. As future works, the performance of the tracking algorithm should be quantitatively measured using, for example, the CLEAR MOT metrics [25]. At this stage of work, only the trajectories of the different pedestrians in the scene are extracted. However, in order to construct a complete system for surveillance and abnormal event detection applications, these trajectories need firstly to be described using feature vectors. Then, a machine learning approach should be developed in order to allow the system to autonomously detect the suspicious people. In addition, trajectories alone might not be sufficient but need to be combined with velocity and acceleration information, which might be also computed in the compressed domain.

Acknowledgment. The generation of the proposed dataset using thermal cameras is supported by MIRTECHNOLOGIES SA, Chemin des Eysines 51, 1226 Nyon, CH.

References

1. Wu, S., Oreifej, O., Shah, M.: Action recognition in videos acquired by a moving camera using motion decomposition of Lagrangian particle trajectories. In: 2011 IEEE International Conference on Computer Vision (ICCV), pp. 1419–1426. IEEE (2011)
2. Wang, H., Schmid, C.: Action recognition with improved trajectories. In: Proceedings of the IEEE International Conference on Computer Vision, pp. 3551–3558 (2013)
3. Park, S.-M., Lee, J.: Object tracking in mpeg compressed video using mean-shift algorithm. In: Proceedings of the 2003 Joint Conference of the Fourth International Conference on Information, Communications and Signal Processing and Fourth Pacific Rim Conference on Multimedia, vol. 2, pp. 748–752. IEEE (2003)
4. Babu, R.V., Ramakrishnan, K., Srinivasan, S.: Video object segmentation: a compressed domain approach. IEEE Trans. Circuits Syst. Video Technol. **14**(4), 462–474 (2004)
5. Yeo, C., Ahammad, P., Ramchandran, K., Sastry, S.S.: Compressed domain real-time action recognition. In: 2006 IEEE 8th Workshop on Multimedia Signal Processing, pp. 33–36. IEEE (2006)
6. Biswas, S., Babu, R.V.: H.264 compressed video classification using histogram of oriented motion vectors (HOMV). In: 2013 IEEE International Conference on Acoustics, Speech and Signal Processing (ICASSP), pp. 2040–2044. IEEE (2013)
7. Käs, C., Nicolas, H.: An approach to trajectory estimation of moving objects in the H.264 compressed domain. In: Wada, T., Huang, F., Lin, S. (eds.) PSIVT 2009. LNCS, vol. 5414, pp. 318–329. Springer, Heidelberg (2009). https://doi.org/10.1007/978-3-540-92957-4_28
8. Kantorov, V., Laptev, I.: Efficient feature extraction, encoding and classification for action recognition. In: Proceedings of the IEEE Conference on Computer Vision and Pattern Recognition, pp. 2593–2600 (2014)
9. Zhang, B., Wang, L., Wang, Z., Qiao, Y., Wang, H.: Real-time action recognition with enhanced motion vector CNNs. In: Proceedings of the IEEE Conference on Computer Vision and Pattern Recognition, pp. 2718–2726 (2016)
10. Poularakis, S., Avgerinakis, K., Briassouli, A., Kompatsiaris, I.: Efficient motion estimation methods for fast recognition of activities of daily living. Sig. Process. Image Commun. **53**, 1–12 (2017)
11. Avgerinakis, K., Briassouli, A., Kompatsiaris, I.: Recognition of activities of daily living for smart home environments. In: 2013 9th International Conference on Intelligent Environments (IE), pp. 173–180. IEEE (2013)
12. Karakasis, E., Bampis, L., Amanatiadis, A., Gasteratos, A., Tsalides, P.: Digital elevation model fusion using spectral methods. In: 2014 IEEE International Conference on Imaging Systems and Techniques (IST) Proceedings, pp. 340–345. IEEE (2014)
13. Davis, J.W., Keck, M.A.: A two-stage template approach to person detection in thermal imagery. In: Seventh IEEE Workshops on Application of Computer Vision, WACV/MOTIONS 2005, vol. 1, pp. 364–369, January 2005
14. Torabi, A., Massé, G., Bilodeau, G.-A.: An iterative integrated framework for thermal-visible image registration, sensor fusion, and people tracking for video surveillance applications. Comput. Vis. Image Underst. **116**, 210–221 (2012)
15. Arodź, T., Kurdziel, M., Popiela, T.J., Sevre, E.O., Yuen, D.A.: Detection of clustered microcalcifications in small field digital mammography. Comput. Methods Programs Biomed. **81**(1), 56–65 (2006)

16. Achanta, R., Hemami, S., Estrada, F., Susstrunk, S.: Frequency-tuned salient region detection. In: IEEE International Conference on Computer Vision and Pattern Recognition (CVPR 2009), pp. 1597–1604 (2009)

17. Matas, J., Chum, O., Urban, M., Pajdla, T.: Robust wide-baseline stereo from maximally stable extremal regions. Image Vis. Comput. **22**(10), 761–767 (2004)

18. Tun, W.N., Tyan, M., Kim, S., Nah, S.-H., Lee, J.-W.: Marker tracking with AR drone for visual-based navigation using SURF and MSER algorithms, pp. 124–125 (2017)

19. Sun, X., Ding, J., Dalla Chiara, G., Cheah, L., Cheung, N.-M.: A generic framework for monitoring local freight traffic movements using computer vision-based techniques. In: 2017 5th IEEE International Conference on Models and Technologies for Intelligent Transportation Systems (MT-ITS), pp. 63–68. IEEE (2017)

20. Kumar, A., Gupta, S.: Detection and recognition of text from image using contrast and edge enhanced mser segmentation and OCR. IJOSCIENCE (Int. J. Online Sci.) Impact Factor: 3.462 **3**(3), 07 (2017)

21. Khosravi, M., Hassanpour, H.: A novel image structural similarity index considering image content detectability using maximally stable extremal region descriptor. Int. J. Eng. Trans. B: Appl. **30**(2), 172 (2017)

22. Alyammahi, S.M.R., Salahat, E.N., Saleh, H.H.M., Sluzek, A.S., Elnaggar, M.I.: Hardware architecture for linear-time extraction of maximally stable external regions (MSERs). US Patent 9,740,947, August 22 2017

23. Śluzek, A.: MSER and SIMSER regions: a link between local features and image segmentation. In: Proceedings of the 2017 International Conference on Computer Graphics and Digital Image Processing, p. 15. ACM (2017)

24. Ma, Y., Wu, X., Yu, G., Xu, Y., Wang, Y.: Pedestrian detection and tracking from low-resolution unmanned aerial vehicle thermal imagery. Sensors **16**(4), 446 (2016)

25. Bernardin, K., Stiefelhagen, R.: Evaluating multiple object tracking performance: the CLEAR MOT metrics. EURASIP J. Image Video Process. **2008**, 246309 (2008)

An Image Processing Framework for Automatic Tracking of Wave Fronts and Estimation of Wave Front Velocity for a Gas Experiment

Samee Maharjan[✉], Dag Bjerketvedt, and Ola Marius Lysaker

Department of Process, Energy and Environmental Technology,
University College of Southeast Norway, Porsgrunn, Norway
`samee.maharjan@usn.no`

Abstract. This work presents an image processing framework designed to automatically track the wave front in a sequence of images from a high speed film. A watershed algorithm is used for segmentation and contouring, while an active contour model is used for controlling the flexibility and the rigidity of the contour. The velocity of the wave front is calculated by estimating the displacement of the front in two frames, divided by the time difference between the frames. The calculated velocity is compared with the sensor measurements. Further, the calculated velocities can be used to estimate thermodynamic properties like the Mach number, the pressure and the temperature across the wave. With the purposed framework, these properties can be estimated along the entire wave front. Otherwise, these thermodynamic properties are limited to either theoretical values or to sparse measurements from sensors. The experiment is done by using a shock tube and the film is captured by a high speed camera using the shadowgraph system.

Keywords: Image processing application · Watershed ·
Front tracking · Active contour model

1 Introduction

Image segmentation is one of the important and most explored field in image processing. Among the numerous methods of image segmentation, watershed algorithm which is based on mathematical morphology of an image is well known and widely used, especially for boundary contouring and edge detection [1]. The watershed method takes an image as a topographic surface, where the graylevel values of the image corresponds to the altitude of a surface (minimum being the deepest). The algorithm was first introduced by Digabel and Lantuéjoul [2] and further modified by Beucher and Lantuéjoul [3,4]. Initially, the algorithm was highly suffering by over segmentation due to the large number of local minima present in an image. To overcome with the problem of over segmentation, Meyer

© Springer Nature Switzerland AG 2019
L. Chen et al. (Eds.): RFMI 2017, CCIS 842, pp. 45–55, 2019.
https://doi.org/10.1007/978-3-030-19816-9_4

and Beucher proposed a strategy known as marker-controlled segmentation [5]. More on the application of watershed method in grayscale images and overall review of the marker controlled segmentation can be found in [6,7].

The active contour or snake model was first developed by Kass et al. in 1988 [8]. The snake model is an essential part in image processing and computer vision applications, mainly used for shape modeling [9] and motion tracking [10]. A snake is a moving curve within an image, which eventually lie itself around the surface/edge of the desired object. For the present work, an open contour model developed in [11] is used.

In general, shock waves appear in many flow fields, for example, at the wings of an airplane, in explosions, fired bullets, exhaust of engines etc. The study of the structure and the properties of a shock wave and its boundary layer interactions has been the point of interest during World War II [12,13]. Shock wave initiates when the speed of the wave exceeds the speed of sound in the meduim. It is characterized by the fact that across the shock regions, the gas properties like the pressure, the temperature, and the gas density increases drastically. The major cause for shock initiation is detonation, but sources could also be explosion or lighting. The study of shock waves is a key component in the field of aerospace and oil and gas industry as it could provide necessary information for designing better aircraft and safety equipment. Generation of a shock wave through detonation and its properties can be studied in [14].

Image processing technology has become a valuable tool in the field of gas combustion and fluid mechanics. However, most of the time, the use of images are limited to visualize the structure of the waves [12]. There is a lack of an image processing framework which manage to extract information of the wave properties. One challenging task is to capture this extremely high-speed phenomena. The generated waves propagate at a speed of 200 m/s and above, and the reactions of interest are completed within a microsecond. Therefore, a special high-speed camera designed for capturing these phenomena is needed. In addition, the high speed images from a gas experiment can vary rapidly from frame to frame due to the continuous chemical reaction, which demands a robust framework. In the past, a few work has been done based on numerical simulation and thermodynamic differential equations [15]. However, to obtain a tolerable accuracy using numerical models is a CPU demanding task. The main goal of the paper is to design a complete image processing framework, which pre-process/filter the images and automatically track the wave front in these images. The tracked fronts are then used to estimate the velocity of the wave.

The rest of the paper is organized as follows. Section 2 gives a brief description on the experimental setup for the generation of a shock wave. The methodology behind image filtering, front tracking and post processing is described in Sect. 3, which is followed by Sect. 4 in which the procedure for calculating velocity from the tracked fronts is presented. The results from the framework are shown in Sect. 5. Lastly, the conclusion and some possible further work is discussed in Sect. 6.

2   Experimental Set Up

The shock wave was generated in the laboratory using a pure CO_2 gas and a shock tube, with the initial pressure and temperature of 10 kPa and 274 K respectively. A shock tube is one of the most used and essential laboratory instrument for study of the fluid mechanics and gas combustion [16]. A shock tube typically is a closed tube that consists of two chambers, one with a high pressure known as the donor section and another with fairly low pressure known as the acceptor section. Figure 1 shows the schematic representation of a shock tube with its pressure distribution. The shock propagation is captured at the closed end of the acceptor section. Due to the boundary layer following behind the incoming shock, the reflected shock wave bends around the boundary creating an oblique shock. An oblique shock makes a certain angle with the boundary of the tube known as a shock angle. Hence, a single reflected shock wave can be divided into two parts: a normal shock and an oblique shock (see Fig. 2). This paper focus on the reflected shock wave, hence the notation 'shock wave' refers to the reflected shock wave onwards.

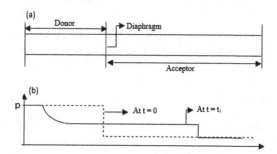

Fig. 1. (a) Schematic representation of the shock tube (b) pressure distribution along the tube at $t = 0$ and $t = t_1 \neq 0$.

Some of the images from the high speed film capturing the shock wave propagation are presented in Fig. 2. The growing of the oblique shock is clearly visible in the images. A shadowgraph system [17] is used for capturing the wave propagation.

3   Methodology

In this section, the four parts of the image processing framework are described. For simplicity, only the lower halves of the images are taken for further processing as the phenomena is almost identical at both the top and the bottom boundary.

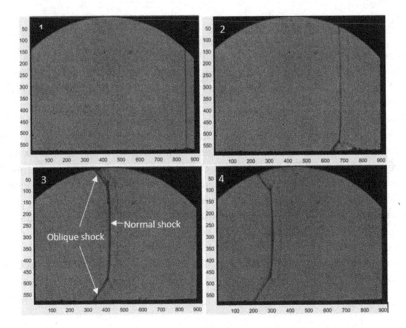

Fig. 2. Some of the raw images from the high speed film showing the reflected shock wave propagation. The shock wave travels from left to right, as shown in frames 1–4.

3.1 Pre-processing

The pre-processing of an image not only reduce the variations of noise present in the image, but also reduce the problem of over segmentation of an image. The pre-processing framework presented here consists of 3 steps. The first step is the background subtraction. An image was formed by making an average image based on all the images prior to the front propagation, and this image was then successively subtracted from all the images with a visual front. The background subtracted images are normalized to intensity level [0–1] in the second step. The third step is filtering of noise from the normalized image. The filtering is done by using the log transformation of the image followed by the $[2 \times 2]$ median filter [18].

3.2 Segmentation

The filtered image is changed into a binary image by using Otsu method [19] followed by the morphological operation 'closing'. The closing of the binary image [5] enhanced the edges of an object as well as filling the tiny gaps found close to the edges. The sequence of images in Fig. 3 shows the output from each step of the pre-processing operation of an image from the high speed film.

Generally, the watershed segmentation is not performed directly to the original image due to over segmentation. In this work, the distance transformed

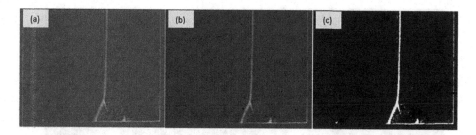

Fig. 3. (a) Background subtracted normalized image (b) filtered image (c) thresholded binary image.

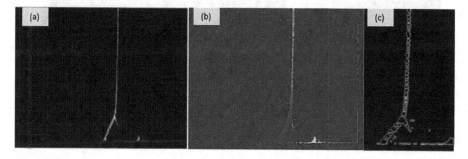

Fig. 4. (a) Distance transformed image (b) watershed output (c) morphologically removed image with initial contour.

image [20] is used for the segmentation. The distance transformed image is suitable when the edge of the object is diffuse, but visuable. Figure 4(a) and (b) respectively shows the distance transformed image and the output of the watershed transformation of Fig. 3. The watershed algorithm uses 8 neighbourhood pixels for the catchment building and consecutive flooding [21].

3.3 Front Tracking/Contouring

To represent of the front in the segmented image, the morphological operation 'remove' is done. This operation removes all the internal pixels in an object, but keep all the edge pixels unchanged [22]. By using a priori information of the direction of the wave propagation, a contour point is placed at the first position where the intensity value changes from 0 to 1. The search starts from the left to the right i.e. opposite direction of propagation. The points are tracked for all the rows and the contour is created by simply joining them. If the size of an image is $[m, n]$, the contour can now be represented as a vector of size $[m, 1]$. The initial contour plotted in the morphologically removed image is shown in Fig. 4(c).

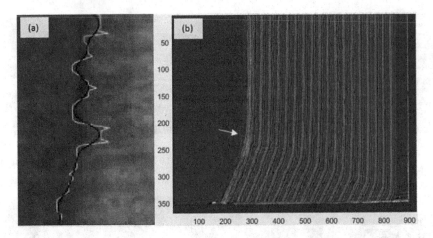

Fig. 5. (a) This subsection of the front is selected from the area pointed with a white arrow in (b), initial contour (green) and final smoothed contour (red). (b) final fronts from the high speed film tracked by the framework. (Color figure online)

3.4 Post Processing

It can be seen from Fig. 5(a) that the initial contour (green) has a ragged shape. Thus, a proper module for smoothing the curve was needed. By using a snake model [11], the smoothing was done locally using only on a few neighbouring points. A basic active contour model or snake model defined in [8] is a controlled continuity parametric curve, formed within an image, where the snake is initialized manually by set of x-y points. However, for this work the contour from the watershed segmentation is taken as an initial snake, eliminating any human interactions. By representing the position of the snake parametrically as $P(s) = (x(s), y(s))$, its energy function is defined as in (1)

$$E_{snake} = \int_s E_{int}(P(s)) + E_{ext}(P(s))ds. \tag{1}$$

The first term in (1), E_{int} is an internal energy and the second term, E_{ext} is the external energy function. An open active contour model developed in [11] which is used to smooth the curve. Figure 5(a) shows the contour from watershed (green) and the smoothed contour (red) by the snake model. It also shows convergence of the contour to the actual wave front around the pointed part in Fig. 5(b)). Figure 5(b) shows the 100 final fronts of the shock wave tracked by the designed framework in the sequence of images of a high-speed film.

4   Velocity Calculation

By estimating the displacement of the front in two frames combined with the framing frequency of a camera (which will give the time difference between the

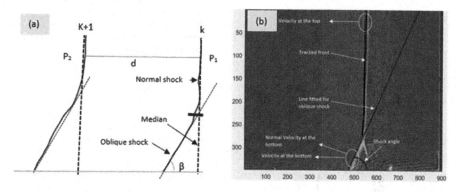

Fig. 6. (a) Schematic sketch of two consecutive fronts with the fitted lines, the median and the shock angle. (b) A raw image with actual tracked front and fitted line for the oblique shock. (Color figure online)

frames), the velocity can then be calculated. For the present work, the frequency of a camera is 500 kfps and the pixel to meter scaling is approx. 1 px = (0.0001 ± 5%) m. The velocity of a front at point $P_1 = (x_1, y_1)$ (x_1 and y_1 represents row and column) in image k can be estimated by using the point $P_2 = (x_1, y_2)$ of the front in the consecutive image $k + 1$. If a displacement is $d = | P_2 - P_1 |$, then velocity v will be,

$$v = \frac{d \times 0.0001}{0.2 \times 10^{-5}} m/s. \tag{2}$$

One of the raw image from the film with the tracked front (red) and the line formed for the oblique shock (blue) is shown in Fig. 6(b). The shock angle β can be estimated by forming a line (equation) for the oblique shock, therefore the contour needs to be divided into two sections; normal shock (upper) and oblique shock (lower). For this, a median of top 100 points of the tracked front (red) is used. The separating point is chosen to be situated where the front starts to deviate from a median in an increasing order. The equation for the oblique shock is formed by using all the points below the separating point shown in Fig. 6(b) by a blue line. Figure 6(b) also point out the desired calculations from the tracked front and the fitted line. The top and bottom velocities are calculated by taking 10 points on each of them (highlighted by an oval structure). The normal velocity is then estimated by using velocity at the bottom v and shock angle β i.e. $v \sin\beta$. The calculated velocity is then used to estimate the Mach number at that point. A Mach number M is the ratio between the velocity of the wave and the speed of sound in the medium. By using the Mach number along with the initial temperature and pressure, the final pressure and temperature can be estimated with the use of shock relationships. More about the Mach number, its importance and implementation along with the shock relationships can be found in [23].

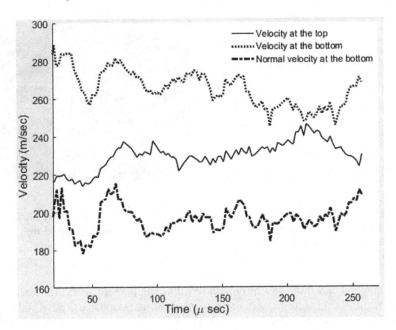

Fig. 7. Average velocity calculated for each frame at the top, bottom and average normal velocity at the bottom plotted along the time.

5   Results

The velocity at the top and the bottom of the front along with the normal velocity at the bottom as pointed in Fig. 6(b) are plotted in Fig. 7 for each front. Please notice that the time start from the first frame considered and is estimated from the frame rate of the camera which gives 2 μsec per frame.

The calculated average velocity is compared with the experimental results that was calculated from the readings of the pressure transducers. The method of calculating velocity and other thermodynamic properties from the pressure transducers and all the experimental results will be published in a separate publication (in progress). The results are also compared to the similar work done by using pattern matching and segmented regression in [24]. The overall comparison is shown in Table 1.

The comparison shows that the designed framework produces results within a necessary precision. The difference between the experimental result (pressure transducer readings) and the result from the framework is 11 m/s (top) and 1 m/s (bottom). The error of the framework due to misplacement of the contour by 1 pixel leads to deviation of approx. 5.23 m/s. Even though, individual velocity along the front may vary with the experimental value, overall average seems to match well (Fig. 8).

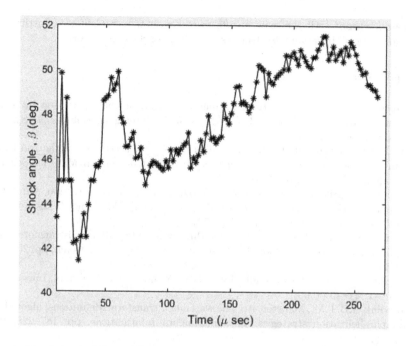

Fig. 8. Shock angle (β) at the foot of all the tracked fronts plotted along the time.

Table 1. Comparison between results from different methods.

Exp.no		Average velocity at the top	Average velocity at the bottom	Av. Shock angle (degree)
2516	Pressure transducer results	216 m/s	266 m/s	48
	Results from [24]	229 m/s	262 m/s	50
	Results from the designed framework	227 m/s	267 m/s	48.9

6 Conclusion and Further Work

From the results presented in Sect. 5, it can be concluded that the designed framework produces results in accordance with the pressure transducer measurements. Furthermore, the velocity at each point along the front can now be calculated by using the process described in Sect. 4. The procedure and results of estimating thermodynamic properties of gas like the Mach number, the pressure and temperature ratios by using this framework will be presented in a different publication [25].

Acknowledgment. All the experiments were conducted at California Institute of Technology in collaboration with University College of Southeast Norway.

References

1. Beucher, S., Bilodeau, M.: Road segmentation and obstacle detection by a fast watershed transformation. In: Proceedings of the Intelligent Vehicles '94 Symposium, pp. 296–301 (1994)
2. Digabel, H., Lantuéjoul, C.: Iterative algorithms. In: Proceedings of the 2nd European Symposium Quantitative Analysis of Microstructures in Material Science, Biology and Medicine, pp. 85–89 (1978)
3. Beucher, S., Bilodeau, M.: Use of watersheds in contour detection. In: International Workshop on Image Processing: Real-Time Edge and Motion Detection/Estimation, France, pp. 17–21 (1979)
4. Beucher, S., Centre De Morphologie Mathmatique: The watershed transformation applied to image segmentation. In: Scanning Microscopy International, pp. 299–314 (1991)
5. Beucher, S., Meyer, F.: Morphological segmentation. J. Vis. Commun. Image Represent. **1**, 21–46 (1990)
6. Roerdink, J.B.T.M., Meijster, A.: The watershed transform: definitions, algorithms and parallelization strategies. In: Fundamenta Informaticae, pp. 187–228. IOS Press (2001)
7. Vincent, L., Soille, P.: Watersheds in digital spaces: an efficient algorithm based on immersion simulations. IEEE Trans. Pattern Anal. Mach. Intell. **13**, 583–598 (1991)
8. Kass, M., Witkin, A., Terzopoulos, D.: Snakes: active contour models. Int. J. Comput. Vis. **1**, 321–331 (1988)
9. Terzopoulos, D., Fleischer, K.: Deformable models. Visual Comput. **4**, 306–331 (1988)
10. Peterfreund, N.: Robust tracking of position and velocity with Kalman snakes. IEEE Trans. Pattern Anal. Mach. Intell. **21**, 583–598 (1999)
11. Maharjan, S., Gaathaug, A.V., Lysaker, O.M.: Open active contour model for front tracking of detonation waves. In: Proceedings of the 58th Conference on Simulation and Modelling, pp. 174–179. Linköping University Electronic Press, Linköping (2017)
12. Mark, H.: The Interaction of a Reflected Shock Wave with the Boundary Layer in a Shock Tube. Cornell University, Ithaca (1958)
13. Courant, R., Friedrichs, K.O.: Supersonic Flow and Shock Waves. Interscience Publishers, New York (1948)
14. Nikiforakis, N., Clarke, J.F.: Numerical studies of the evolution of detonations. Math. Comput. Model. **24**, 149–164 (1996)
15. Glimm, J., Grove, J.W., Li, X.L., Zhao, N.: Simple front tracking. In: Contemporary Mathematics, pp. 133–149 (1999)
16. Glass, I.I., Patterson, G.N.: A theoretical and experimental study of the shock tube. J. Aeronaut. Sci. **22**, 73–100 (1955)
17. Settle, G.H.: Schlieren and Shadowgraph Techniques: Visualizing Phenomena in Transparent Media. Springer, Berlin (2001). https://doi.org/10.1007/978-3-642-56640-0
18. Lim, J.S.: Two-Dimensional Signal and Image Processing. Prentice-Hall Inc., Upper Saddle River (1990)

19. Otsu, N.: A threshold selection method from gray-level histograms. IEEE Trans. Syst. Man Cybern. **9**, 62–66 (1979)
20. Paglieroni, D.W.: Distance transforms: properties and machine vision applications. CVGIP: Graph. Models Image Process. **54**, 56–74 (1992)
21. Meyer, F.: Topographic distance and watershed lines. Signal Process. **38**, 113–125 (1994)
22. Gonzalez, C.R., Woods, E.R.: Digital Image Processing. Prentice-Hall, Upper Saddle River (2000)
23. Law, C.K.: Combustion Physics. Cambridge University Press, New York (2010)
24. Siljan, E., Maharjan, S., Lysaker, M.: Wave front tracking using template matching and segmented regression. In: Proceedings of the 58th Conference on Simulation and Modelling, pp. 326–331. Linköping University Electronic Press, Linköping (2017)
25. Maharjan, S., Bjerketvedt, D., Lysaker, O.M.: Estimation of Mach Number and Wave Properties of a Reflected Shock Using Image Processing (in process)

The Algorithm and Software for Timber Batch Measurement by Using Image Analysis

Andrey V. Mehrentsev[1] and Artem V. Kruglov[2(✉)]

[1] Ural State Forest Engineering University,
Sibirsky Tract, 37, 620100 Yekaterinburg, Russia
mehrentsev@yandex.ru
[2] Ural Federal University, Mira Street, 19, 620004 Yekaterinburg, Russia
avkruglov@urfu.ru

Abstract. This paper is devoted to the investigation and development of the round timber batch measurement technique on the basis of abuts detection and calculation of their diameters. The algorithm of abuts contours detection and refinement relies on the modified radial symmetry object detection. The meanshift clustering, Delaunay triangulation, Boruvka's minimum spanning tree algorithm, watershed and Boykov-Kolmogorov graph cut algorithm are implemented at the further stages of the algorithm. The testing of the algorithm gives its TPR value at 96.2% which is much higher than other unsupervised training methods. The software for the round timber batch volume measurement was developed on the base of the algorithm. An error of the software measurement in comparison with manual piece-by-piece approach is less than 7.07% with an average error of 4.9%. It meets the requirements of industry standards so the offered technique can be successfully applied in the activity of forest enterprises.

Keywords: Round timber · Volume measurement · Photogrammetry ·
Abut detection · Image processing · Radial symmetry · Mobile application

1 Introduction

The problem of the accurate accounting of raw materials and products is one of the most significant in respect to a constant struggle to minimize production costs. There are many different methods of measuring the timber volume, which differ from each other both in terms of physical principles and methods of volume management. The peculiarity of round timber is a high level of measurement error, which leads to a shortage or surplus in the revision of timber residues in warehouses and fluctuations in the consumption of timber during processing. Most methods for measuring the volume of round timber were developed more than 60 years ago [1]: piece-by-piece volume measurement, geometric group measurement, weight group measurement, etc.

The idea of the given method is to obtain the images of the timber batch ends with further processing of the photography by specialized software. During the image processing, the software produces:

– automatic detection of all visible abuts in each image;
– reconstruction of the 3D spatial structure of the timber batch;

– calculation of the quantitative characteristics of each log and a batch as a whole.

The software for the mobile measurement of the round timber is designed on the basis of the described method and suitable for calculating a volume and geometry of timber batches. The software is designed to conduct operations with maximum possible automatic performance, however, the tools for manual editing of the processing result are also provided. The flow chart of the software processing is given in Fig. 1.

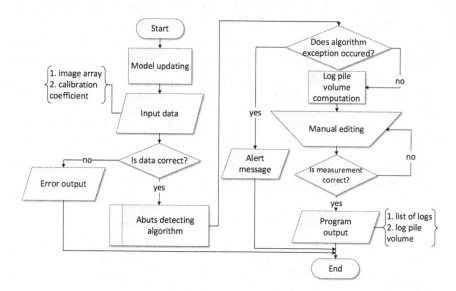

Fig. 1. Software processing flow chart.

2 Development of the Algorithm for the Automatic Abut Detection

As far as the algorithm for the automatic detection of the log abuts is the key feature of the software and the method in all it will be described more thoroughly within this paper.

The problem of the log abuts detection in the images was observed in several researches [2–6], and some of them have found practical implementation as a part of the applicable measuring system [5, 6]. Presented in those papers detection techniques could be divided into two categories. First group includes methods based on the machine learning. In [4] Herbon et al. describe the iterative algorithm for detection and segmentation which uses the descriptors of interest points based on histogram of oriented gradients (HOG) [7] in combination with Haar features and local binary patterns (LBP) at the stage of the log abut detection. Gutzeit and Voskamp in [3] applied Viola-Jones algorithm means for implementation of the cascade of the classifiers where each of them is the assembly of weak classifiers; the features for the detection algorithm are the rectangular Haar ones. Second group are the unsupervised training methods which used the assumptions of the form and size of logs [2, 6]. In general, these methods are based on the Hough transform [8–11] or its modifications and used to detect log abuts in the image in the form of circles or ellipses.

In the context of the given task the most appropriate detection method in terms of the computational cost and requirements to the possible distortions of the target objects is the one based on the evaluation of the fast radial symmetry transformation [12]. This method show high efficiency for the images with a priory known radii, low level of the form distortions and upon condition that the searching radii spread in a small range. However, it has some disadvantages that should be eliminated:

– The signal/noise ratio of the cumulative accumulator is significantly reduced with a large range of radii, resulting in complicacy of the potential circle centers detecting;
– Necessity of scanning the output for each radius after detecting of the potential circle centers in full transform output to compare responses in detected points for radii refinement.
– Choosing the optimal threshold for analyzing the spikes of the full transform output for specific image.

Thus for the abuts detection task the modification of the radial symmetry object detection method was implemented in reliance on the above (see Fig. 2).

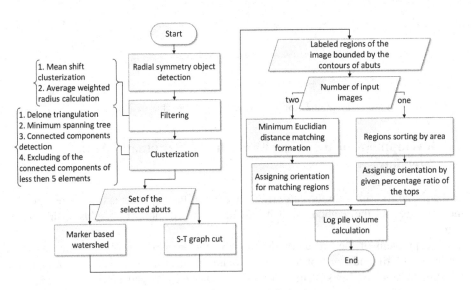

Fig. 2. Algorithm control-flow chart.

2.1   Object Detection

The detection stage involves the finding in the image all possible target objects which meet a number of criteria. The aim of the detection is to obtain the primary input data about measuring objects and select the necessary sets of features for further classification and segmentation. Analysis of the considerable number of the batch images shows that the most abuts have approximately circular form (Fig. 3).

a   b

Fig. 3. Examples of the timber batch images.

The magnitude projection image is not constructed as far as detector decisions are made on the basis of the modified orientation projection image analysis. First stage of the detection is the Sobel operator implementation for the boundary pixels recognition, which estimates the magnitude and the direction of gradient vector. The voting boundary pixels are the ones with the high value of the gradient magnitude. After that the gradient vector direction is estimated for each boundary pixel in order to calculate the center of circle of the specific radius.

At second stage the search of the local maximum in the orientation projection is implemented. The algorithm splits the set of search radii into non-overlapping ranges to provide invariance to the image scale and target objects form distortions. Each range covers the specific scale interval and has its own size of the filter. It was decided to calculate the specific size of the scanned aperture as function of search radius according to the formula:

$$A_r = \begin{cases} [\log_{10} Sq_r] & for\ odds \\ [\log_{10} Sq_r] + 1 & otherwise \end{cases} \tag{1}$$

where [] – integral part of a number, Sq_r - area of the circle of radius r.

The idea of the optimal threshold selection is that it can be evaluated from the result of the algorithm implementation to the image of the same size and brightness arrangement as the initial one but containing no radial symmetry objects. The value of the optimal threshold depends on initial image entropy, thereat the threshold for the segmentation of the initial image orientation projection can be selected as following:

$$T_r = \max(\tilde{O}_r) + A_r^2 \tag{2}$$

where $\max(\tilde{O}_r)$ – global maximum of the «noise» projection image scanned by A_r.

A_r in the formula (1) can be interpreted as correction scale coefficient. The descriptor of the region of interest of specific radius r with the scale invariance is calculated as following

$$D_r(x, y) = O_r(x, y) - T_r \qquad (3)$$

where $O_r(x, y)$ – local maximum with coordinates (x, y) in the projection image of radius r scanning with aperture A_r, T_r – optimal threshold for the radius r.

Thus the offered method solves two problems: the search of the target objects with radial symmetry and the computation of their descriptors with scale invariance. It means that the value of the interest point for orientation projection of radius r_1 is the same as the local maximum in accumulator of radius $r_2 (r_1 \neq r_2)$. The greater the value of the descriptor (weight of the object) the more accurate the target object form matches the circle. This approach allows selection of the best candidates among the obtained objects. The result of the modified detection algorithm is shown in Fig. 4a and c. Inasmuch as cross-correlation of the near-by search radii has negative impact on the result (there are many overlapping circles in the Fig. 4a and c) as well as prominent medulla of the abuts, the filter function should be introduced.

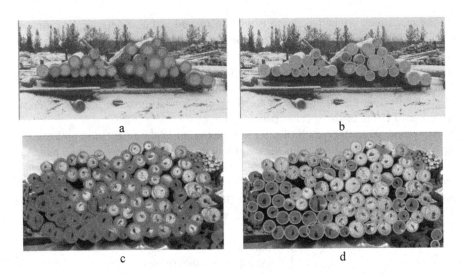

a

b

c

d

Fig. 4. Implementation of the modified detection algorithm

The meanshift clustering [13] is implemented to the output transform of the modified detection algorithm. The average weighted radius is calculated for each cluster:

$$r_{aw} = \sum_{i=1}^{n} r_i \cdot \omega_i / \sum \omega_i \qquad (4)$$

where n – cluster cardinality, ω_i – weight function: $\omega_i = l_{r_i} \cdot n_{r_i}$
where l_{r_i} – radius, n_{r_i} – number of radius of given length in the cluster.
Result of the filtration is shown in Fig. 4b and d.

2.2   Clustering

Clustering solves the problem of grouping the set of the objects obtained at the previous stage into the disjoint subsets of the target and nontarget objects. For the problem of the timber batch volume measurement the aim is to divide the detected objects into two subsets – «batch» and «non-batch». In such a way the image regions which are selected at the detection stage but not related to the target objects will be excluded before the segmentation and measuring.

Firstly it is necessary to construct the feature set and metrics based on the purpose of the clustering. The useful assumption is that the logs in a batch displayed in a feature space as a closely adjacent points. It is evident that the closer objects to each other the higher probability of their belonging to the same group. Thus the geometrical similarity metric (log density) was introduced to solve the clustering problem. This metric defines weather the log belongs to the batch or not. Among the existing clustering methods [14] the graph one was selected due to its clarity and simplicity.

The following algorithm is implemented to the set of the detected objects:

1. Iterative Delaunay triangulation [15] with dynamic caching [16],
2. Finding the minimum spanning tree through Borůvka's algorithm [17];
3. Cut of the tree along edges until the condition (5) is reached.

$$\max_{(v,u)\in E} c(v, u) < 2 \cdot \max(r_{aw}) \tag{5}$$

where E – set of the graph edges, $c(v, u)$ – weight of the edge (its length in this case), r_{aw} – the average weighted radius (4)

4. The criteria for the obtained connected components $G(V_i)$ to be included into the final sample $G(V)$ is the following:

$$G(V) = \bigcup G(V_i) : |G(V_i)| \geq 5 \tag{6}$$

The result of the clustering is shown in Fig. 5.

a   b

Fig. 5. Structure of the batch determined by the graph algorithm.

2.3   Segmentation

Segmentation is carried out to refine the contour of each abut and to extract feature set for further timber batch volume measurement. The segmentation algorithm relies on the combination of two methods: marker-based watershed [18] and Boykov-Kolmogorov algorithm of the minimum s-t graph cut [19]. Watershed algorithm is used to specify the regions where abuts are located. At that an approximate boundary of each object is known as far as it is the average weighted radius r_{cp} that should be rectified.

For min-cut/max-flow algorithm the area for source node selected within less than $1/2\,r_{aw_i}$ whereas the sink node area is farther than $3/2\,r_{aw_i}$ from mass center d_i. The conclusive region corresponding with abut in the image is determined by the combination of the watershed and s-t cut outputs:

$$G(V)_i = G(S)_i \bigcap W_i \tag{7}$$

where $G(V)_i$ – region of the abut i, $G(S)_i$ – region of the abut i according to the s-t cut output, W – watershed basin containing marker i.

3   Manual Editing

After the automatic algorithm execution some abuts may be undetected while other objects in the image may be detected incorrectly, so the manual editing should be implemented. In order to add new object in the image the tool "+" should be selected. Then the new object will be added after clicking in the image area. Deleting of the objects is implemented by selecting "–" tool and clicking objects in the image. In order to exit from current mode user should click the active tool again. Addition of the objects is implemented on the basis of the Lee algorithm [20]. Also manual editing allows user to resize objects when they are activated. In this case the anchor points of the ellipse become available so user can stretch, rotate or relocate it. Also the tools for additional log parameters adjusting become available: abut number, timber species, log length and orientation (see Fig. 6).

Automatic orientation (top or butt) is assigned for each abut according to the following rules:

In case of two images processing the orientation is determined by comparison of two abuts for each log and bigger one is labeled as butt whereas smaller – as top.

In case of one image processing orientation is assigned selectively on the basis of the area of the image regions related to abuts and specified percentage ration of the top abuts. In this mode the manual editing of the orientation is provided: after the particular abut is selected the tools "Top" and "Butt" (displayed as letters "K" and "B" respectively, see Fig. 6) are appeared in the workspace and user can assign the orientation of the abut.

Fig. 6. Manual editing tools for specific abut: abut number, timber species, log length and orientation

4 Testing and Results

The testing of the algorithm was carried out on the tablet Samsung Galaxy Tab 3 GT0P5210 16 Gb 10,1". Requirements to the picture taking are the following: camera is parallel to the abuts plane, the batch is located at the center of the frame with space between the frame edge and the nearest abut. There were 940 measurement of the 632 piles under the different conditions during the algorithm testing.

Results of the testing show that the offered algorithm based on the modified radial symmetry detection method reaches higher performance in comparison with methods based on linear classifiers and weak classifiers cascades. Also the offered algorithm is outperformed the methods based on Hough transformation (see Table 1).

Table 1. Comparison of the methods

Method	TPR (σTPR), %	Method	TPR (σTPR), %
LBP [4]	95,8(3,7)	LBP+HAAR+HOG [4]	98,4(2,1)
HOG [4]	77,9(10)	CHT+LCM [3]	90,8(9,4)
LBP+HOG [4]	96,0(3,1)	CHT [3]	84,8(11,6)
HAAR [4]	95,1(3,8)	LCM [3]	89,7(9,8)
HAAR+HOG [4]	96,0(3,5)	**Our**	**96,2(4,1)**

On the other hand the algorithm is inferior to the methods described in [4] when the last are strengthened by the combined classifiers and considered the abuts textural information. In spite of high rate of TPR this method has much higher computational complexity which is sensitive for its implementation for mobile devices.

After the analyzing of the algorithm output the results of the round timber batch measurement manually edited by the software tools were compared against piece-by-piece measurement (see Fig. 7).

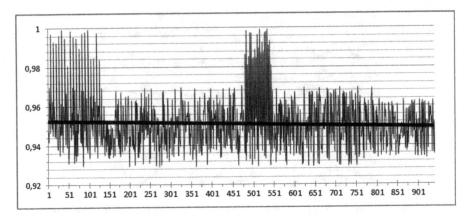

Fig. 7. Relative accuracy of the algorithm output in comparison with manual piece-by-piece measurement.

5 Conclusion

As a result of the proposed methodology, the measurements of the round timber will be made faster in comparison with other approaches (manual measurement, weighing), whereas their results will become more reliable (re-verification of the measurement, reducing the possibility of falsification). Mobility and speed of the given solution allow user to perform measurements in places of logging, on the truck, during the shipment-acceptance or sending for further processing. That is, to account for raw materials at every stage of its life cycle. Implementation of the developed software makes it possible to automate previously unavailable parts of the production process, which leads to higher labor discipline of personnel, lower costs for traditional (paper) communications between company divisions (an average of 67%) [21] and a decrease in the time of accounting operations (an average of 36%, in the range from 0 to 90%).

The maximum error of the software for the timber batch volume measurement is less than 7.07% with an average error of 4.9% (see Fig. 7). The tolerance of the measurement of the same batch from the different viewpoints is less than 1%. Thus, the method of the timber batch measurement using the developed algorithm can be successfully applied in the activity of forest enterprises as far as industry standards establish the maximum volume measurement error for the round timber accounting in the range between ±3% and ±12%.

References

1. Samoylov, A.N.: Classification and determination of the major trends in round timber measurement. Sci. J. KybGAU **24**(8), 114–120 (2006)
2. Galsgaard, B., Lundtoft, D.H., Nikolov, I., Nasrollahi, K., Moeslund, T.B.: Circular hough transform and local circularity measure for weight estimation of a graph-cut based wood stack measurement. In: IEEE Winter Conference on Applications of Computer Vision, Waikoloa, HI, pp. 686–693 (2015)

3. Gutzeit, E., Voskamp, J.: Automatic segmentation of wood logs by combining detection and segmentation. In: Bebis, G., et al. (eds.) ISVC 2012. LNCS, vol. 7431, pp. 252–261. Springer, Heidelberg (2012). https://doi.org/10.1007/978-3-642-33179-4_25
4. Herbon, C., Tönnies, K., Stock, B.: Detection and segmentation of clustered objects by using iterative classification, segmentation, and gaussian mixture models and application to wood log detection. In: Jiang, X., Hornegger, J., Koch, R. (eds.) GCPR 2014. LNCS, vol. 8753, pp. 354–364. Springer, Cham (2014). https://doi.org/10.1007/978-3-319-11752-2_28
5. Knyaz, V.A., Maksimov, A.A.: Photogrammetric technique for timber stack volume control. Int. Arch. Photogram. Remote Sens. Spat. Inf. Sci. **XL-3**, 157–162 (2014)
6. Knyaz, V.A., Vizilter, Y., Zheltov, S.Yu.: Photogrammetric techniques for measurements in woodworking industry. Int. Arch. Photogram. Remote Sens. Spat. Inf. Sci. Proc. **XXXIII**, 42–47 (2004). Part B5/2
7. Misra, A., Takashi, A., Okatani, T., Deguchi, K.: Hand gesture recognition using histogram of oriented gradients and partial least squares regression. In: MVA2011, IAPR Conference on Machine Vision Applications; Nara, Japan (2011)
8. Cheng, H.D., Guo, Y., Zhang, Y.: A novel Hough transform based on eliminating particle swarm optimization and its applications. Pattern Recogn. **42**(9), 1959–1969 (2009)
9. Cauchie, J., Fiolet, V., Villers, D.: Optimization of an Hough transform algorithm for the search of a center. Pattern Recogn. **41**(2), 567–574 (2008)
10. Mochizuki, Y., Torii, A., Imiya, A.: N-point hough transform for line detection. J. Vis. Commun. Image Represent. **20**(4), 242–253 (2009)
11. Fornaciari, M., Prati, A., Cucchiara, R.: A fast and effective ellipse detector for embedded vision applications. Pattern Recogn. **47**(11), 3693–3708 (2014)
12. Loy, G., Zelinsky, A.: Fast radial symmetry for detecting points of interest. IEEE Trans. PAMI **25**(8), 959–973 (2003)
13. Comaniciu, D., Meer, P.: Mean shift: a robust approach toward feature space analysis. IEEE Trans. PAMI **24**(5), 603–619 (2002)
14. Mandel, I.D., Klasternyy Analiz, M.: Finansy i Statistika, 186 p. (1988)
15. Skvortsov, A.V.: Triangulyatsiya Delone i ee primenenie. Tomsk: Izd-vo Tom. un-ta, 128 p. (2002)
16. Skvortsov, A.V., Mirza, N.S.: Algoritmy postroeniya i analiza triangulyatsii. – Tomsk: Izdvo Tom.un-ta, 168 p. (2006)
17. Erzin, A.I., Kochetov, Yu.A.: Zadachi marshrutizatsii: ucheb. posobie/Novosib. gos. un-t. – Novosibirsk: RITsNGU, 95 p. (2014)
18. Roerdink, J.B.T.M., Meijster, A.: The watershed transform: definitions, algorithms and parallelization strategies. Fundamenta Informaticae **41**, 187–228 (2001)
19. Boykov, Y., Kolmogorov, V.: An experimental comparison of min-cut/max-flow algorithms for energy minimization in vision. IEEE Trans. PAMI **26**(9), 1124–1137 (2004)
20. Cormen, T.H., Leiserson, C.E., Rivest, R.L., Stein, C.: Introduction to Algorithms, 3rd edn. The MIT Press, Cambridge (2009)
21. The Benefits of MES: A Report from the Field. MESA International. http://www.cpdee.ufmg.br/~seixas/PaginaII/Download/DownloadFiles/pap1.pdf. Access 21 Feb 2017

Deep Learning on Image and Shape Data

Stereo Matching Confidence Learning Based on Multi-modal Convolution Neural Networks

Zehua Fu[(✉)], Mohsen Ardabilian, and Guillaume Stern

Universite de Lyon - Ecole Centrale de Lyon, LIRIS UMR 5205,
69134 Lyon, France
zehua.fu@doctorant.ec-lyon.fr,
{mohsen.ardabilian,guillaume.stern}@ec-lyon.fr

Abstract. In stereo matching, the correctness of stereo pairs matches, also called confidence, is used to improve the dense disparity estimation result. In this paper, we propose a multi-modal deep learning approach for stereo matching confidence estimation. To predict the confidence, we designed a Convolutional Neural Network (CNN), which is trained on image patches from multi-modal data, namely the source image pairs and initial disparity maps. To the best of our knowledge, this is the first approach reported in the literature combining multiple modality and patch based deep learning to predict the confidence. Furthermore, we explore and compare the confidence prediction ability of multiple modality data. Finally, we evaluate our network architecture on KITTI data sets. The experiments demonstrate that our multi-modal confidence network can achieve competitive results while compared with the state-of-the-art methods.

1 Introduction

Stereo matching is a fundamental problem in stereo vision. For two images of different views on the same scene, taken by cameras with horizontal displacement, the task of stereo matching is to find the corresponding pixels between the left and right images. The distance between the corresponding points is called disparity and the set of all disparities in the image is called disparity map. Despite decades of improvement, stereo matching still suffers from various issues, such as occlusion, ambiguity and extreme lighting conditions, which lead to incorrect stereo matches. In order to improve dense disparity estimation, several methods have been proposed to rate the correctness of matches. These methods are also called confidence measures.

According to the taxonomy proposed by Scharstein and Szeliski [1], stereo matching algorithms perform the following four steps (or subset of them): (1) Matching cost computation; (2) Cost aggregation; (3) Disparity computation/optimization and (4) Disparity refinement. The framework above produce several different types of data, including inputs and intermediate results, such

© Springer Nature Switzerland AG 2019
L. Chen et al. (Eds.): RFMI 2017, CCIS 842, pp. 69–81, 2019.
https://doi.org/10.1007/978-3-030-19816-9_6

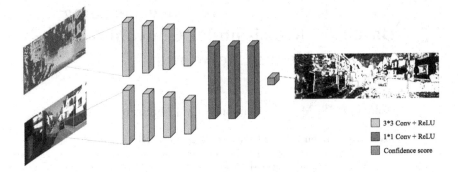

Fig. 1. The architecture of the proposed RGBD-LFN. By given two patches of different modalities including initial disparity map and RGB image, our goal is to estimate the confidence to correct matches on the current center pixel of patches. (Color figure online)

as input RGB image pairs, matching cost volumes (MCVs) and initial disparity maps (IDMs), which are achieved by directly applying Winner Take All (WTA) strategy after matching cost computation. In early studies of confidence measures, approaches were designed and examined to estimate the reliability of corresponding matches in stereo matching [2–4]. From the perspective of the used data type, manually designed measures can be categorized into three groups: (1) Confidence measures based on MCVs. In this category most approaches are related to the minimum, the second minimum matching cost, or a combination of them, e.g. Naive Peak Ratio (PKRN), Maximum Likehood Measure (MLM) and Left-Right Difference (LRD). (2) Confidence measures utilizing IDMs. Can be found in this category, approaches such as Left-Right Consistency (LRC), Variance of the Disparity Values (VAR) and the Median Deviation of Disparity Values (MDD). (3) Confidence measures employing source images pairs. As few approaches in this category, we give, as example, Magnitude of the Image Gradients Measure.

Hand-crafted confidence measures such as PKRN, MLM perform well on correct matches detection [4] but they have some weaknesses. They should be designed carefully with expertise and knowledge on stereo matching. Besides, most of them are only well suited for certain challenges. For example, Matching Score Measure (MSM) is the best choice for occlusion detection, while it has poor performance near discontinuities [4].

To alleviate the weakness of separate measures, some authors [5–8] focus on feature combination approaches. Both Ensemble [5] and GCP [6] selected several confidence measures as feature vectors and applied random forests to train a regression classifier. After that, Park and Yoon [7] analyzed the specialty of various confidence measures and selected the effective ones by permutation importance through a regression forest framework. Then with the feature vectors of selected measures, they trained another random forest and used it to predict the confidence of correct correspondence. Their experimental results proved that the proposed regression forest could effectively select important confidence measures and their confidence estimation method outperformed method Ensemble [5] and GCP [6]. More recently, Poggi and Mattoccia [9] explored hand-crafted features for streaking detection in stereo matching. They proposed an ensemble classifier trained by feature vectors similar to [5–8] while achieved better results with time complexity of O(1).

Although joint features used for learning are thoughtfully formulated and selected, it is hard to make sure that all discriminating information has been taken into consideration. Recently, convolutional neural networks (CNNs) became popular in computer vision tasks because of their outstanding feature learning abilities [10–13]. CNNs were first introduced to confidence prediction of correct matches in stereo matching by Zhong et al. [14]. They proposed a siamese network [15] architecture, with two weight-shared sub-networks for both left and right image patches respectively for feature extraction. Following [14], Seki and Pollefeys [16] designed a 2-channel input patches for CNN based confidence learning. The design of input patches was inspired by left right consistency (LRC) measure with an assumption that the consistently matched pixels are correct. At the same time, Poggi and Mattoccia [17] proposed a patch-based CNN, learn confidence features of centre pixels by square patches from disparity maps.The experimental results indicate that both methods above are more efficient than the method proposed by Park and Yoon [7]. After that, Poggi et Mattoccia [18] proposed a deep learning based methodology to improve the effectiveness of the current top-performing confidence methods. Their experiments of 23 state-of-the-art confidence measures on three datasets discovered the local consistency in confidence map and demonstrated that this property can be learned by a deep network. Recently, Poggi et al. [19] summarized state-of-the-art stereo confidence measures and updated their review and quantitative evaluation based on Hu and Mordohai's work [4].

The contribution of this paper is mainly twofold. (1) we explore the confidence prediction ability of different types of data in stereo matching (e.g. source image pairs, MCVs and IDMs); (2) propose a novel CNN method which utilizes multi-modal data, including IDMs and referenced RGB images, as inputs. We explore and study two types of multi-modal CNNs on detecting disparity errors in stereo matching. Experimental results prove that our multi-modal approach can reach the state-of-the-art result on both KITTI2012 and KITTI2015 dataset.

The rest of this paper is organized as follows. Section 2 discusses how we select input data from stereo matching procedure, then describes two types of designed networks. Section 3 presents experimental results of confidence accuracy on challenging datasets and analyzes the results of different performances while comparing with other methods. Section 4 draws the conclusion to this paper.

2   Proposed Method

In this section, we will begin with the background of proposed methods. Then we will discuss which types of stereo data can be used to train CNN networks

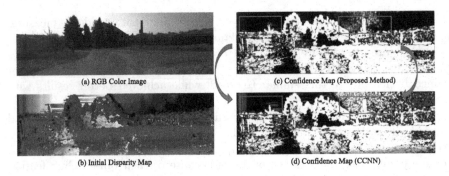

(a) RGB Color Image
(c) Confidence Map (Proposed Method)

(b) Initial Disparity Map
(d) Confidence Map (CCNN)

Fig. 2. Confidence quality result comparison of CCNN [17] and our proposed method on K12 Frame 99. Black pixels in (c) and (d) are considered as low confidence points.

for confidence estimation. For more than one modalities, there are several ways to construct networks and combine features. Therefore, we explore and test two kinds of models. Besides, training details will be mentioned at the end of this section.

2.1 Background

From the observation that the state-of-art confidence CNNs [16,17] are all using disparity maps as inputs while there are several different kinds of data available in the stereo matching framework. In the early experiments, we trained the CNNs from patches of each data type that mentioned in Sect. 1. The structure of CNNs we used here are similar to Fig. 3(a). From the results, we found that patches from both the entire matching cost volumes, patches combined minimum and second minimum matching cost as 2-channels almost do not have the ability to predict confidence, as these models did not converge in training stage. However, the latter one achieves good performance while producing manual features such as PKRN. We also found that CNN trained by initial IDM patches is equipped with high ability to differentiate incorrect matches while CNN trained by RGB image patches only have a very weak capacity (Fig. 2).

Based on those observations, we trained a multi-modal Network to locate the error matches in IDMs. As shown in Fig. 1, for every pixel in an IDM, we extract patches centered at current pixel both from IDM and related RGB image, then forward it to our MN, predicting the match correctness of current pixel.

2.2 Deep Network Architecture

According to Sect. 2.1, the initial disparity patches with one channel and its referenced RGB image patches with three channels are considered to be the inputs of the neural network. We explore two architectures with different fusion stages and fusion methods.

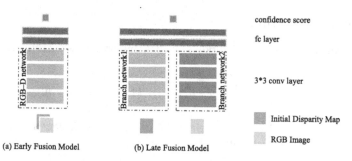

(a) Early Fusion Model   (b) Late Fusion Model

Fig. 3. Two architectures designed by different fusion stage. Architecture (a) is an early fusion structure which using RGB-Disparity 4-channel patches as input. For architecture (b), the features of two modalities are trained separately by two CNN branches without sharing weight. Then, the extracted features have a late fusion and forward to a decision network. (Color figure online)

RGB-D Early Fusion Network (RGBD_EFN): This type of network simply considers IDM and referenced RGB image of an input pair as a 4-channel image. As shown in Fig. 3(a), the network only has one branch during feature extraction, consisting of several convolutional and rectified linear unit(ReLU) layers. The following decision module consists simply of a number of fully connected layers with one output as the feature fusion network.

RGB-D Late Fusion Network (RGBD_LFN): As shown in Fig. 3(b), it contains two sub-networks composed by convolutional layers and ReLU layers. The sub-networks extract feature vectors separately without sharing weights as siamese networks do, as we want to learn specific features of input data crossing domains. After being simply fused, the extracted feature vectors are forward propagated through several units of fully connected layers followed by ReLU layers. The last fully connected layer is followed by a sigmoid criterion to normalize the final result between 0 and 1, namely our confidence measure.

For both two networks above, each network has the fully connected (FC) layers. These FC layers will be replaced by fully convolutional layers with 1×1 kernels following Zbontar et LeCun [20]. We take the advantage that for those fully convolutional layers as the input size are not limited during test stage. So that we can predict the confidence of a sample through single forward pass rather than predicting patch by patch throughout the whole image. Besides, we also add paddings to all convolution layers to keep the size of images during prediction.

2.3 Details of Learning

Optimization. We train all models with a binary cross-entropy (BCE) loss term,

$$Loss_{BCE} = -\sum_{i=1}^{N}(y_i \cdot log(\hat{y}_i) + (1-t) \cdot log(1-\hat{y}_i)) \tag{1}$$

where y_i is the ground truth of i-th training sample, defining by the absolute difference from IDM to ground truth disparity map, $y_i \in \{0,1\}$. $\hat{y}_i$ is the network output for the i-th training sample.

All networks are trained by mini-batch stochastic gradient descent (Mini-batch SGD) with batch-size, momentum term set to 128, 0.9 respectively. We trained for 15 epochs with the learning rate set to 0.003 at the beginning and decreased to 0.0003 at 11-th epoch. Weights are initialized by Xavier initialization method [21].

Preprecessing. During data preparation, patches size was set to 9×9. The number of convolution layers is set to 4. The number of fully connected layers and decision residual blocks are set to 3. In convolution layers, filter size is set to 3×3 with no padding. It is noteworthy that we just kept patches with valid non-occlusion disparity ground truth. For labeling the training data, the ground truth of confidence was set according to the central pixel disparity of the patch, as shown in Fig. 1. Before sending to the network, we normalized each channel of RGB images and IDMs to $[0,1]$.

All networks were implemented with torch7 [22] and cuDNN library [23].

3 Experiments

In this section, we introduce the challenging dataset and the evaluation methods we used at the very beginning. Then we design two experiments to evaluate proposed algorithms. In the first one, we compare the performance of the two proposed multi-modal confidence architectures. After that, we compare our best architecture with several state-of-the-art confidence methods. In the last experiment, we explored how training set size influences the confidence prediction accuracy.

3.1 KITTI Datasei

We evaluate the performance of our method on the KITTI 2012 (K12) dataset [24,25] and KITTI 2015 (K15) dataset [26]. K12 and K15 contain images from scenarios with varying weather conditions of a mid-size city, including rural areas and highways. The acquisition of K12 and K15 datasets were managed by two cameras (each of them has two units to capture the color images and grayscale images separately) settled on the top of a moving car, with a distance of 54 cm roughly. The stereo benchmark of K12 dataset consists of 194 training and 194 test rectified image pairs with a resolution of 1240×375 pixels, while the K15 dataset consists of 200 training and 200 test rectified image pairs with the same resolution. The training sets of both datasets contain semi-dense ground truth with sub-pixel accuracy but test sets not. Comparing with K12, K15 dataset contains more labels with dynamic objects like moving vehicles and denser labels with reflective regions like car glasses.

The disparity ground truths of KITTI datasets range from 1 to 255. According to the benchmark instructions, the correct estimation of a point is considered as the disparity error is less than 3. For the stereo confidence measures, we set the pixel-wise ground truth to 1 if the absolute differences between ground truth disparities and the initial disparities are no more than 3. Otherwise, the confidence values are set to 0.

3.2   Evaluation Methodology

In order to evaluate the performance of our methods and compare the results with other state-of-the-art methods. We apply sparsification curves and its area under the curve (AUC) to benchmark quantitative accuracy refer to [4,5,7,8]. For a confidence map of a given method, all effective pixels (pixels with ground truth) are sorted by descending confidence. Then the ordered pixels are divided into m equal parts (e.g, $m = 100$). Each time we pick the part with the lowest confidence of them and put down the bad pixel rate of the rest parts (bad pixel defined as differences larger than ± 3). In this way, we plot the sparsification curves. In the ideal case, all pixels with incorrect correspondence will be removed before correct ones, resulting in the optimal curves. The area under the optimal curve, namely optimal AUC, defined as:

$$A_{opt} = \int_{1-\varepsilon}^{1} \frac{d_m - (1 - \varepsilon)}{d_m} = \varepsilon + (1 - \varepsilon)ln(1 - \varepsilon) \qquad (2)$$

where ε presents the disparity error of current initial disparity map. Apparently, lower AUC values indicate better ability to predict confidence.

We using Δk to evaluate the improvement of method k [18]. As shown in Eq. 3, AUC_{opt} presents the average optimal AUC value on each test dataset. Our baseline here is CCNN [17], which presented as AUC_{CCNN}.

$$\Delta k = \frac{AUC_{ccnn} - AUC_k}{AUC_{ccnn} - AUC_{opt}} \qquad (3)$$

By using the defined AUC value, we evaluate our proposed method on K12 and K15 datasets with two stereo matching cost methods.

- SAD(Sum of Absolute Differences): A typical stereo algorithm. The MCVs are computed by using the absolute difference between two image intensities patches (9×9) from corresponding locations.
- MC-CNN [20]: A popular deep learning stereo method. A network is trained to calculate the matching cost by comparing the corresponding image patches. We used the pre-trained network (trained on K12, fast version) provided by authors.

After computing MCVs by two methods above, a *winner take all strategy* was simply applied to get the IDMs that we need.

3.3 Confidence Prediction Performance

We use AUC values to measure the confidence prediction abilities. First of all, for training learning-based classifiers, we split K12 dataset with ground truth (194 frames in total) into the training set (frames 0–93) and test set (frames 94–193). The whole K15 (frames 0–199) dataset is used as test set as suggested in [19]

Table 1. Confidence evaluation results with two matching cost algorithms on K12, K15 datasets. The first two rows are the comparison of alternative models. The following rows are comparisons with state-of-the-art methods(CCNN [17], CCNN$^+$ [18]). In order to prove the advantages of join RGB and disparity data cues, we also add CCNN* which used the similar structure except for the input modalities. ε is the average confidence error rate for each test dataset.

Measure	AUC_k	Δ_k	AUC_k	Δ_k
(a) Confidence evaluation with MC-CNN matching cost				
	K12 ($\varepsilon = 17.12\%$)		K15 ($\varepsilon = 17.46\%$)	
RGBD_LFN	0.02362	28.98%	0.03208	15.13%
RGBD_EFN	0.02372	27.00%	0.03340	3.05%
CCNN*	0.02503	2.05%	0.0337	0.20%
CCNN$^+$	0.02489	4.68%	0.03306	6.12%
CCNN	0.02514	-	0.03373	-
Optimal	0.0199		0.0228	
(b) Confidence evaluation with SAD matching cost				
	K12 ($\varepsilon = 36.89\%$)		K15 ($\varepsilon = 32.79\%$)	
RGBD_LFN	0.1061	45.77%	0.0921	8.89%
RGBD_EFN	0.1073	41.03%	0.0949	-2.39%
CCNN*	0.1157	8.16%	0.0933	3.90%
CCNN$^+$	0.1169	3.72%	0.0939	1.62%
CCNN	0.1178	-	0.0943	-
Optimal	0.0922		0.0699	

Alternative Models: For figuring out which designed multi-modal architecture works better on the confidence prediction task, we compared the proposed two multi-modal networks. The first part of Table 1 shows the average AUC values and Δk of each architecture by using MC-CNN and SAD matching cost. We can see that both RGBD_LFN and RGBD_EFN achieve good results on K12 dataset, while on K15 RGBD_LEF shows better generalization ability. Finally, we chose RGBD_LEF as it has the better performance.

Comparisons with State-of-the-Art Methods: To analyze the capability of our multi-modal method on predicting correct matches, we compared our method with two learning based methods proposed recently, CCNN [17], CCNN+ [18]. Besides, we also add a model named CCNN*, which has the same structure with CCNN but use the same numbers of convolutional layers and fc layers as ours (CCNN: 64 conv layers, 100 fc layers; CCNN*: 112 conv layers, 384 fc layers). Again, all methods are trained on the same datasets mentioned above.

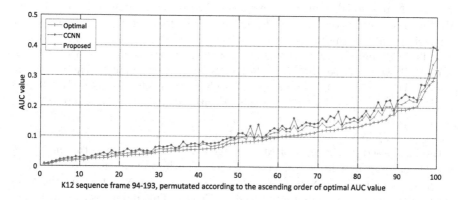

Fig. 4. Comparison of AUC values for 100 frames of K12 training image pairs with SAD MCVs. AUC values of the same method are sorting in the ascending order according to optimal AUC values. Here we selected CCNN [17] as a comparative item, which is trained by initial disparities patches only.

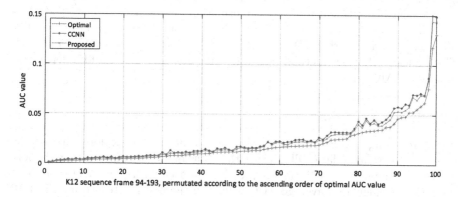

Fig. 5. Comparison of AUC values for 100 frames of K12 training image pairs with MC-CNN MCVs. AUC values of the same method are sorting in the ascending order according to optimal AUC values. Here we selected CCNN [17] as a comparative item, which is trained by initial disparities patches only.

Figure 6 shows a comparison of AUC values of the state-of-the-art learning based method CCNN and ours with SAD matching cost method on K12. AUC values of each method are sorted by the ascending orders of optimal AUC values. The curves of both two methods in Fig. 6 wave with the similar trend to optimal AUC values. But the gap between optimal AUC and other two becomes larger when optimal AUC values increase. Refer to [7], it is more challenging to predict the confidence while the gap between optimal and predicted AUC values growing. From the figure, we can see clearly that the difference between our method and CCNN method becomes more obvious in the ascending order of optimal AUC values. So the comparison of AUC from different methods leads us to the conclusion that our method is more robust than CCNN (Figs. 4 and 5).

While Comparing with other state-of-the-art methods as shown in Table 1, first of all, we can see that our RGBD_LFN method achieves the minimum average AUC above all. Observing the evaluation results between CCNN and CCNN*, we can find that CCNN model with increasing parameters can not provide significant improvement. We can also notice that our method is much better than CCNN* presented by Δ_k. It means that the improvement of our method is caused by the joint of RGB image features, rather than the increasing of convolutional and fully connected layers. The improvement of our method is much better than CCNN$^+$, an upgrade version of CCNN, learned the local consistency in confidence map produced by CCNN. This indicates that although the leveraging information from neighborhood points can help to improve the effectiveness of confidence measures, many contents can not be learned due to the ambiguity of wrong disparities. For example, the texture less and repeat texture surface like walls, sky and greenbelts, resulting to peak regions or lots of noises in disparity maps as shown in Fig. 6, or dark places like shadows, leading to failure of matching cost calculation (wrong and small disparity values). The disparity maps based CCNN often failed in those regions. However, with the complement of RGB features, more information can be used to learn the edges in such kind of areas mentioned above. Finally, our method achieves the best performance with Both SAD and MC-CNN MCVs on K12 and K15 datasets. This indicates that our method has good generalization ability and independent to different MCVs.

3.4 Training Set Size

As we are using a deep learning method, we would like to explore whether the rising size of training data will improve the performance of confidence prediction. Hence we trained our network on the K12 dataset with incremental training samples and calculated average AUC values on the rest fourteen frames in K12 dataset. We use ratio described in Eq. 4 to evaluate the improved performance with the training size ranges from 20 to 180.

$$ratio = \frac{AUC_k}{AUC_{opt}} \qquad (4)$$

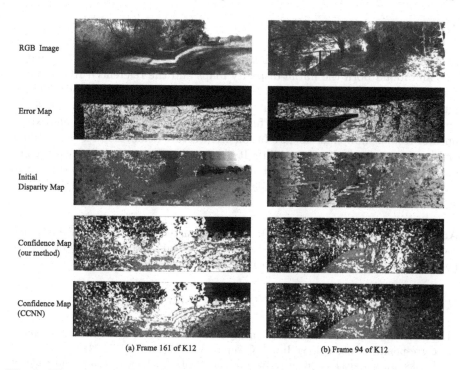

RGB Image

Error Map

Initial
Disparity Map

Confidence Map
(our method)

Confidence Map
(CCNN)

(a) Frame 161 of K12   (b) Frame 94 of K12

Fig. 6. The comparison of confidence maps with SAD on two most challenge K12 frames, which have the highest optimal AUC values. Notice that in error maps, red points are the low confidence labels. In the predicted confidence maps, darker points have lower confidence values. On each confidence map, we picked low confidence points using a threshold of 0.5. Then if the estimations are correct, we painted pixels in green, otherwise, we painted them in red. (Color figure online)

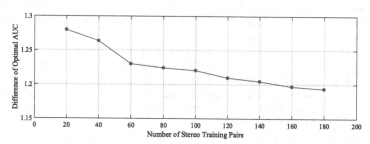

Fig. 7. The influence of training data size on performance, presenting as ratio between average AUC values of our method on K12 with SAD MVCs and average optimal AUC values.

Figure 7 shows the results of our experiment. We note that the ratio decreases fast with the growing training set size. Then curve becomes almost stable after training set size up to 160.

4   Conclusion

In this paper, we explored the confidence prediction potential of different modalities and found both the initial disparity maps and the referenced RGB images have the capabilities. Based on this discovery, we proposed a multi-modal Convolutional Neural Network (CNN) for confidence estimation. We design and study on two architectures with different fusion stages and fusion methods. The experimental results show that the late fusion architecture achieves lower AUC values and has better generalization ability. It also has better performance while compared with several state-of-the-art methods. Overall, our approach shows the potential of feature fusion for confidence prediction in stereo matching, which is worthwhile for further research.

Acknowledgement. We would like to thank Park and Yoon [7] for sharing his source code and also evaluation code. We also want to thank Seki and Pollefeys [16] for providing guidance on how to implement their algorithms.

References

1. Scharstein, D., Szeliski, R.: A taxonomy and evaluation of dense two-frame stereo correspondence algorithms. Int. J. Comput. Vis. **47**(1), 7–42 (2002)
2. Banks, J., Corke, P.: Quantitative evaluation of matching methods and validity measures for stereo vision. Int. J. Robot. Res. **20**(7), 512–532 (2001)
3. Egnal, G., Wildes, R.P.: Detecting binocular half-occlusions: empirical comparisons of five approaches. IEEE Trans. Pattern Anal. Mach. Intell. **24**(8), 1127–1133 (2002)
4. Hu, X., Mordohai, P.: A quantitative evaluation of confidence measures for stereo vision. IEEE Trans. Pattern Anal. Mach. Intell. **34**(11), 2121–2133 (2012)
5. Haeusler, R., Nair, R., Kondermann, D.: Ensemble learning for confidence measures in stereo vision. In: 2013 IEEE Conference on Computer Vision and Pattern Recognition, pp. 305–312, June 2013
6. Spyropoulos, A., Komodakis, N., Mordohai, P.: Learning to detect ground control points for improving the accuracy of stereo matching. In: Computer Vision and Pattern Recognition 2014, Columbus, Ohio, United States, June 2014
7. Park, M.G., Yoon, K.J.: Leveraging stereo matching with learning-based confidence measures. In: 2015 IEEE Conference on Computer Vision and Pattern Recognition (CVPR), pp. 101–109, June 2015
8. Spyropoulos, A., Mordohai, P.: Correctness prediction, accuracy improvement and generalization of stereo matching using supervised learning. Int. J. Comput. Vis. **118**(3), 300–318 (2016)
9. Poggi, M., Mattoccia, S.: Learning a general-purpose confidence measure based on O(1) features and a smarter aggregation strategy for semi global matching. In: Proceedings - 2016 4th International Conference on 3D Vision, 3DV 2016, vol. 1, pp. 509–518 (2016)
10. Karpathy, A., Toderici, G., Shetty, S., Leung, T., Sukthankar, R., Fei-Fei, L.: Large-scale video classification with convolutional neural networks. In: Proceedings of the 2014 IEEE Conference on Computer Vision and Pattern Recognition, CVPR 2014, Washington, DC, USA, pp. 1725–1732. IEEE Computer Society (2014)

11. Krizhevsky, A., Sutskever, I., Hinton, G.E.: Imagenet classification with deep convolutional neural networks. In: Proceedings of the 25th International Conference on Neural Information Processing Systems, NIPS 2012, USA, Curran Associates Inc. pp. 1097–1105 (2012)
12. Karpathy, A., Toderici, G., Shetty, S., Leung, T., Sukthankar, R., Fei-Fei, L.: Large-scale video classification with convolutional neural networks. In: 2014 IEEE Conference on Computer Vision and Pattern Recognition, pp. 1725–1732, June 2014
13. Dong, C., Loy, C.C., He, K., Tang, X.: Learning a deep convolutional network for image super-resolution. In: Fleet, D., Pajdla, T., Schiele, B., Tuytelaars, T. (eds.) ECCV 2014. LNCS, vol. 8692, pp. 184–199. Springer, Cham (2014). https://doi.org/10.1007/978-3-319-10593-2_13
14. Zhong, Z., Su, S., Cao, D., Li, S., Lv, Z.: Detecting ground control points via convolutional neural network for stereo matching. Multimedia Tools Appl. 1–16 (2016)
15. Bromley, J., Guyon, I., LeCun, Y., Säckinger, E., Shah, R.: Signature verification using a "siamese" time delay neural network. In: Proceedings of the 6th International Conference on Neural Information Processing Systems, NIPS 1993, San Francisco, CA, USA, pp. 737–744. Morgan Kaufmann Publishers Inc. (1993)
16. Seki, A., Pollefeys, M.: Patch based confidence prediction for dense disparity map. In: British Machine Vision Conference (BMVC), vol. 10 (2016)
17. Poggi, M., Mattoccia, S.: Learning from scratch a confidence measure. In: British Machine Vision Conference (BMVC) (2016)
18. Poggi, M., Mattoccia, S.: Learning to predict stereo reliability enforcing local consistency of confidence maps. In: Proceedings of the IEEE Computer Society Conference on Computer Vision and Pattern Recognition (2017)
19. Poggi, M., Tosi, F., Mattoccia, S.: Quantitative evaluation of confidence measures in a machine learning world. In: The IEEE International Conference on Computer Vision (ICCV), October 2017
20. Zbontar, J., LeCun, Y.: Stereo matching by training a convolutional neural network to compare image patches. J. Mach. Learn. Res. **17**, 1–32 (2016)
21. Glorot, X., Bengio, Y.: Understanding the difficulty of training deep feedforward neural networks. In: Proceedings of the International Conference on Artificial Intelligence and Statistics (AISTATS 2010). Society for Artificial Intelligence and Statistics (2010)
22. Collobert, R., Kavukcuoglu, K., Farabet, C.: Torch7: a Matlab-like environment for machine learning. In: BigLearn, NIPS Workshop (2011)
23. Chetlur, S., et al.: cuDNN: efficient primitives for deep learning (2014). CoRR abs/1410.0759
24. Geiger, A., Lenz, P., Urtasun, R.: Are we ready for autonomous driving? The KITTI vision benchmark suite. In: 2012 IEEE Conference on Computer Vision and Pattern Recognition, pp. 3354–3361, June 2012
25. Geiger, A., Lenz, P., Stiller, C., Urtasun, R.: Vision meets robotics: the KITTI dataset. Int. J. Rob. Res. **32**(11), 1231–1237 (2013)
26. Menze, M., Geiger, A.: Object scene flow for autonomous vehicles. In: Conference on Computer Vision and Pattern Recognition (CVPR) (2015)

Multi-person Head Segmentation in Low Resolution Crowd Scenes Using Convolutional Encoder-Decoder Framework

Muhammad Shaban[2], Arif Mahmood[1]([⊠]), Somaya Al-maadeed[1],
and Nasir Rajpoot[2]

[1] Department of Computer Sciece and Engineering, Qatar University, Doha, Qatar
{arif.mahmood,S_alali}@qu.edu.qa
[2] Department of Computer Science, University of Warwick, Coventry, UK
{M.Shaban,N.M.Rajpoot}@warwick.ac.uk

Abstract. Person head detection in crowded scenes becomes a challenging task if facial features are absent, resolution is low and viewing angles are unfavorable. Motion and out-of-focus blur along with headwear of varying shapes exacerbate this problem. Therefore, existing head/face detection algorithms exhibit high failure rates. We propose a multi-person head segmentation algorithm in crowded environments using a convolutional encoder-decoder network which is trained using head probability heatmaps. The network learns to assign high probability to head pixels and low probability to non-head pixels in an input image. The image is first down sampled in encoder blocks and then up sampled in decoder blocks to capture multiresolution information. The information loss due to down sampling is compensated by using copy links which directly copy data from encoder blocks to the decoder blocks. All heads and faces in an image patch are simultaneously detected contrasting to the traditional sliding window based detectors. Compared to the existing state-of-the-art methods, the proposed algorithm has demonstrated excellent performance on a challenging spectator crowd dataset.

Keywords: Person head detection · Head localization ·
Head segmentation

1 Introduction

Person head/face detection is precursor to many high-level tasks such as person detection, crowd counting, person tracking, body pose detection, and action recognition. In crowds, person heads remain more visible while upper bodies are less visible and lower bodies often get occluded by other persons. Therefore, in crowded scenes one may safely assume that if there is a head, there is a person. However, head detection is a challenging problem because of low head

© Springer Nature Switzerland AG 2019
L. Chen et al. (Eds.): RFMI 2017, CCIS 842, pp. 82–92, 2019.
https://doi.org/10.1007/978-3-030-19816-9_7

resolution, out of focus blur and motion blur in crowd images. Moreover, absence of facial features such as eyes, nose and mouth, use of headwear of varying shapes, colors and textures make the head detection problem more tough than the face detection (Fig. 1).

Visual analysis of relatively dense crowds is significantly more difficult compared to images of scenes containing single or few persons. It is due to a set of challenges posed by the crowded environments including severe occlusion, low resolution, and perspective distortions. Thus, head detection in crowded environments is significantly complex while it also offers applications in dense crowd analysis and helps to solve real word problems such as crowd counting. It is important for surveillance, space and infrastructure management of large events such as political, religious, social, and sports gatherings.

Fig. 1. Some sample head/face images in crowded scenes. Low resolution, unfavorable viewing angles, lack of facial features, partial occlusions, and varying shapes and textures of headwear cause performance degradation of approaches based on hand crafted features. The proposed convolutional encoder-decoder network has shown excellent performance in this domain.

In this paper, we propose a convolutional encoder-decoder network for multiple simultaneous head segmentations and detections. Like an auto encoder, the network has the same size of output layer as the data layer. However, unlike auto encoders, we train the network to generate head probability at each output pixel. That is, the network assigns each input image pixel a probability of being a head pixel. In the training data, probability of a pixel exponentially decays with increasing distance from the head center. During training, the network learns the relationship between probability heatmap at the output and patterns in the input images. The network consists of multiple convolutional and de-convolutional layers and successfully segments heads in a moderate sized image patch. We compared the results of the proposed algorithm with Local Binary Pattern (LBP), HOG and Haar based head/face detectors. Even after retraining on the same datasets, these methods have shown lower accuracy than our proposed detector.

84   M. Shaban et al.

Figure 2 (a) shows an example image from the SHOCK dataset showing spectators in an ice hockey match. Figure 2(b) shows a manually marked probability map used as pixel labels. The pixels inside the head bounding boxes are assigned high probabilities of being head pixels. High probabilities are shown in red and low in blue. Central pixel has got maximum probability and as distance from the center increases, probability decreases as per isometric truncated 2D Gaussian having both $\sigma_x = 1$ and $\sigma_y = 1$. Pixels outside the bounding box has been assigned zero probability of being a head pixel. Figure 2(c) shows the probability map predicted by the trained network. The network has assigned each pixel a probability of being the head pixel. In Fig. 2(d), in each detection we find the center of the detection and plot a circle of fixed length for visualization purpose.

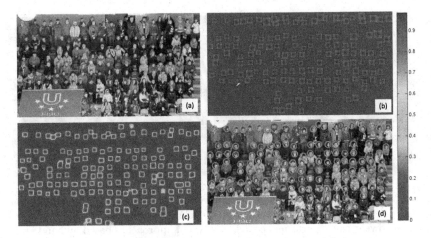

Fig. 2. (a) An example image from SHOCK dataset [5]. (b) A manually marked probability heatmap containing probability of each pixel being a head pixel in the training dataset. Within the head bounding box, probability is 1.00 at the central pixel and 0.85 at the boundary. Variation is according to 2D Gaussian function having $\sigma = 1$ in both directions. Outside head bounding box, probability is zero. (c) Predicted probability map of each pixel being a head pixel. Network has maintained an approximate box shape of high probability blobs. Transition at the box boundary has become smooth. (d) Head localization is performed by estimating the detected head center. Circles of fixed size are plotted around the predicted head centers only for visualization. Green circles are true positives, red are false positives, and black are false negatives. (Color figure online)

The organization of the rest the paper is as follows: related work is in Sect. 2. In Sect. 3 we describe our approach. Section 4 contains the datasets, experiments and results. Finally, we conclude our work in Sect. 5.

2   Related Work

In recent years, significant work has been done on crowd analysis. However, most of the research has focused on high level tasks such as crowd counting [8,15,16] and crowd flow segmentation [1,2]. CNN has recently been used for head detection [4,11,12,21], and person detection [19]. Vu et al. [21] proposed context-aware CNNs to detect person heads, which combine a global and a local model and obtains effective detection rates in movie frames. Their algorithm performs good for high resolution head detection. However, the use of context-aware CNNs suffers from poor recall in crowded scenes especially when the head resolution is low. In the current work, we focus on a complex spectator crowd dataset [5] for low level analysis by head localization. This dataset has been focused by relatively fewer researchers due to low person resolution and large number of persons in each scene. Some scenes contain as many as 160 persons which is significantly higher than ten or even less persons 'crowd' often used to demonstrate results.

Head detection or localization have some similarity with face detection [22], however it poses significant challenges of its own. Especially in crowded scenes facial features may not always be visible. Most of the face detectors [7,13,20] are based on face specific features such as structure of eyes, nose and mouth. In crowded scenes, these features even if visible, may not be strong enough to yield good detection accuracy because of very low resolution of faces. Additionally, face pose varies a lot from frontal to left, right, down and rear causing significant performance degradation of face detectors. Due to such artifacts, hand-crafted features based methods such as [20] have shown quite low performance on head detection task.

Recent success of deep neural networks for image classification [10,18] and segmentation [5,14,17] has motivated us to propose similar network for head detection. Our proposed head detection method is based on a fully convolutional encoder-decoder network.

3   Deep Head Detection (DHD) Algorithm

Deep Head Detection (DHD) algorithm is based on convolutional encoder-decoder network for head segmentation. As discussed in the introduction, in the training data set each image pixel is assigned a 'being head' probability. The network is then trained to predict probability of 'being head' at each test image pixel. The blobs of high values in the generated probability heatmap correspond to heads in the test image. Our approach is different from the typical object detectors which slide a filter on the image and classify the central pixel as object or non-object. We rather use a deep learning based solution that segments all heads in non-overlapped image patches.

3.1   Network Architecture

Network architecture of the convolutional encoder-decoder used for head segmentation is shown in Fig. 3. Like autoencoders, first we perform down sampling in almost first half of the network and then up sampling in the second half of the network. Like residual networks (ResNet) [6] and SegNet [3], we directly copy data from the down sampling layers to up sampling layers to avoid the loss of information due to down sampling. Both down sampling and up sampling paths are arranged in blocks.

Each down sampling block consists of a max-pooling layer followed by two pairs of convolutional and activation layers. In the first block no max-pooling layer is used. We used 2×2 max pooling with no overlapping, $3 \times 3 \times channels$ unpadded convolution filter and *tanh* activation function. We also used dropout layer with 0.5 dropout rate in the last down sampling block to reduce the over-fitting effect.

In each of the up sampling block two pairs of convolution and *tanh* layers are used which is similar to the down sampling blocks. In addition to that, a deconvolution layer followed by a concatenation layer is also included in each up sampling block. In the last up sampling block, a convolution filter of size $(1 \times 1 \times C)$ is used to map output to the required number of classes where C is the total number of classes. In our case, we have only two classes, head or non-head, $C = 2$. Feature map size gets doubled in each down sampling block and gets halved in each up sampling block.

In case of unpadded convolution, input image size becomes crucial because size of each down sampled block must be an integer. The reduction in image size a after each convolution can be computed using the Eq. 1 which depends on filter and stride size.

$$a = n_o - \frac{n_o - f_s + 1}{S}, \tag{1}$$

where n_o, f_s and S are the sizes of the image, convolution filter and stride, respectively.

We derive an Eq. (2) to verify aforementioned constraint before selecting an image size. Moreover, the segmentation mask obtained at the output of the last up-sampling block is smaller than the input image due to same reason (unpadded convolution) but it also has a fixed relation (Eq. (3)) with input image size.

$$n_D = (r_d)^{D-1} \times n_o - 2a\left(\frac{1 - (r_d)^D}{1 - r_d}\right), \tag{2}$$

$$n_U = (r_u)^U \times n_D - 2a\left(\frac{(r_u)^U - 1}{r_u - 1}\right) \tag{3}$$

where r_d and r_u are the down sampling and up sampling ratios, D and U represents the number of down sampling and up sampling blocks.

We tried different number of down sampling and up sampling blocks, and obtained better performance on a validation dataset using four down sampling blocks and three up sampling blocks. The resulting algorithm is named as Deep Head Detector (DHD-4), where 4 are the number of down sampling blocks. Experiments are also performed on DHD-3 and DHD-5 which have similar architecture except the number of down sampling blocks are three and five respectively.

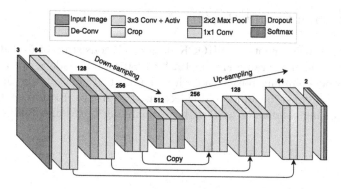

Fig. 3. Deep Head Detector (DHD-4) network architecture: each block consists of a set of layers and each layer represents a specific operation as shown on the top of image. Within a block each layer has the same number of channels as written on the top of each block. Left to right 'copy' arrows show that the last layer of each down sampling block is used during up sampling. Network has 4 down sampling and 3 up sampling blocks, represented as DHD-4 in experiments.

In deep CNN, good initialization of weights is very important to enable the whole network to take part in the learning process. A bad initialization may lead a part of the network to excessively contribute in learning as compared to the rest of the network resulting in poor generalization. We initialize the weights by random numbers drawn from Gaussian distribution with a standard deviation of $\sqrt{(2/N)}$ where N is the total number of incoming nodes of a neuron (rows × columns × *feature map channels*). Final feature map contains the activation scores for each class at each pixel location. We convert these scores into probabilities by using a pixel-wise softmax.

$$p_c(u) = \frac{\exp(f_c(u))}{\sum_{c'=1}^{C} \exp(f_{c'}(u))}, \tag{4}$$

where $f_c(u)$ is the activation score in c^{th} feature map channel at pixel location u, where $u \in \Omega$ and $\Omega \subseteq N^2$, and $p_c(u)$ is the probability of pixel u belonging to the class c.

To measure the deviation of the predicted mask from the ground-truth, we use cross entropy as a cost function

$$cost = -\sum_{u \in \Omega} \sum_{c=1}^{C} l_c(u) \log_2(p_c(u)), \tag{5}$$

where $l_c(u)$ represents the actual probability at pixel u belonging to class c. Equation (5) has been used during training. We used Adam stochastic optimization method [9] for optimization of our model with 0.001 initial learning rate.

4   Experiments and Results

We performed experiments on SHOCK dataset [5] consisting of 60 videos with 900 frames each. The frame size is 1024×1280 and 15 videos are annotated including head bounding boxes. In each video, up to 150 spectators are visible. We randomly divided the annotated videos into two groups, 10 videos for training and 5 for testing. Manually marked head bounding boxes are used as ground truth.

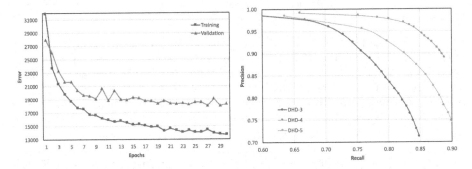

Fig. 4. Left: training and validation error variation of DHD-4 network as given by Eq. (5). Note that 10% of the training data is used for validation purpose. After 30 epochs, error reduction is insignificant. Right: precision-recall based performance comparison of DHD-3, DHD-4 and DHD-5 on SHOCK test dataset. DHD-4 has shown better performance than DHD-3 and DHD-5.

For the training of the proposed deep network, we randomly cropped 10 patches of size 428×428 pixels from each frame of the training videos with frame rate reduced to one frame per second. We do online data augmentation by random horizontal flipping of training patches during each epoch. We train our network for 30 epochs of data. Beyond that error reduction is insignificant (Fig. 4 Left). The down sampling ratio is fixed to 0.50 and the up sampling ratio was fixed to 2.00.

We trained our Deep Head Detector (DHD) network by varying the down sampling and up sampling blocks. DHD-3 network contains three Down Sampling (DS) and two Up Sampling (US) blocks. DHD-4 has four DS and three US blocks. Figure 3 shows DHD-4 network. DHD-5 has five DS and four US blocks. The deeper network DHD-5 exhibited overfitting by learning undesired low level details such as pixel color for positive class instead of learning a useful mixture of high level and low level features. The shallow network DHD-3 was not able to perform good learning and showed relatively more mistakes. DHD 3 had more false negatives while DHD-5 exhibited lot of false positives especially on patches containing skin color such as hands. The network with 4 DS and 3 US blocks, DHD-4 learned a good representation of data and hence performed the best as compare to DHD-3 and DHD-5 (Fig. 4 Right).

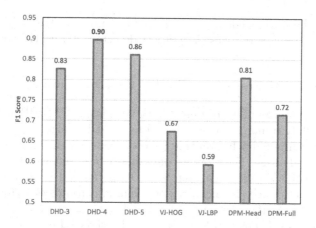

Fig. 5. Comparison of head detection results of different algorithms in terms of F_1 score. The existing algorithms are retrained on the same training dataset as used by the proposed DHD algorithm. Retraining has significantly improved accuracy of these algorithms. All algorithms are tested on the SHOCK dataset. The proposed DHD-4 algorithm has remained the best algorithm

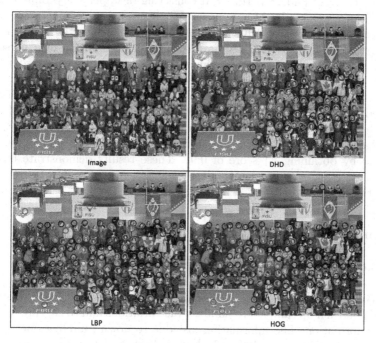

Fig. 6. Visual comparison of the proposed algorithm with the existing state-of-the-art algorithms. LBP and HOG are the head detection results of Viola-Jones detector trained using local binary pattern (LBP) and histogram of oriented gradients (HOG) features respectively. DHD is the head detection results of our proposed DHD-4 algorithm. Green circles are true positive, red are false positive and black are false negatives. (Color figure online)

We compared the head detection results of the proposed DHD algorithm with two variants of Viola and Jones (VJ) object detector [20], using LBP and HOG features using F_1 score.

$$F_1 = 2(\text{Precision} \times \text{Recall})/(\text{Precision} + \text{Recall}).$$

For a fair comparison, we retrained both versions of VJ (LBP and HOG) on the same SHOCK training dataset as used by the DHD algorithm. The generic trained VJ which is publicly available have showed very degraded performance on the SHOCK dataset. Therefore we only report performance of both VJ variants (LBP and HOG) after retraining. VJ-HOG performed better than VJ-LPB, however both performed significantly poor than all variants of DHD algorithm, including DHD-3, DHD-4, and DHD-5. Visual comparison of DHD-4 with VJ-LBP and VJ-HOG is shown in Fig. 6. Red circles show false positives and black circles shown false negatives. Both variants of VJ algorithm have shown significant number of red and black circles.

The proposed DHD algorithm is also compared with two variations of Deformable Part Models (DPM) [23], including the only three parts (head, face, and neck) detector and 18 parts DPM consisting of upper body. Similar to the VJ algorithms, generic DPM has shown very degraded performance on the low resolution crowd images of SHOCK dataset. It is because the DPM was trained by the original authors on Buffy dataset in which resolution of a person, or particularly person head, is many times larger than the person resolution in SHOCK dataset. We, therefore retrained both versions of DPM on the same training dataset as used by the DHD algorithms. Retraining has significantly improved performance of both versions of DPM algorithm. The retrained DPM-head detector was able to obtain F_1 score of 0.81 which is close to the F_1 score 0.83 obtained by DHD-3 algorithm. However, DHD-4 has remained the best algorithm by obtaining F_1 score of 0.90. These results demonstrate that the proposed DHD algorithm is capable to detect low resolution heads in crowded scenes (Fig. 5).

5   Conclusions

In this work a multi-person head segmentation algorithm has been proposed for images of crowded scenes. The proposed Deep Head Detection (DHD) algorithm is based on a convolutional encoder-decoder network. A given image is first down sampled and then up sampled to handle scale variations and to capture multiresolution information. The information lost due to down sampling operations is compensated by using copy links which directly copy data from down sampling blocks to the up sampling blocks. The proposed encoder-decoder network was trained to generate head probability at each pixel of the input image. In the generated probability map, blobs of high values correspond to the heads in the input image. Encoder-decoder networks with different down sampling and up sampling blocks were compared. For the given training dataset, network with four down sampling and three up sampling blocks (DHD-4) was found to be the best performer. DHD networks were evaluated on a challenging spectator crowd dataset containing up to 160 persons in an image. The experiments demonstrated better performance of the proposed algorithm over current state-of-the-art for the task of head detection in crowded scenes where resolution of each person is low. The proposed DHD network has the potential to obtain even higher accuracies if network training is improved particularly by using better data augmentation techniques.

Acknowledgments. This work was made possible by NPRP grant number NPRP 7-1711-1-312 from the Qatar National Research Fund (a member of Qatar Foundation). The statements made herein are solely the responsibility of the authors.

References

1. Ali, S., Shah, M.: A Lagrangian particle dynamics approach for crowd flow segmentation and stability analysis. In: IEEE Conference on Computer Vision and Pattern Recognition, CVPR 2007, pp. 1–6. IEEE (2007)
2. Andrade, E.L., Blunsden, S., Fisher, R.B.: Hidden Markov models for optical flow analysis in crowds. In: 18th International Conference on Pattern Recognition, ICPR 2006, vol. 1, pp. 460–463. IEEE (2006)
3. Badrinarayanan, V., Kendall, A., Cipolla, R.: SegNet: a deep convolutional encoder-decoder architecture for image segmentation. arXiv preprint arXiv:1511.00561 (2015)
4. Bai, Y., Ghanem, B.: Multi-scale fully convolutional network for face detection in the wild. In: 2017 IEEE Conference on Computer Vision and Pattern Recognition Workshops (CVPRW), pp. 2078–2087. IEEE (2017)
5. Conigliaro, D., et al.: The S-HOCK dataset: analyzing crowds at the stadium. In: Proceedings of the IEEE Conference on Computer Vision and Pattern Recognition, pp. 2039–2047 (2015)
6. He, K., Zhang, X., Ren, S., Sun, J.: Deep residual learning for image recognition. In: Proceedings of the IEEE Conference on Computer Vision and Pattern Recognition, pp. 770–778 (2016)
7. Hsu, R.L., Abdel-Mottaleb, M., Jain, A.K.: Face detection in color images. IEEE Trans. Pattern Anal. Mach. Intell. **24**(5), 696–706 (2002)
8. Idrees, H., Saleemi, I., Seibert, C., Shah, M.: Multi-source multi-scale counting in extremely dense crowd images. In: Proceedings of the IEEE Conference on Computer Vision and Pattern Recognition, pp. 2547–2554 (2013)
9. Kingma, D., Ba, J.: Adam: a method for stochastic optimization. arXiv preprint arXiv:1412.6980 (2014)
10. Krizhevsky, A., Sutskever, I., Hinton, G.E.: ImageNet classification with deep convolutional neural networks. In: Advances in Neural Information Processing Systems, pp. 1097–1105 (2012)
11. Li, H., Lin, Z., Shen, X., Brandt, J., Hua, G.: A convolutional neural network cascade for face detection. In: Proceedings of the IEEE Conference on Computer Vision and Pattern Recognition, pp. 5325–5334 (2015)
12. Li, Y., Dou, Y., Liu, X., Li, T.: Localized region context and object feature fusion for people head detection. In: 2016 IEEE International Conference on Image Processing (ICIP), pp. 594–598. IEEE (2016)

13. Lienhart, R., Maydt, J.: An extended set of Haar-like features for rapid object detection. In: Proceedings of 2002 International Conference on Image Processing, vol. 1, pp. I–900. IEEE (2002)
14. Long, J., Shelhamer, E., Darrell, T.: Fully convolutional networks for semantic segmentation. In: Proceedings of the IEEE Conference on Computer Vision and Pattern Recognition, pp. 3431–3440 (2015)
15. Rabaud, V., Belongie, S.: Counting crowded moving objects. In: 2006 IEEE Computer Society Conference on Computer Vision and Pattern Recognition, vol. 1, pp. 705–711. IEEE (2006)
16. Rodriguez, M., Laptev, I., Sivic, J., Audibert, J.Y.: Density-aware person detection and tracking in crowds. In: 2011 IEEE International Conference on Computer Vision (ICCV), pp. 2423–2430. IEEE (2011)
17. Ronneberger, O., Fischer, P., Brox, T.: U-Net: convolutional networks for biomedical image segmentation. In: Navab, N., Hornegger, J., Wells, W.M., Frangi, A.F. (eds.) MICCAI 2015. LNCS, vol. 9351, pp. 234–241. Springer, Cham (2015). https://doi.org/10.1007/978-3-319-24574-4_28
18. Simonyan, K., Zisserman, A.: Very deep convolutional networks for large-scale image recognition. arXiv preprint arXiv:1409.1556 (2014)
19. Stewart, R., Andriluka, M., Ng, A.Y.: End-to-end people detection in crowded scenes. In: Proceedings of the IEEE Conference on Computer Vision and Pattern Recognition, pp. 2325–2333 (2016)
20. Viola, P., Jones, M.J.: Robust real-time face detection. Int. J. Comput. Vis. 57(2), 137–154 (2004)
21. Vu, T.H., Osokin, A., Laptev, I.: Context-aware CNNs for person head detection. In: Proceedings of the IEEE International Conference on Computer Vision, pp. 2893–2901 (2015)
22. Yang, S., Luo, P., Loy, C.C., Tang, X.: Wider face: a face detection benchmark. In: Proceedings of the IEEE Conference on Computer Vision and Pattern Recognition, pp. 5525–5533 (2016)
23. Yang, Y., Ramanan, D.: Articulated pose estimation with flexible mixtures-of-parts. In: 2011 IEEE Conference on Computer Vision and Pattern Recognition (CVPR), pp. 1385–1392. IEEE (2011)

CrossEncoder: Towards 3D-Free Depth Face Recovery and Fusion Scheme for Heterogeneous Face Recognition

Wuming Zhang[✉] and Liming Chen

LIRIS Laboratory, Ecole Centrale de Lyon, Ecully, France
{wuming.zhang,liming.chen}@ec-lyon.fr

Abstract. As a worthwhile trade-off between fully 2D and fully 3D based face recognition (FR), 2D/3D asymmetric face recognition has recently emerged which involves matching two face representations from these two alternative modalities. Different from most previous work which rely on accurately registered 3D face templates, we address this issue by proposing a novel multi-task deep convolutional neural network (CNN) architecture based on 2.5D images. With an autoencoder-like pipeline and a specially formulated criterion, our approach is capable of parallelizing real-time 2.5D face image reconstruction and discriminative face feature extraction. Further, through both qualitative and quantitative experiments on commonly used FRGC 2D/3D face database, we demonstrate that our framework could achieve satisfactory performance on both tasks while being drastically efficient.

Keywords: Heterogeneous face recognition · Deep learning · 3D reconstruction

1 Introduction

Heterogeneous face recognition (HFR) [12] has rightfully received considerable attention due to the exploding growth of face data through a variety of imaging modalities: near-infrared, forensic sketch, range image, just to name a few. The underlying assumption of HFR is that different visual observations of one specific subject are implicitly correlated. We can thereby construct or learn a common representation to enable cross-modal identification. While facing the increasingly complex scenarios where gallery set and probe set may contain partially or even totally different modalities, HFR grants us the possibility to go beyond the conventional boundaries and make the recognition system more flexible and powerful.

Commonly known as an important branch of HFR, 2D/3D asymmetric face recognition copes with a scenario where 3D face models, including both texture and shape, present in gallery set while only 2D face images are involved in probe set, or inversely. The motivation behind this framework is that the use of 3D

© Springer Nature Switzerland AG 2019
L. Chen et al. (Eds.): RFMI 2017, CCIS 842, pp. 93–109, 2019.
https://doi.org/10.1007/978-3-030-19816-9_8

data may cut both ways: 3D information is reasonably beneficial for refinement of robust FR because 2D face image is essentially a outgrowth projection of 3D shape onto 2D plane, re-introducing the informative depth value into research could efficiently alleviate the impact of nuisance factors such as illumination and occlusion, this additional dimension, on the other hand, could adversely impose a heavy burden on registration and computational cost. Likewise, when it comes to most practical circumstances, non-intrusive and convenient 3D face acquisition for an unknown person remains another challenge due to its specific requirement for equipment and environment. Considering the above arguments, it becomes natural to strike a balance between fully 3D and fully 2D based architecture. To this end, 2D/3D asymmetric FR was proposed with the core idea of limiting the deployment of 3D data to where it really helps, which means we can avail ourselves of 3D face shape in gallery set as complementary information, and at the online evaluation stage it simply takes a 2D image of the person who needs to be identified.

Over the past decade, a few attempts have been made to propose impressive asymmetric 2D/3D FR algorithms. It is worth noticing that among these researches, some take complete face model as 3D data while the others only process pseudo-3D, also known as 2.5D image, for heterogeneous comparison with ordinary photographic image. Using full 3D model could be advantageous to handle pose variations other than frontal pose due to its capacity of rotating face model in 3D space to fit the real pose. Nevertheless, 2.5D based methods hold advantage with its ease of implementation and outstanding performance when dealing with frontal pose scenarios as considered in many large 3D face datasets, such as FRGC, BU3D and Bosphorus.

In addition to its efficiency and effectiveness, the fact that 2.5D still retains the characteristic of acting as an image endows 2.5D based methods with more flexibility and attractiveness for combination with other powerful 2D based techniques. For example, Huang et al. [7] proposed Oriented Gradient Map (OGM) as a lighting-robust feature which could describe both local texture changes and local geometry variations from 2D/2.5D image pairs. Similar with approaches reported in [8] and [24], they all utilized a projection technique to find a common subspace on which the comparison between cross-modal features could be proceeded, such as Canonical Correlation Analysis (CCA), Kernel CCA (KCCA) and Multiview Smooth Discriminant Analysis (MSDA). However, all these transformations are linear and shallow, which therefore makes them partially restricted for a nonlinear representation.

Motivated by the considerations described above, and the deep learning development process, in this paper we resort to one of the most representative and frontier technology, the deep CNN for driving advances in our task. As illustrated in Fig. 1, we learn an autoencoder-like network architecture, instead of taking the input 2D face image itself as reconstruction objective, its corresponding 2.5D is considered as the target in order to reconstruct 2.5D for 2.5D/2.5D FR in the evaluation stage, and meanwhile a discriminative objective function is integrated in the feature layer which aims to generate an intermediate feature output for 2D/2D FR. The dual FR phases would be ultimately combined to compute a fusion score between gallery and probe.

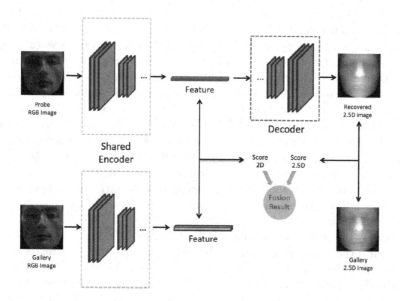

Fig. 1. The proposed framework takes one single RGB face image as input and serves two purposes: (i) extract discriminative feature through well-trained encoder and (ii) reconstruct a 2.5D range image after decoder. The dual output will be used in the final fusion phase of FR.

In summary, this paper makes following contributions:

- We propose a novel 2D/3D asymmetric FR method by combining powerful deep CNN and conventional face matching techniques.
- Different from many existing approaches, our method only makes use of 2.5D range images, thus requires very few preprocessing steps and greatly improves system efficiency.
- The objective is twofold in our framework: 2.5D face image reconstruction from a single color image and discriminative feature extraction for robust 2D/3D FR.
- The proposed method achieves satisfactory performance on the challenging 2D/3D datasets FRGC ver2.0.

2   Related Work

2.1   2D-3D Heterogeneous FR

As a pioneer and cornerstone for numerous subsequent 3D Morphable Model (3DMM) based methods, Blanz and Vetter [4] built this statistical model by merging a branch of 3D face models and then densely fit it to a given facial image for further matching. Toderici et al. [22] located some predefined key landmarks on the facial images in different poses, and then roughly align them to a frontal 3D model to achieve recognition target; Riccio and Dugelay [18] also established a dense correspondence between the 2D probe and the 3D gallery using geometric invariants across face region. Following this framework, a pose-invariant asymmetric 2D-3D FR approach [29] was proposed which conducts a 2D-2D matching by synthesizing 2D image from corresponding 3D models towards the same pose as a given probe sample. This approach was further extended and compared with work of Zhao et al. [30] as a benchmarking asymmetric 2D-3D FR system on the UHDB face database [1], a complete version of their work was recently released in [9]. Though the above models achieved satisfactory performance, unfortunately they all suffer from high computational cost and long convergence process owing to considerable complexity of pose synthesis, and their common assumption that accurate landmark localization in facial images was fulfilled turns out to be another tough topic. More recently, learning based approaches have significantly increased on 2D/3D FR. Huang et al. [7] projected the proposed illuminant-robust feature OGM onto the CCA space to maximize the correlation between 2D/3D features; instead, Wang et al. [24] combined Restricted Boltzmann Machines (RBMs) and CCA/kCCA to achieve this goal. The work of Jin et al. [8], called MSDA based on Extreme Learning Machine (ELM) as aforementioned, aims at finding a common discriminative feature space revealing the underlying relationship between different views. These approaches take well advantage of learning model, but would encounter weakness when dealing with non-linear manifold representations.

2.2   3D Face Reconstruction

3D face reconstruction from single/multiple images or stereo video has been a challenging task due to its nonlinearity and ill-posedness. A number of prevailing approaches addressed this problem based on shape-subsapce projections, where a set of 3D prototypes are fitted by adjusting corresponding parameters to a given 2D image and most of them were derived from 3DMM [4] and Active Appearance Models [15]. Alternative models were afterwards proposed as well which follow the similar processing pipeline by fitting 3D models to 2D images through various face collections or prior knowledge. For example, Gu and Kanade [6] fit surface 3D points and related textures together with the pose and deformation estimation. Kemelmacher-Shlizerman et al. [10] considered the input image as a guide with a single reference model to achieve 3D reconstruction. In recent work of Liu et al. [13], two sets of cascaded regressors are implemented and correlated via a 3D-2D mapping iteratively to solve face alignment and 3D face reconstruction simultaneously. Likewise, using generic model remains a decent solution as well for 3D face reconstruction from stereo videos, as presented in [5]. Despite of strikingly accurate reconstruction result reported in the above researches, the drawback of relying on single or a large number of well-aligned 3D training data is observed and even enlarged here, because as far as we know 3D prototypes are necessary for almost all reconstruction approaches.

3 Our Approach

In this section, we elaborate an integrated 2D/3D asymmetric FR system. To begin with, we first recapitulate the framework of AutoEncoder (AE) upon which our work is based. Then we will demonstrate the details of how implementing an end-to-end CNN could solve a heterogeneous FR problem. Inspired by some up-to-the-minute work, a bunch of weighted loss functions are specifically defined for the dual tasks, followed by some discussions.

3.1 Autoencoder

Generally considered as an efficient coding algorithm for dimensionality reduction, a conventional auto-encoder framework is composed of two main parts: encoder f and decoder g. Given an input $x \in \mathbf{R}^d$, the encoder f defines a deterministic mapping $\mathbf{R}^d \to \mathbf{R}^{d'}$:

$$y = f(x) = s(Wx + b) \tag{1}$$

where $y \in \mathbf{R}^{d'}$ denotes the d'-dimension coding representation in hidden layer, s is the nonlinear activation function, $W \in \mathbf{R}^{d' \times d}$ and $b \in \mathbf{R}^{d'}$ stand for weight matrix and bias term, respectively. Not surprisingly, the newly generated y normally falls in low dimensional vector space which helps avoid the curse of dimensionality compared with using directly the original data, moreover, this compression could help eliminate noise factors as well. To ensure that y retains the latent characteristics of x, the decoder g, inversely, re-map the hidden representation into $\mathbf{R}^d$:

$$z = g(y) = s(W'y + b') \tag{2}$$

where $z \in \mathbf{R}^d$ denotes the output of network, and similarly, $W' \in \mathbf{R}^{d \times d'}$ and $b' \in \mathbf{R}^d$ are weight matrix and bias term respectively for decoder. Auto-encoder then sets the target of network output exactly the same as input, which implies that the obtained feature y is highly correlated with input x. The training process is thus entirely unsupervised by minimizing the reconstruction error throughout the whole training set $\{x_1, x_2, ..., x_n\}$:

$$\{\hat{W}, \hat{b}, \hat{W}', \hat{b}'\} = \arg \min_{W, b, W', b'} \sum_{i=1}^{n} \|x_i - z_i\|^2 \tag{3}$$

More recently, a surge of variants of AE have emerged to help improve conventional AE for learning more informative representations. Masci et al. [14] develop convolutional auto-encoder which targets specifically 2D image structure in order to benefit from local correlation in an image. Sparse auto-encoder [11] imposes sparsity on hidden layers by adding a penalty term in loss function, similarly, contractive auto-encoder [19] introduces another regularizer which enables the learned model to be robust against slight variations of input data.

Despite of its effectiveness in dimensionality reduction, the self-reconstruction characteristic of auto-encoder is always neglected, the decoding phase serves more as a regularization term in order that data are compressed without losing the principle components. The explanations are twofold: (i) conventional auto-encoder aims to reconstruct an output which is exactly the same as input, making it meaningless to make use of reconstruction result due to duplication, (ii) like all other dimensionality reduction approaches, auto-encoder is inevitably lossy, thus suffers from low resolution and noise.

Fortunately, some researches take a further step. Vincent et al. [23] first proposed the concept of denoising auto-encoder (DAE) for reconstructing an image from its corrupted version. The emergence of multi-layer deconvolution network [27,28] provided a powerful tool for projecting feature activation in a certain layer back to the input pixel space, which is actually helpful for improving convolutional auto-encoder capacity other than self-reconstruction. In the next subsections, we will introduce our heterogeneous 'auto-encoder', namely cross-encoder, which reconstructs a 2.5D face image from its related 2D color image.

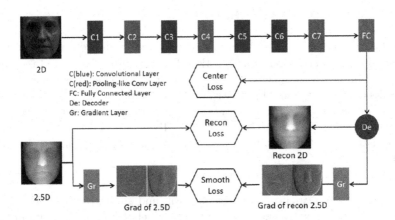

Fig. 2. Architecture and training process of the proposed cross-encoder framework. A $3 \times 98 \times 98$ 2D image is fed into the system with its corresponding 2.5D image as the target. The kernel sizes of C1 is 6×6, and its stride is 3. C3, C5 and C6 own the same kernel size 3×3 and the same stride 1. All convolutional layers in red, i.e. C2, C4 and C7, keep the kernel size as 2×2 and stride as 2, in this way they play the role of pooling layers in other networks. The output vector representation of fully connected layer is 4096-dimension. The structure of decoder is omitted here because it simply reverses the structure of encoder. All convolultional layers are followed by a ReLU layer and a batch normalization layer. (Color figure online)

3.2 Discriminative Cross-Encoder

Intuitively, 2D and 3D representations could be regarded as two views of human face, one can easily establish a connection in mind between a photographic image and its corresponding 3D model simply through visual observation. Inspired by this internal correspondence and the reconstruction ability of auto-encoder, we are encouraged to build an end-to-end learning pipeline which could achieve a straightforward transfer from 2D to 2.5D.

Following the main idea of conventional auto-encoder, the cross-encoder stacks a bank of filters at its encoder stage, and symmetrically project the low dimensional feature representation back to an image of the original size step-by-step at its decoder stage. As detailed in Fig. 2, our framework differs from existing AE and its variants in three respects:

1. Initially proposed as a data compression algorithm, auto-encoders are inevitably lossy. This shortcoming is partly neglected for compression task since the reconstruction quality would not be further considered, whereas it becomes significantly crucial and needs to be carefully remedied in our 2.5D reconstruction task. To run a mile from huge information loss, we construct alternative convolution layers which function as pooling layers in other networks, the feasibility of taking this step was evidenced by Springenberg et al. [21] which supported that pooling operations do not always improve performance on CNNs and could be simply replaced by fully convolutions. In our work, this trick helps to effectively avoid large portion of informationless regions caused by pooling operation, especially in upsampling stage. A conceptual illustration of how a pooling-like conv layer differs from conventional max-pooling layer is shown in top row of Fig. 3.

2. A common observation occurs lately in connection with the ever-advancing development of feature visualization and other CNN based image generation techniques: the checkerboard artifacts [16]. This strange pattern seems unfortunately to be a default drawback for all deconvolution work, however, the effect could be alleviated to a certain extent by some workarounds. First, to avoid the uneven overlap which is prone to the checkerboard artifact, we carefully design our network to be sure that the kernel size in each conv layer could be divided by the stride and then the neighboring pixels after upsampling are supposed to be equally rendered. We subsequently add a fixed convolution layer which calculates the gradient of reconstructed output after the decoder. With this layer we are capable to impose a smooth prior within this framework by minimizing the difference between gradient maps of reconstructed 2.5D and ground truth 2.5D. This additional layer, conjointly with aforementioned pooling-like convolutional layer, helps to attenuate the checkerboard artifacts and make the output image naturally smoother, this effect could be intuitively perceived in bottom row of Fig. 3.

3. Until quite recently, the trend of using deep CNN focus mainly on maximizing inter-class differences since it was originally designed and optimized for classification purpose of object, scene or action which are label-specific, whereas the face task imposes a higher requirement for discriminative capacity. To

this end, Wen et al. [25] proposed an efficient and easy-to-implement loss which encourages the discriminability of features, namely center loss. This mini-batch based loss function updates the center of each class, which is the person identity in FR, during each iteration and minimizes the intra-person distances in order that two images of the same person would lead to two similar representations after FC layer. Unlike the way it was used in [25], Softmax function is not included in our framework, instead, we fuse this loss with the aforementioned two errors which could avoid learning zero features for all samples.

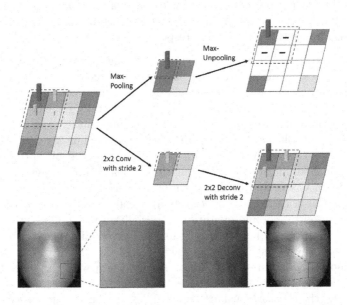

Fig. 3. The difference of processing method (top) and output effect (bottom) between a conventional max-pooling layer and a pooling-like convolutional layer with kernel size 2×2 and stride 2. In the bottom row, the left two images which benefit from pooling-free network and gradient layer presents a smoother surface with invisible checkerboard effect compared with the right-hand side images which results from a conventional CNN.

Note that we intend to take advantage of hidden layer output as a 2D based discriminative feature other than using only reconstructed result, a conventional loss function based on pairwise distance between reconstructed 2.5D and target is not enough. In the next subsection we define and detail two additional criteria in connection with the proposed framework.

3.3   Multi-criterion Mechanism

Prerequisite. Given n pairs of 2D/2.5D face images collected from m identities in the training batch during the tth iteration $\{(X_1^{2d}, X_1^{2.5d}), (X_2^{2d}, X_2^{2.5d}), ...,$

$(X_n^{2d}, X_n^{2.5d})\}$ with their labels $\{Y_1, Y_2, ..., Y_n\}$ where $Y_i \in \{1, 2, ..., m\}$. The corresponding 4096-d hidden layer output are $\{Z_1, Z_2, ..., Z_n\}$, and their reconstructed results are denoted as $\{\hat{X}_1^{2.5d}, \hat{X}_2^{2.5d}, ..., \hat{X}_n^{2.5d}\}$. Note that for a certain iteration, it is possible that only a part of m identities occur in the batch, here m refers to the total number of persons in the whole training dataset.

Reconstruction Loss. Known as a frequently used measure between predictions and observations, Mean Square Error (MSE) computes the mean of the square of their differences. In our case, this crucial loss could be interpreted as an averaged error between ground truth and reconstruction:

$$L_r = \frac{1}{n}\sum_{i=1}^{n}\|X_i^{2.5d} - \hat{X}_i^{2.5d}\|^2 \tag{4}$$

Center Loss. To effectively reduce the intra-class variations in hidden layer, the objective function L_c to be minimized is defined as the sum of distances between each flattened feature Z_i and its identity-related center C_{Y_i}. Different from other losses, this term is more like a learnable layer because the center of each class is updated during back-propagation at every iteration in order to gradually approximate the best cluster center. The loss function and update strategy of centers at iteration t are as follows:

$$L_c = \frac{1}{2n}\sum_{i=1}^{n}\|Z_i - C_{Y_i}^t\|^2 \tag{5}$$

$$C_j^{t+1} = C_j^t - \rho \cdot \frac{\sum_{i=1}^{n} \mathbf{1}_{\{i|Y_i=j\}}(C_j^t - X_i^t)}{max(1, \sum_{i=1}^{n} \mathbf{1}_{\{i|Y_i=j\}})} \tag{6}$$

where $\mathbf{1}_A(x)$ is an indicator function which will return 1 if $x \in A$ and returns 0 otherwise, ρ denotes the learning rate for updating centers which counteracts the negative effect of mislabelled samples and outlier data.

Smooth Loss. For this purpose, we compute and concatenate the gradient maps g_x and g_y of reconstructed 2.5D face image through the gradient layer which involves two fixed filters $f_x = [-1, 0, 1]$ and $f_y = [-1; 0; 1]$ along two image dimensions respectively. The gradient of $\hat{X}_i^{2.5d}$ simply follows the operation:

$$\nabla\hat{X}_i^{2.5d} = \begin{bmatrix} g_x \\ g_y \end{bmatrix} = \begin{bmatrix} f_x * \hat{X}_i^{2.5d} \\ f_y * \hat{X}_i^{2.5d} \end{bmatrix} \tag{7}$$

where $*$ represents the convolution operator. In a similar way the gradient of ground truth depth image is calculated as well, and we accumulate the differences of gradients across the whole training set as follows:

$$L_s = \frac{1}{n}\sum_{i=1}^{n}\|\nabla X_i^{2.5d} - \nabla\hat{X}_i^{2.5d}\|^2 \tag{8}$$

The final representation of our loss function combines the above three criteria:

$$L = L_r + \lambda_c L_c + \lambda_s L_s \tag{9}$$

where λ_c and λ_s are multipliers for center loss and smooth loss. The algorithm of mini-batch gradient descent is further applied to minimize this joint loss.

4   Experiments

To intuitively demonstrate and evaluate the effectiveness of the proposed framework, we conduct extensive experiments for 2D/3D asymmetric face recognition on several publicly available databases. Besides the reconstructed 2.5D depth image, our method also achieves acceptable performance despite only using 2.5D images instead of holistic 3D face models.

4.1   Dataset Collection

Collecting 2D/2.5D image pairs presents itself as a primary challenge when considering deep CNN as a learning pipeline. Unlike the tremendous boost in dataset scale of 2D face images, massive 3D face data acquisition still remains a bottleneck for the development and practical application of 3D based FR techniques, from which our work is partly motivated.

In this work, three large scale and publicly available 3D face databases are gathered for generating training/validation/evaluation splittings. Considering the significance of face alignment and adequate training data, we detail the preprocessing step and data augmentation method along with the database overview.

BU3D: To improve the accuracy of handling subtle facial behavior by using only 2D video or 2D static images, BU3D [26] was originally constructed for analyzing facial expressions in 3D space. It contains 2500 two-views' texture images and 2500 geometric shape models, correspondingly, from 100 female and male subjects with a variety of ethnic backgrounds, facial expressions and age ranges. All scans are included in our training stage, where 2250 sessions are involved in training set and the rest 250 are supposed to be validation set.

Bosphorus: Intended for multi-task 2D and 3D face analysis, Bosphorus [20] contains 4666 single-view scans from 105 subjects which involve pose variations and occlusions as well as expressions. In view of the fact that the proposed approach deals with frontal pose and occlusion-free reconstruction, we retain 2896 face models of which the variation is solely determined by expressions. 2500 of them are integrated in training set while the others go to the validation set.

FRGC: Over the last decade, the FRGC Ver2.0 face database [17] has held the field as one of the most commonly used benchmark dataset. FRGC consists of 50,000 recordings divided into training/validation sets, here we concentrate mainly on the validation set which contains 4003 sessions collected from 466 subjects from 2003 to 2004. We carry out our evaluation framework on this database and three different protocols are adopted for comparative research.

Preprocessing: To generate 2.5D range image from original 3D shape, we either proceed a direct projection if the point cloud is pre-arranged in grids (Bosphorus/FRGC) or adopt a simple Z-buffer algorithm (BU3D). Furthermore, to ensure that all faces are of the similar scale, we resize and crop the original image pairs to $(3\times)98 \times 98$ while fixing their inter-ocular distance to a certain value. Especially, to deal with the missing holes and unwanted body parts (shoulder and ears, for example) in FRGC, we first locate the face region based on 68 automatically detected landmarks [3], then apply a linear interpolation algorithm to approximate the default value of each hole pixel by averaging its non-zero neighboring points. Some face samples in FRGC Ver2.0 before and after preprocessing are illustrated in Fig. 4.

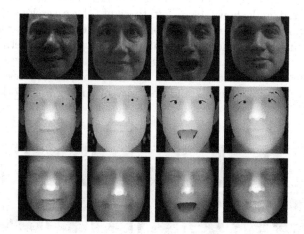

Fig. 4. Some face examples of 2D texture and 3D depth image in the FRGC Ver2.0 face database. Top: 2D texture samples. Center: 3D depth images before preprocessing. Bottom: 3D depth images after filling holes and face region cropping. Note that the texture images shown above are correspondingly preprocessed following the same rule with depth images.

Data Augmentation: Though three mainstream 3D face datasets are gathered in preparation stage, they are still too few to fit a deep CNN as proposed in our work. Therefore the data augmentation approach is applied to approximate samples and thus increase the variability of the original dataset. In this work, we take a few simple transformations to achieve this goal: (1) horizontal flipping. Each 2D/2.5D pair is equally flipped in the left-right direction. (2) small amount of shifting. We iteratively carry out 3×3 1-pixel shiftings around the center area of the image.

4.2 Implementation Details

We perform our network architecture on the Torch framework. The cross-encoder model is trained with the architecture as per Sect. 3.2 With regards to the choice of hyperparameters, unless otherwise specified, we adopt the following setting: the learning rate μ begins with 1 and is divided by 5 every 10 epochs, although we found that $\mu = 1$ may cause the loss to explode while dealing with raw FRGC training set, the preprocessing pipeline solves the problem perfectly; the momentum m is initially set as 0.5 until it is increased to 0.9 at the 10th epoch; the weights for center loss λ_c and smooth loss λ_s are respectively set to 0.1 and 0.7 with the learning rate for updating class centers $\rho = 0.3$.

4.3 Reconstruction Results

Figure 5 illustrates the results of the reconstruction obtained for face images in the FRGC Ver2.0 face database. Seven examples from different subjects are randomly selected and shown from left to right, these sessions are collected across a wide range of illumination environments and expression variations. They thereby give hints on the generalization ability of the proposed method. For each sample we first portray the original 2D texture with the corresponding 2.5D depth image as ground truth, followed by the reconstructed results whereby we demonstrate the effectiveness and necessity of adding a smooth loss in our framework.

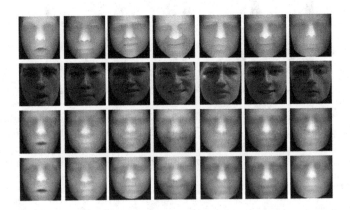

Fig. 5. Reconstruction results of FRGC samples with varying illumination situations and expressions. From top to bottom: ground truth 2.5D image, RGB texture image, reconstructed 2.5D from cross-encoder without gradient layer and reconstructed 2.5D from fully cross-encoder. (Color figure online)

We observe that the reconstructed 2.5D face images are consistently similar to the ground truth while retaining exactly the original expression. Especially, the reconstruction results hold their intensity value at the same level irrespective of lighting variations in the input RGB images, which could be proved if we compare the last two examples, this observation implies that the lighting effect could be normalized during the process of the well-learned cross-encoder. Furthermore, when we take a closer examination of the two reconstruction results in Col. 3 and Col. 4, the comparison provides a further evidence that the implementation of the simple gradient layer, i.e. the smooth loss L_s is beneficial for obtaining a natural output with few checkerboard artifacts, meanwhile the boundaries between different textures, such as lips, become more consist with the ground truth. Though the reconstruction results appear more like a blurred version compared with the ground truth, which results from the lossy transformation of cross-encoder as well as auto-encoder, they remain recognizable and could be set as a baseline performance for further improvement.

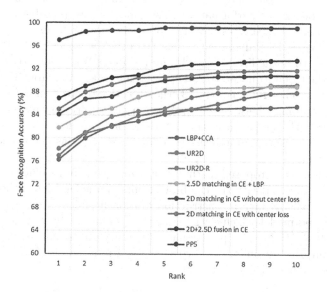

Fig. 6. CMC curves for recognition accuracy on FRGC Ver2.0 face database following the protocol defined in [9]. Here UR2D and UR2D refer to the approaches proposed in their paper and PP5 are results given by a FR software [2].

4.4   2D-3D Asymmetric FR

Compared with 2D/2D and 3D/3D FR experiments, very few attempts have been made on 2D/3D asymmetric FR. For convenience of comparison, we conduct the quantitative experiments on the FRGC Ver2.0 face database by following three recent and representative protocols reported respectively in [8,9,24]. These protocols mainly differ in gallery and probe splittings, and it is noticeable that in none of these protocols was there any overlap between our training and test set for evaluating the generalization capacity of the proposed method. In addition, we add LBP+CCA method for each experiment as a baseline to derive a more intuitive evaluation.

To highlight the effectiveness of the proposed method, we simply adopt the cosine similarity of 4096-d hidden layer features as 2D-2D matching scores, the LBP histogram features are extracted from depth images and Chi-square distance between them is computed as 3D-3D matching scores. As for the score fusion stage, all scores are normalized to [0,1] and fused by a simple sum rule.

The comparison results are illustrated in Fig. 6 through which we could gain the observation that our method achieves a higher accuracy than most baseline approach and the fusion between learned discriminative feature and 2.5D-2.5D matching effectively helps improve the performance. The accuracy increase gained by adding center loss to the framework also reflected the significance of the joint loss. Unfortunately, the proposed framework seems uncompetitive against state-of-the-art performance, this could be interpretable at three levels: (1) our method integrates very few preprocessing steps except for a rough eye location based face alignment, while the other methods make the most of 3D prototypes to normalize pose and illumination, (2) as a supervised learning method, the lack of adequate 2D/2.5D pairs remains an inevitable bottleneck for learning a more powerful classifier, (3) the objective of cross-encoder is twofold, hence the compromise between reconstruction and discriminative feature learning, together with the intrinsic characteristic of being lossy in cross-encoder, might requires a more comprehensive architecture, such as deeper network, as an improvement.

Nevertheless, the proposed method is advantageous in its efficiency and 3D-free reconstruction capacity. To the best of our knowledge, this is the first time to investigate a 2.5D face reconstruction approach which is free of any forms of 3D prototype models, including 3D meshes, point clouds and statistical 3D shape models. With less computational complexity on 2D images, it takes only 1.6 ms to complete an online forward pass for a mini-batch of 125 images, i.e. 0.0128 ms per image (Tables 1 and 2).

Table 1. Recognition accuracy on FRGC with protocol of [8].

2D/3D FR method	Accuracy
LBP+CCA	0.7851
2.5D matching in CE + LBP	0.8029
2D matching in CE without center loss	0.8200
2D matching in CE with center loss	0.8531
2D+2.5D fusion in CE	0.8646
MSDA+ELM [8]	**0.9680**

Table 2. Recognition accuracy on FRGC with protocol of [24].

2D/3D FR method	Accuracy
LBP+CCA	0.7851
2.5D matching in CE + LBP	0.8133
2D matching in CE without center loss	0.8400
2D matching in CE with center loss	0.8600
2D+2.5D fusion in CE	0.8733
GRBM+rKCCA [24]	**0.9600**

5   Conclusion

In this paper, we have presented a novel deep CNN framework as a fusion scheme for 2D/2.5D heterogeneous face recognition. This approach combines the reconstruction capacity of conventional auto-encoder and the discriminative feature extraction for cross-modality learning. The extensive experiments have convincingly evidenced that this framework successfully reconstructs recognizable 2.5D from single 2D while being adaptive and sufficient for HFR. Our future work will be concentrated on network improvement and super-resolution realization. Besides, this architecture could hopefully be generalized to other heterogeneous FR tasks, such as visible light vs. near-infrared and 2.5D vs. forensic sketch, which provides an interesting and promising prospect.

References

1. UHDB11 face database (2009).http://cbl.uh.edu/URxD/datasets/
2. PittPatt face recognition software development kit (PittPatt SDK) v5.2 (2011)
3. Asthana, A., Zafeiriou, S., Cheng, S., Pantic, M.: Incremental face alignment in the wild. In: Proceedings of the IEEE Conference on Computer Vision and Pattern Recognition, pp. 1859–1866 (2014)
4. Blanz, V., Vetter, T.: Face recognition based on fitting a 3D morphable model. IEEE Trans. Pattern Anal. Mach. Intell. **25**(9), 1063–1074 (2003)
5. Chowdhury, A.R., Chellappa, R., Krishnamurthy, S., Vo T.: 3D face reconstruction from video using a generic model. In: Proceedings of 2002 IEEE International Conference on Multimedia and Expo, ICME 2002, vol. 1, pp. 449–452. IEEE (2002)
6. Gu, L., Kanade, T.: 3D alignment of face in a single image. In: 2006 IEEE Computer Society Conference on Computer Vision and Pattern Recognition (CVPR 2006), vol. 1, pp. 1305–1312. IEEE (2006)
7. Huang, D., Ardabilian, M., Wang, Y., Chen, L.: Oriented gradient maps based automatic asymmetric 3D–2D face recognition. In: 2012 5th IAPR International Conference on Biometrics (ICB), pp. 125–131. IEEE (2012)
8. Jin, Y., Cao, J., Ruan, Q., Wang, X.: Cross-modality 2D–3D face recognition via multiview smooth discriminant analysis based on ELM. J. Electr. Comput. Eng. **2014**, 21 (2014)

9. Kakadiaris, I.A., et al.: 3D–2D face recognition with pose and illumination normalization. Comput. Vis. Image Underst. **154**, 137–151 (2016)
10. Kemelmacher-Shlizerman, I., Basri, R.: 3D face reconstruction from a single image using a single reference face shape. IEEE Trans. Pattern Anal. Mach. Intell. **33**(2), 394–405 (2011)
11. Le, Q.V.: Building high-level features using large scale unsupervised learning. In: 2013 IEEE International Conference on Acoustics, Speech and Signal Processing, pp. 8595–8598. IEEE (2013)
12. Li, S.Z.: Encyclopedia of Biometrics: I–Z, vol. 1. Springer, Heidelberg (2009)
13. Liu, F., Zeng, D., Zhao, Q., Liu, X.: Joint face alignment and 3D face reconstruction. In: Leibe, B., Matas, J., Sebe, N., Welling, M. (eds.) ECCV 2016. LNCS, vol. 9909, pp. 545–560. Springer, Cham (2016). https://doi.org/10.1007/978-3-319-46454-1_33
14. Masci, J., Meier, U., Cireşan, D., Schmidhuber, J.: Stacked convolutional autoencoders for hierarchical feature extraction. In: Honkela, T., Duch, W., Girolami, M., Kaski, S. (eds.) ICANN 2011. LNCS, vol. 6791, pp. 52–59. Springer, Heidelberg (2011). https://doi.org/10.1007/978-3-642-21735-7_7
15. Matthews, I., Xiao, J., Baker, S.: 2D vs. 3D deformable face models: Representational power, construction, and real-time fitting. Int. J. Comput. Vis. **75**(1), 93–113 (2007)
16. Odena, A., Dumoulin, V., Olah, C.: Deconvolution and checkerboard artifacts (2016). http://distill.pub/2016/deconv-checkerboard/
17. Phillips, P.J.: Overview of the face recognition grand challenge. In: 2005 IEEE Computer Society Conference on Computer Vision and Pattern Recognition (CVPR 2005), vol. 1, pp. 947–954. IEEE (2005)
18. Riccio, D., Dugelay, J.-L.: Geometric invariants for 2D/3D face recognition. Pattern Recognit. Lett. **28**(14), 1907–1914 (2007)
19. Rifai, S., Vincent, P., Muller, X., Glorot, X., Bengio, Y.: Contractive auto-encoders: explicit invariance during feature extraction. In: Proceedings of the 28th International Conference on Machine Learning (ICML 2011), pp. 833–840 (2011)
20. Savran, A., et al.: Bosphorus database for 3D face analysis. In: Schouten, B., Juul, N.C., Drygajlo, A., Tistarelli, M. (eds.) BioID 2008. LNCS, vol. 5372, pp. 47–56. Springer, Heidelberg (2008). https://doi.org/10.1007/978-3-540-89991-4_6
21. Springenberg, J.T., Dosovitskiy, A., Brox, T., Riedmiller, M.: Striving for simplicity: the all convolutional net. arXiv preprint arXiv:1412.6806 (2014)
22. Toderici, G., et al.: Bidirectional relighting for 3D-aided 2D face recognition. In: 2010 IEEE Conference on Computer Vision and Pattern Recognition (CVPR), pp. 2721–2728. IEEE (2010)
23. Vincent, P., Larochelle, H., Bengio, Y., Manzagol, P.-A.: Extracting and composing robust features with denoising auto encoders. In: Proceedings of the 25th International Conference on Machine Learning, pp. 1096–1103. ACM (2008)
24. Wang, X., Ly, V., Guo, R., Kambhamettu, C.: 2D–3D face recognition via restricted Boltzmann machines. In: 2014 International Conference on Computer Vision Theory and Applications (VISAPP), vol. 2, pp. 574–580. IEEE (2014)
25. Wen, Y., Zhang, K., Li, Z., Qiao, Y.: A discriminative feature learning approach for deep face recognition. In: Leibe, B., Matas, J., Sebe, N., Welling, M. (eds.) ECCV 2016. LNCS, vol. 9911, pp. 499–515. Springer, Cham (2016). https://doi.org/10.1007/978-3-319-46478-7_31
26. Yin, L., Wei, X., Sun, Y., Wang, J., Rosato, M.J.: A 3D facial expression database for facial behavior research. In: 7th International Conference on Automatic Face and Gesture Recognition (FGR 2006), pp. 211–216. IEEE (2006)

27. Zeiler, M.D., Fergus, R.: Visualizing and understanding convolutional networks. In: Fleet, D., Pajdla, T., Schiele, B., Tuytelaars, T. (eds.) ECCV 2014. LNCS, vol. 8689, pp. 818–833. Springer, Cham (2014). https://doi.org/10.1007/978-3-319-10590-1_53
28. Zeiler, M.D., Taylor, G.W., Fergus, R.: Adaptive deconvolutional networks for mid and high level feature learning. In: 2011 International Conference on Computer Vision, pp. 2018–2025. IEEE (2011)
29. Zhang, W., Huang, D., Wang, Y., Chen, L.: 3D aided face recognition across pose variations. In: Zheng, W.-S., Sun, Z., Wang, Y., Chen, X., Yuen, P.C., Lai, J. (eds.) CCBR 2012. LNCS, vol. 7701, pp. 58–66. Springer, Heidelberg (2012). https://doi.org/10.1007/978-3-642-35136-5_8
30. Zhao, X., et al.: Benchmarking asymmetric 3D–2D face recognition systems. In: 2013 10th IEEE International Conference and Workshops on Automatic Face and Gesture Recognition (FG), pp. 1–8. IEEE (2013)

Neural Approach for Context Scene Image Classification Based on Geometric, Texture and Color Information

Ameni Sassi[1]([✉]), Wael Ouarda[1], Chokri Ben Amar[1], and Serge Miguet[2]

[1] REGIM-Lab.: REsearch Groups in Intelligent Machines,
University of Sfax, ENIS, BP 1173, 3038 Sfax, Tunisia
{ameni.sessi.tn,wael.ouarda,chokri.benamar}@ieee.org
[2] LIRIS, Université de Lyon, UMR CNRS 5202, Université Lumiére Lyon 2,
5 av. Mendès-France, Bât C, N 123, 69676 Bron, Lyon, France
serge.miguet@univ-lyon2.fr

Abstract. Revealing the context of a scene from low-level features representation, is a challenging task for quite a long time. The classification of landscapes scenes to urban and rural categories is a preliminary task for landscapes scenes understanding. Having a global idea about the scene context (rural or urban) before investigating its details, would be an interesting way to predict the content of that scene. In this paper, we propose a novel features representation based on skyline, colour and texture, transformed by a sparse coding using Stacked Auto-Encoder. To evaluate our proposed approach; we construct a new database called SKYLINEScene Database containing 2000 images of rural and urban landscapes with a high degree of diversity. Many experiments were carried out using this database. Our approach shows it robustness in landscapes scenes classification.

Keywords: Deep neural network · Auto-encoder ·
Scene classification · Skyline and curvature

1 Introduction

Having a wider idea about the preference of people for the skyline of the cities where they live or they want to visit, is an important issue in social urbanism. This study was in the framework of a sustainable city project SKYLINE. The main purposes of that project is the identification and the systematic-analyze of the landscapes perceptions of the general public and practitioners by corresponding the aspects taken from the skyline photographs and the perceptions collected from an interesting number of audiences within European cities (The example of London and Lyon). One of our distant goals is to objectify the effect of natural elements such as vegetation and mountains on the representations of urban landscapes using a photo-questionnaire system.

The first step to achieve our goals is to reveal, from a landscape photo, if it represents a city or a rural scene, by scanning the whole skyline. The Skyline

© Springer Nature Switzerland AG 2019
L. Chen et al. (Eds.): RFMI 2017, CCIS 842, pp. 110–120, 2019.
https://doi.org/10.1007/978-3-030-19816-9_9

could be defined as the silhouette describing a place, or in other words, the profile of some cities or towns or different places. The nature of a skyline is an important cue on evaluating the landscapes perceptions. So, classifying a landscape scenes into urban and rural ones would be a sufficient first step for our purposes. This study is dedicated to the classification of landscapes scenes based on a deep neural approach with a new combination of some features which are geometric, texture and color.

The rest of the paper is composed of four major sections. The first one exposes some related works. Then, in the second part, we will describe our proposed neural approach for landscapes classification. After that we present our constructed database and some first results evaluating our proposed approach. The last section contains the conclusions about the realized works and some perspectives that will be the goal of a future work.

2   Related Works

Natural scenes classification is an interesting task for a variety of applications of computer vision (content-based image retrieval systems [5], pattern recognition, image understanding...). This topic can touch many facets of computer vision like scene segmentation or labelling, scene parsing or object detection [4].

The work [3] proposed a hybrid holistic/semantic approach for natural scenes classification. Using the Hierarchical Matching Pursuit (HMP) to learn holistic features and the Semantic Spatial Pyramid SSP to represent the spatial object information, this work combined these two strategies with a support vector machine (SVM) to propose a scene classification methodology. Their hybrid approach reached a global accuracy of 78.2% using a dataset of 700 images containing six natural scenes (forests, coasts, rivers/lakes, plains, mountains, and sky/clouds). Another work touching the facet of scene parsing [14] proposed an approach for outdoor scenes classification. The first step in their process is to generate Spatially Constrained Location Prior (SCLP). The second one is the prediction of class probabilities using visual feature based classifiers. This last step is followed by the propagation of contextual class votes based on SCLP to reach the final step which is the integration of visual feature based class probabilities and contextual class votes. The visual features used in that work were the RGB histograms in addition to the texton and SIFT histograms. They adopted the SVM with radial basis function kernel as a classifier. The performance of the proposed approach in [14] was evaluated in two datasets (The Stanford Background and SIFT Flow) and gave a global accuracy of 81.2% and a class accuracy of 71.8% for the first dataset. Reviewing the approaches that combine object detection and scene classification, we found out that work [13] that proposes CRF (conditional random field) models reasoning jointly about object detection, image labelling and scene classification. To create the unitary potentials (composing their holistic model) for the scenes, they used a standard bag-of-words spatial pyramid with a sparse coding dictionary on RGB histograms, color moment invariants, SIFT features and colorSIFT, and trained a linear one-vs-all SVM classifier. The scene classification accuracy reached in this work was 80.6% on the MSRC-21 dataset (origMSRC).

3 Proposed System

As shown in the Fig. 1 the proposed system is composed of three main processing steps: (1) the features extraction from landscapes images based on the skyline and the texton, (2) the training of a deep neural network (sparse autoencoders), and (3) the classification process based on the extracted visual features.

We used a deep neural network to achieve the task of skylines classification based on the geometric and the texture-color features. Thus, we train a neural network using two hidden layers. These hidden layers are trained individually using autoencoders. After that, for the classification process, we compared the results using a support vector machine and a softmax classifier.

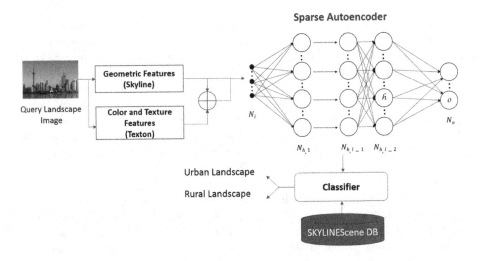

Fig. 1. Architecture of the proposed system

3.1 Features Extraction

3.1.1 Skyline's Geometric Description

Based on the sky line extracted from landscapes scenes, we took out suitable measurements allowing to distinguish between rural landscapes and urban landscapes.

The Straight Lines Classification. The idea was to take a look at the skyline as a polyline and determine if there is an important number of straight lines. So, we begin by extracting the straight line segments based on the Douglas-Peucker approximation algorithm [11]. Then, we compute the resulting segments length.

After that, we create categories based on segments length distribution; and then counting segments by length category to get a histogram presenting the number of segments on each category of segments length. The limits of categories' intervals follow the form of geometric sequence and it depend on three main elements which are: (i) the shortest segment length within the approximated skyline, (ii) the number of the categories itself, and (iii) the height of the landscape image. The used sequence helps in having an appropriate histogram for each landscape image and avoids getting categories with no segments. An example of the obtained histograms is shown in Fig. 2(c).

To characterize each skyline with concrete values, we generate histograms with different distribution in order to highlight the linkage between the number of segments per skyline and their length and get a significant value of the mean segments size (Fig. 2(d)). The mean segments size, derived from these cumulated histograms, and the length of the longest segment on the skyline could be an indicative couple of values that describes the skyline in a global way: the skyline is almost artificial or natural. The obtained values and more details are illustrated on [12]. These values are illustrated in the second and third column of the Table 1 for some samples of skylines.

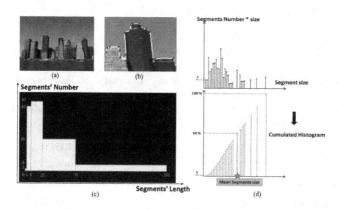

Fig. 2. (a) The cityscape of New York (b) The polygonal approximated segments of the skyline (c) The segments classification histogram (d) Modified cumulated histogram

The Curvature Analysis. By examining the skyline curve, we can affirm that the curvature goes through a lot of changes. It is clear that the mountain peaks, the indentation created by a vegetation, and the structure of a building have very different values of curvature. To calculate the curvature, we admit the formula (1) where the skyline is the curve defined by (2).

$$k(t) = \frac{\dot{x}(t)\ddot{y}(t) - \ddot{x}(t)\dot{y}(t)}{(\dot{x}^2(t) + \dot{y}^2(t))^{3/2}} \tag{1}$$

$$c = (x(t), y(t)) \tag{2}$$

To well determine the geometric features along the skyline and select the most important key points, we used the curvature scale-space description CSS. This descriptor was at the first time introduced by [7] and used for a variety of applications such as: the shape similarity retrieval [6] and the corner detection [8]. The process comprises the computation of the curvature values for a curve that has to be smoothed progressively on each scale via Gaussian kernels. So, we have a different set of curvatures values at each smoothing scale. The skylines, we get in different smoothing scales for different rural landscapes images, depict an important number of key points that replicate the fast variation in the curvature, nevertheless, these points vanished from low smoothing scales. In contrast, for urban landscapes, the corners of buildings or any remarkable point fight till high scales of smoothing. To interpret these notes with values, we represented the waning of the key points' number across different scales of smoothing as scatter plots (Fig. 3). The concrete number describing these graphics we picked, is the percentage of key points that resist until the middle smoothing scale. To validate our observations, these percentages for cityscapes should be higher than the ones we got for rural landscapes [12]. Some percentages for diverse landscapes are shown in Table 1. These plotted curves validate the short lifetime of the key points across the scales in rural landscapes, unlike, the case for urban landscapes where these points persist until very high scales.

Table 1. Geometric descriptive values for some skylines

Landscape image	Index of the mean segments size	Longest segment	% Percentage of resisting key points at the middle scale
New York	24	68	14.444444
Dubai	40	114	10.465116
London	24	50	8.928571
Rural landscape 1	18	41	3.773585
Rural landscape 2	16	23	6.703911
Rural landscape 3	19	26	4.83871

3.1.2   Colour and Texton for Skylines

Colour and texture are frequently used as low-level features for image classification. Looking at the part of the image under the skyline, we can notice that the colour and the texture presenting buildings are different from the ones describing mountains or vegetation. Then, the colour and the texture could be discriminative features to distinguish between landscapes with urban skyline and rural landscapes. Searching on recent works proposing a combination between colour and texture features, we found this one [1] that suggests to compute the image textons following the original definition [2] and adding the color information. Starting with the definition of texton as blob attributes, this work proposed a texture representation based on Bag of Words framework, that represents the texture-colour image content.

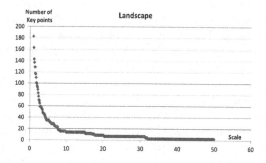

Fig. 3. The lifetime of skyline key points over smoothing scales

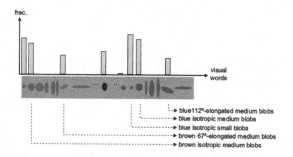

Fig. 4. A schematic representation of the JTD [1]

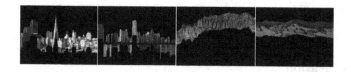

Fig. 5. The under-skylines images

For the colour-texture representation of our landscapes images, we applied the co-joint texton descriptor (JTD). This descriptor is defined as the probability density function of a bidimensional random variable (C, S); C concerns the quantised colour texton space and S concerns the quantised shape texton space. The Fig. 4 depicts an example of a JTD descriptor. This colour texture descriptor were applied to our SKYLINEScene database to represent the part under skyline and not the whole image, as shown in the Fig. 5.

3.2 Deep Neural Network Training

The deep architecture used in our system was a stacked auto-encoders architecture that has a series of inputs, outputs and hidden layers. So for that, we have used the nonlinear auto-encoders (Fig. 6) to construct each hidden layer of the deep neural network. The input layer of the first hidden layer (first auto-encoder) is the input layer for the all network. Starting from the second hidden layer (Second autoencoder), there is always reconstructing of the output of the previous layer. Namely, for each layer, we have reconstructed features using a number of neuron smaller than the number of neuron of the previous one. Using this method, we have constructed a deep neural network with two hidden layers using the extracted geometric skyline features. We have trained the two hidden layers individually using two unsupervised autoencoders. The objective of the reconstruction of features and reducing the number of neuron of each hidden layer is to force the network to learn only the most important features and achieve a dimensionality reduction and separate the maximum between features of classes [9,10]. Finally, we obtained an unsupervised neural network which is shown in the Fig. 6.

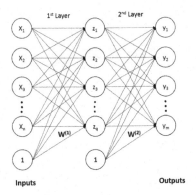

Fig. 6. Unsupervised neural network architecture

3.3 Classification

3.3.1 The SVM Classifier

The simple Support Vector Machines Classifier performs with low complexity than other kernels such as sigmoid, radial basis function, polynomial. For the SVM classification the challenge is to find the appropriate hyper plane that separates the data in two classes. The used architecture of multiSVM aims to construct two groups separated by the optimal hyper plane. We can find more than one hyper plane. In fact, another problem appear when the data are not in linear possibility of separation. The strength of SVM classifier compared to the Neural Network method is that the SVM is capable to overcome with the convergence problem in a local minimum of the optimization function. It scales relatively well to low dimensional data and the trade-off between classifier complexity and error can be explicitly controlled.

3.3.2   The Softmax Classifier

The SoftMax classifier denoted as SMC is a supervised model which generalizes logistic regression as

$$f_{w^{(3)}}(z) = \frac{1}{1 + exp(-W^{(3)^T} z)} \tag{3}$$

where $f_{w^{(3)}}$ is a sigmoid function having as parameters $W^{(3)}$. When the input z of the softmax classifier is a high-level representation of the skyline features learned by the Stacked Sparse Auto-Encoder, the Softmax's parameter $W^{(3)}$ is trained with the set explained in (4) to minimize the cost function. By minimizing the cost function with respect to $W^{(3)}$ via the gradient descent based approach, the parameter $W^{(3)}$ can then be determined.

$$\left\{ h^{(2)}(k), y(k) \right\}_{k=1}^{N} \tag{4}$$

4   Experiments and Results

In this section, we evaluate our proposed approach on SKYLINEScene database. The photographs taken into consideration in our constructed database are the ones showing the global view of cities or rural places. We experiment, first, the use of the geometric features extracted from the sky Line to get the classification accuracies. To find the Auto-Encoder neural network architecture that gives the best accuracies results, we have experimented three architectures with a final SoftMax layer. The results are summarized in Table 2. To reveal if the SVM classifier gives better results than the SoftMax classifier, we make some tests using different SVM kernel functions. The experimental configuration for the SVM classifier is as follow: the dataset is randomly divided into ten folds; one fold for the test and the lasting nine folds for training. The average performance of ten folds testing data is reported. The parameters of SVMs are set by two-fold cross-validation on the training data. The reported overall performance is the average accuracy of the two classes. Table 3 illustrates the accuracies and the standard deviation values for three different kernel functions.

Table 4 shows the classification accuracy obtained using our proposed neural approach based on the combination of the geometric, the color and the texture features from Skylines. These accuracies show up the usability of the geometric features extracted from skylines in the classification of landscapes scene since this horizon line is a very specific feature to landscapes images. Combining the geometric features with the texton ones, the classification accuracy reaches 84.92%.

To have a global vision about the performance of our proposed system for context scene classification, we summarized in the Table 5 the related works mentioned in the state of the art. We can notice that there is obviously differences between the number of classes and also the images per classes. Our approach proves it robustness in landscapes scenes classification behind the existing approaches.

Table 2. Classification accuracies using a softmax classifier

Architecture		Accuracies	Urban accuracy	Rural accuracy
1st HL	2nd HL			
300	150	**85.78%**	88.12%	83.7%
30	15	85.7%	88.44%	83.3%
20	10	85.68%	88.34%	83.32%

Table 3. Classification accuracies using an SVM classifier

kernel function	Accuracy	Standard deviation
Linear	82.86%	0.006
RBF (sigma $=5$)	**83.87%**	0.007
Polynomial (3 planes)	78.09%	0.0381

Table 4. Classification accuracies depending on features

Features vector	Accuracy	Standard deviation
Geometric (Skyline)	83.87%	0.007
Color and texture (Texton)	62.97%	0.0012
Geometric+color+texture	**84.92%**	0.001

Table 5. Comparison of our system with the state of the art related works

Works	Datasets	Image per class	Scene classes	Total images	Image size	Results
[13]	MSRC-21	$\sim$13	21	591	320×213	80.6%
[3]	Natural scene dataset	$\sim$100	6	700	480×720	78.2%
[14]	The Stanford background	$\sim$90	8	715	320×240	81.2%
Our approach	SkylineScene	1000	2	2000	320×240	84.92%

5 Conclusions

This paper introduce a new neural approach for landscapes scenes classification based on a very specific feature which is the skyline and the color-texture features. To represent these combination of low-level features, we build a sparse stacked Auto-Encoders architecture to have a new structure of our input data. The new SKYLINEScene database, containing a specific collection of rural and urban landscapes photographs, was created to evaluate our approach. The classification accuracies reached are very competitive and they confirm that the skyline is a significant geometric feature for landscapes scenes.

Our work with the geometric features of the skyline should be expanded by using other tools to describe better the skyline. The results obtained using our skyline-based approach to classify landscapes scenes will be compared with similar works based on a variety of local and global features.

Acknowledgements. The authors would like to acknowledge the financial support of this work by grants from General Direction of Scientific Research (DGRST), Tunisia, under the ARUB program.

This work was funded by the "ANR-12-VBDU-0008 - Skyline" project of the "Agence Nationale de la Recherche (ANR)", and by the LabEx "Intelligence des mondes Urbains - IMU".

References

1. Alvarez, S., Vanrell, M.: Texton theory revisited: a bag-of-words approach to combine textons. Pattern Recognit. **45**(12), 4312–4325 (2012)
2. Bergen, J.R., Julesz, B.: Rapid discrimination of visual patterns. IEEE Trans. Syst. Man Cybern. **13**(5), 857–863 (1983)
3. Chen, Z., Chi, Z., Fu, H.: A hybrid holistic/semantic approach for scene classification. In: 22nd International Conference on Pattern Recognition, ICPR 2014, Stockholm, Sweden, 24–28 August 2014, pp. 2299–2304 (2014)
4. Lazzez, O., Ouarda, W., Alimi, A.M.: Age, gender, race and smile prediction based on social textual and visual data analyzing. In: Madureira, A.M., Abraham, A., Gamboa, D., Novais, P. (eds.) ISDA 2016. AISC, vol. 557, pp. 206–215. Springer, Cham (2017). https://doi.org/10.1007/978-3-319-53480-0_21
5. Lazzez, O., Ouarda, W., Alimi, A.M.: Understand me if you can! Global soft biometrics recognition from social visual data. In: Abraham, A., Haqiq, A., Alimi, A.M., Mezzour, G., Rokbani, N., Muda, A.K. (eds.) HIS 2016. AISC, vol. 552, pp. 527–538. Springer, Cham (2017). https://doi.org/10.1007/978-3-319-52941-7_52
6. Mokhtarian, F., Abbasi, S.: Shape similarity retrieval under affine transforms. Pattern Recognit. **35**(1), 31–41 (2002)
7. Mokhtarian, F., Mackworth, A.K.: Scale-based description and recognition of planar curves and two-dimensional shapes. IEEE Trans. Pattern Anal. Mach. Intell. **8**(1), 34–43 (1986)
8. Mokhtarian, F., Suomela, R.: Robust image corner detection through curvature scale space. IEEE Trans. Pattern Anal. Mach. Intell. **20**(12), 1376–1381 (1998)
9. Nasri, H., Ouarda, W., Alimi, A.M.: ReLiDSS: Novel lie detection system from speech signal. In: 2016 IEEE/ACS 13th International Conference of Computer Systems and Applications (AICCSA), pp. 1–8 (2016)

10. Ouarda, W., Trichili, H., Alimi, A.M., Solaiman, B.: Towards a novel biometric system for smart riding club. J. Inf. Assur. Secur. **11**(4) (2016)
11. Ramer, U.: An iterative procedure for the polygonal approximation of plane curves. Comput. Graph. Image Process. **1**(3), 244–256 (1972)
12. Sassi, A., Ben Amar, C., Miguet, S.: Skyline-based approach for natural scene identification. In: 13th IEEE/ACS International Conference of Computer Systems and Applications, AICCSA 2016, Agadir, Morocco, 29 November–2 December 2016, pp. 1–8 (2016)
13. Yao, J., Fidler, S., Urtasun R.: Describing the scene as a whole: joint object detection, scene classification and semantic segmentation. In: CVPR, pp. 702–709. IEEE Computer Society (2012)
14. Zhang, L., Verma, B., Stockwell, D.R.B., Chowdhury, S.: Spatially constrained location prior for scene parsing. In: 2016 International Joint Conference on Neural Networks, IJCNN 2016, Vancouver, BC, Canada, 24–29 July 2016, pp. 1480–1486 (2016)

Self-learning Framework with Temporal Filtering for Robust Maritime Vessel Detection

Amir Ghahremani$^{(\boxtimes)}$, Egor Bondarev, and Peter H. N. de With

Eindhoven University of Technology, Eindhoven, The Netherlands
A.Ghahremani@tue.nl

Abstract. With the recent development in ConvNet-based detectors, a successful solution for vessel detection becomes possible. However, it is essential to access a comprehensive annotated training set from different maritime environments. Creating such a dataset is expensive and time consuming. To automate this process, this paper proposes a novel self learning framework which automatically finetunes a generic pre-trained model to any new environment. With this, the framework enables automated labeling of new dataset types. The method first explores the video frames captured from a new target environment to generate the candidate vessel samples. Afterwards, it exploits a temporal filtering concept to verify the correctly generated candidates as new labels for learning, while removing the false positives. Finally, the system updates the vessel model using the provided self-learning dataset. Experimental results on our real-world evaluation dataset show that generalizing a fine-tuned Single Shot Detector to a new target domain using the proposed self-learning framework increases the average precision and the F1-score by 12% and 5%, respectively. Additionally, the proposed temporal filter reduced the noisy detections in a sensitive setting from 58% to only 5%.

Keywords: Maritime surveillance · Vessel detection · Convolutional networks (CNN) · ConvNet · Self-learning · Automated dataset creation

1 Introduction

With recent advances in automated surveillance systems, maritime and harbor authorities start actively exploiting machine vision techniques. In such an advanced systems, an important application is to monitor the maritime environment against contingent hazards jeopardized by unknown pathless watercrafts. In order to realize this, surveillance systems have to process and analyze the visual data collected by cameras deployed along the shorelines.

Surveying the conventional visual monitoring methodologies, object detection is routinely regarded as the first main task [1,2]. Common historic methods have achieved robust results by exploiting regional variations of pixels, as a

© Springer Nature Switzerland AG 2019
L. Chen et al. (Eds.): RFMI 2017, CCIS 842, pp. 121–135, 2019.
https://doi.org/10.1007/978-3-030-19816-9_10

distinctive indication of moving object presence (e.g. background subtraction approaches) [3,4]. However, the fluctuating nature of water as a dominant background for a typical maritime scene leads to failure when using such conventional detection methods. Additionally, a maritime surveillance camera does not only capture water, but also land pieces and infrastructure. Consequently, irrelevant objects moving in non-water regions would initiate or cause false positives. As a strategy for handling this challenge, irrelevant objects could be neglected using methods proposed to extract clusters of water pixels as regions of interest [5]. However, falsely detected/missed regions triggered by complex scenes and scenarios still expose the system to detect unrelated objects. Moreover, maritime scenes often contain stationary vessels next to the shorelines, which are not detected either.

Contemporary development in convolutional neural networks (ConvNets) have substantially refashioned automated object detection procedures by deliberately seeking for the anticipated target patterns according to their inherent properties [6,7]. ConvNet detectors principally pursue the following scheme: feature extraction, bounding box generation, and classification. Among the state-of-the-art detectors, Single Shot Detector (SSD) [8] exceedingly outperforms its competitors in terms of speed and achieves satisfactory detection accuracy. In [8], the network has been successfully evaluated on several classical benchmark image sets. Although the manifold categories of objects are covered in those datasets, after investigating the samples, one can notice that images have a low resolution and are predominantly encompassing the intended object. Moreover, the challenging outdoor surveillance cases like complex background, miscellaneous weather conditions, divergent occlusion scenarios, multiple various-sized objects, different object distances to cameras, are not represented in classical benchmark samples. However, our research is based on the European APPS research project, aiming at industry-oriented Advanced Plug & Play Smart surveillance systems, where we consider all previously mentioned complex maritime surveillance scenarios.

Within the discussed setting, our objective is to enhance object detection with improved analysis based on deep learning. However, in first experiments, testing a pre-trained ConvNet model on the scenes having different characteristics from the original training set often failed to provide acceptable results. Consequently, the development of scene-specific object detectors has recently emerged as an attractive research topic pursued in many state-of-the-art publications [9–12]. These specific methods commonly attempt to automatically assemble appropriate samples from a target domain and then re-train the available model. In accordance with this, our main contribution is to extend the SSD to the ship detection problem and design a new transfer learning framework to achieve high precision in detection at a low false negative rate.

In this paper, we aim at exploiting ConvNets to detect vessels on genuine maritime surveillance image sequences. Initially, we found out that specific datasets dedicated to one harbor often cover a few camera viewpoints only (sometimes even from the same location) and show vessel types that are partly restricted and dominant for the related specific industrial harbor area. As a consequence, the training with such datasets leads to a specific detector that is not suited for a broad set of harbor areas because of limitations in camera setup and intrinsic parameters, which all leads to a lower performance for other environments.

In this paper, we therefore generalize the finetuned SSD on arbitrary scenes, scenarios and vessel types, and we propose a novel self-learning framework for maritime surveillance applications. The proposed system adopts the following blueprint. Firstly, it generates candidate samples from a new dataset using the finetuned vessel-oriented SSD architecture. These supplementary images are captured by a different camera in varying setups based on disparate locations and having various contexts. Secondly, the generated false positive candidates are discarded by endorsing the samples labeled as correct. To perform this, a dual-condition criterion is employed: (a) evaluate the confidence score of detections, and (b) apply a temporal filtering strategy to investigate the dynamics of the detected box over the sequence. Finally, the network enriches the verified sample set by adding images from successfully learned source data. This preserves the system from losing the already learned useful source information. Additionally, the model will be corrected on the source samples which unexpectedly prompt false detections. We evaluate the method on an annotated image set from various locations in several cities and suburbs in the Netherlands (including Amsterdam and Rotterdam) and Turkey (Istanbul). The images of this dataset are extracted from videos captured at different day/year-times. These images include objects with divergent size, captured from different camera positions and setups, appearing occlusions, object truncations, etc. Figure 1 illustrates a few examples extracted from this dataset.

This paper is organized as follows. Section 2 provides an overview on related work. Section 3 explains the proposed method. Section 4 presents the experimental results and validation. Section 5 concludes the paper.

2   Related Work

This section provides a brief overview on the research work on ConvNet transfer learning that performs the finetuning to adapt the object detector to the specific scenes.

Deep-learning based classifiers are widely exploited in many practical applications [6] because of their advantageous. Furthermore, also for ConvNets, this development has encouraged industry-oriented researchers to deploy them even in products. As a basic requirement, ConvNets need to be trained by suitable training sets. However, challenging practical cases are often not represented in the data produced in a laboratory. If those datasets are limited, semi-supervised and weakly-supervised learning-based methods can be exploited.

Self-learning aims to automatically sample data from a target domain and finetune a detector for the specific visual patterns. The main assumption is that finetuning a generic pre-trained detector with automatically extracted labels from an arbitrary set of target domain images, would adapt the detector to the target environment conditions. In [9], the transfer learning methods tuning a detector to a specific target domain, are categorized into three main groups.

Fig. 1. Six example images from evaluation set.

The methods falling into the first group [13], adjust the source learning parameters to enhance the model accuracy in an objective scope. These methods exploit prior knowledge about source data like visual information. The second group [14] aims at reducing the dissimilarities between the source and target domains by exploiting techniques for adapting distributions, i.e. to manipulate the marginal and conditional distributions to reduce the data dimension in both domains. In order to improve the ConvNet performance on a target domain, the third category of methods [9] enhances the training set by appending appropriate samples from the target domain. With this definition, our work belongs to the third group, since it automatically labels the data from the target domain.

Augmenting the complete source dataset with new samples extracted from a target environment increases the size of the training set and requires more iterations to convergence [13]. The work in [15] deploys a combination of the source samples together with new samples from a target scene. The method proposed in [11] collects only new samples from a target domain to produce the transfer learning dataset. Obviously, this method looses the advantageous information of the source data. In [16], the method gathers new samples from a target domain and combines those with the beneficial source samples only. Other methods exploit information like visual cues and contextual attributes, motion features, to enrich the training set by selecting useful samples from a target domain [17]. Additionally, the method in [10] deploys a sequential Monte Carlo filter to specialize a generic classifier to the specific scenes.

SSD (Single Shot Detector) is a feedforward ConvNet that evaluates the presence of an object instance in the pre-defined default bounding boxes, followed by a non-maximum suppression stage to produce the final detection. This detector allows to omit the region proposal generation stage, encapsulating all the computations in a single network. As stated in [8], SSD achieves 76.9% mAP on the PASCAL dataset. This ConvNet has also proved to be a fast general object detector, which is essential for real-time surveillance applications.

In this paper, we extend the SSD network to address multiple vessel detection problems. Firstly, the SSD network is pre-trained using the VGG-16 model [18] and will be finetuned on more than 48,000 maritime images. Then, we follow a bootstrapping procedure to improve the efficiency of the finetuned model on the training set. Additionally, we propose a novel target-domain specialization framework to automatically adapt the network to any dataset, captured by cameras with different intrinsic and setup. We also provide a challenging evaluation set, which consists of 1,041 annotated maritime surveillance images.

3   Architecture Pipeline

3.1   System Overview

Figure 2 illustrates the architecture of the proposed system, containing two main stages. In the first stage, an initial deep model of vessels is trained on top of the SSD using an image set collected from the current domain. We refer to these images as the initial dataset in the remainder of this paper. Since the main idea of this work is to propose a robust self-learning framework to generalize an initial model (pre-trained on the current domain) to a new target domain, it is not important which initial dataset is used in the first stage. It can be a generic benchmark dataset (e.g. PASCAL), or it can be collected and labeled from the current domain by the user. As mentioned before, we specifically focus on the vessel detection problem as part of our research for maritime surveillance within the industry-oriented APPS project. Therefore, we generate our initial model by finetuning a pre-trained PASCAL-based VGG model, using a non-public vessel-oriented dataset.

The second stage provides a self-learning block, which automatically selects the useful data from both the initial and the target-domain samples and finetunes the network. In the remainder of this paper, we will refer to these images as the "self-learning dataset". The second stage is divided into three sub-stages. The first and second sub-stage find those images from the initial dataset that result in false and true detections, respectively, to establish the self-learning set. The third sub-stage produces the candidate samples from the target domain and verifies them through a temporal filtering approach. Finally, the vessel model is updated with the self-learning set. The following subsections explain the dataflow and individual architectural modules in detail.

3.2   Deep Vessel Detection Model

A captured scene from a typical maritime environment contains various kinds of objects and structures (e.g. cars on the shorelines, bridges, buildings, etc.). In order to robustly detect all kinds of vessels independent from the surrounding environment, we employ ConvNet networks. For a surveillance application, the system should detect ships in real-time. Moreover, it should be robust against the real-world noisy data. Therefore, in this work, we have adopted the SSD detector. Here, the VGG model is used as the base model. We first finetune the network on a vessel-oriented image set. The system uses this as the initial model and supplies this to the second stage.

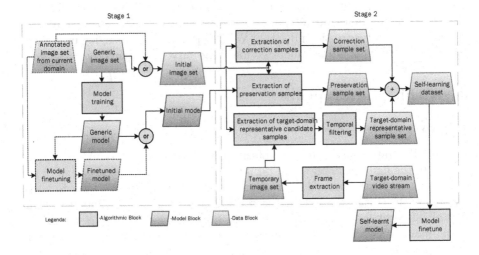

Fig. 2. Architecture of the proposed self-learning method.

3.3   Self-learning Process

The lack of labeled training data is a critical challenge for exploiting ConvNets in practical surveillance applications. Additionally, the performance of a trained deep detector often drops when testing for the new target domain, mainly when the scene structure or the camera characteristics change. To handle these challenges, self-learning has emerged as an interesting research topic among the state-of-the-art work.

In this second stage, we propose a novel self-learning data-augmentation framework for maritime surveillance applications. The input of this stage is the initial vessel-oriented model. Here, we aim at automated creation of the self-learning dataset to correct the initial vessel model and adapt the model to the new target domain. This second stage consists of three main parts, each appending new samples to the self-learning dataset.

Correction Samples. The SSD is trained on the initial dataset during the first stage. However, when we apply the network to the initial vessel-oriented training images, we face high amounts of false positives/negatives. This is a common machine learning problem and often happens since both the labeled objects and the background produce similar features at the training phase. Nevertheless, after exploring the false detections, we have found several unexpected cases, where the vessel is clearly in front of the camera. Therefore, the system starts generating the self-learning dataset by adding randomly selected samples from the initial images causing false detections.

Useful Source Samples. After applying the initial vessel model to the initial set, we observe plenty of images yielding just true positives. Obviously, the lack of those frames in the self-learning dataset deprives the system from useful information. Therefore, the system enriches the self-learning dataset using a random set of images including only those detected vessels. This ensures that the useful information from the source training set will be present among the self-training images.

Target-Domain Adaptation Samples. Although the initial dataset includes more than 48,000 images covering several types of the weather conditions, all images share a similar background and are captured by the same camera. Consequently, both the precision and detection rate drop when the network is applied to a new target domain (i.e. images captured by a different camera or from a new environment containing new vessel types and/or background). In order to address this problem, we have employed a self-learning process.

First, we alternatively extract random frames from the new target domain to make another image set, which is referred to as the temporary set. The system automatically generates a large number of candidate labels from the temporary set for the target-domain adaptation purpose. Since the network is already fine-tuned for vessel detection, it detects most of the watercrafts located at a close distance to the camera. A small fraction of far vessels are also detected. Detection misses mostly occur on vessels positioning far away from the camera. However, we have noticed that the absence of missed detections in the self-learning dataset does not affect the finetuning performance, since those missed vessels are typically detected in the next frames.

An important aspect is temporal filtering of the candidate labels. Briefly, the proposed self-learning framework first applies the initial model to the new target domain to produce the annotation labels. However, since the initial model is trained on the initial dataset, it does not generate the label for most of the desired new target-domain objects. In order to increase the number of annotated objects, we perform the detection with a low confidence score. Nevertheless, such a score results in more noise regions. However, we have noticed that false positive detections rarely happen for water clusters. Many false positives arise on the shorelines, bridges, buildings, e.g. on the objects that have special vessel-like structures. In order to refute the false detections, we propose to extract and use information from the frame sequence. Since the near-shoreline regions remain mostly/partly stationary during short intervals (a few seconds), the proposed system removes those false detections by performing a temporal filtering technique to discard the detected boxes with non-dynamic content. The filter considers the average value of the subtracted pixels over the entire bounding box to investigate the variation in the region through the short-time intervals. If the calculated variation is higher than the noise threshold (T_N), the detected bounding box is maintained as a true label. Otherwise, the system neglects the box.

Although the proposed temporal filter removes most of the false detections, still few labels of background regions remain among the correct labels with vessels. However, since the final signal-to-noise ratio is fairly high (see the Sect. 4), these defect labels do not considerably affect the framework performance. Additionally, the temporal filtering sometimes removes vessels moving at a far distance from the camera, since in short-time intervals those vessels' pixels do not change. This case can also happen for vessels standing next to the shorelines, especially when the water is not wavy. However, since we do not need to label all the visible vessels, this case is not critical. Concluding, according to the experimental results provided in the following section, the ratio between the correctly removed false detections and the incorrectly removed true positives, is rather high. Moreover, the ratio between removed background labels and the background labels remaining after the filtering, is also high.

In addition to the false detection boxes, the proposed system also ignores the objectless frames (i.e. the frames without detected vessels). At the end, the remaining frames will be added to the self-learning dataset. As the last step, the network will be finetuned with a low learning rate on the self-learning dataset.

4   Empirical Validation

This section begins with providing an overview on the experimental materials and process. Afterwards, we validate the proposed framework.

4.1   Experimental Process

A. Datasets

Botlek Dataset: In the first stage, the VGG-based SSD network is finetuned on our vessel-oriented initial dataset. Since this image set was captured from the Botlek region in the port of Rotterdam, we will refer to it as the Botlek dataset in the sequel of this paper. The Botlek dataset consists of 48,364 samples, which are extracted from videos shot in the Botlek region. The videos cover 6 different viewpoints on the region. Since the recordings were running for several months, a vast variety of weather conditions and daytimes are represented in this dataset. The camera model used in the recordings is Axis Q1604, which is a surveillance camera providing a resolution of $1,536 \times 2,048$ pixels, at 25 fps. Figure 3 illustrates three Botlek example frames.

Evaluation Dataset: To improve robustness of the finetuned network, we have recorded several videos from various locations in many waterways (lakes, channels, rivers, sea sides) in the Netherlands (including Amsterdam and Rotterdam) and Turkey (Istanbul). These videos were recorded during different day/year-periods. The videos contain a vast variety of camera setups embracing different viewpoints and heights. Additionally, several vessel types and detection scenarios are represented, including multiple occluded vessels with divergent sizes and distances to the cameras. Furthermore, water region-types like rivers, lakes, and under-bridges are covered. For the recordings, we have used the Canon D5500 camera with $1,080 \times 1,920$ pixel resolution. We have separated 50 videos for evaluation, randomly extracted 1,041 images and manually annotated those to make an evaluation dataset. It is important to mention that the videos used in the evaluation set are exclusively detached from the rest of the data.

Fig. 3. Three example images from the Botlek dataset.

Temporary Dataset: After separating the mentioned 50 videos for the evaluation set, we select another set of 20 videos from our new recordings to represent the new target domain. Then, we alternatively extract random frames with short-time differences from these videos to make the temporary set. Although a minority of these images contain similar background as the evaluation set samples, many different scenes are also included.

B. Architecture realization details

PASCAL-SSD: Our SSD network is configured based on an image resolution of 512×512 pixels. We compared the performance of the VGG-based SSDs pre-trained with the PASCAL VOC, COCO, and ILSVRC datasets on the evaluation set. Since the PASCAL-trained SSD produced the best detection results, we use this model as the basis for our work and will refer to this combination of network as PASCAL-SSD in the remainder of this paper. The model is pre-trained for 240,000 iterations.

Botlek-SSD: At the first stage, we finetune the PASCAL-SSD on the Botlek dataset for 196,855 iterations. A 25-% fraction of the images is used as test data and the rest of the images as training data. We start the finetuning at a learning rate of 0.001 and decrease the rate by a factor of 10 after 143,000 iterations. The finetuning is stopped when the final loss converges to 1.06. We call the resulting model Botlek-SSD, which will be supplied to the second stage.

Self-Learned SSD: As mentioned in the architecture section, generation of the triple self-learning training set is the main task of the second stage. To this end, first the Botlek-SSD performs the detection on the Botlek training set. Despite the 99-% precision rate with 59,759 correctly detected boxes, still 470 false positive and 10,438 false negative boxes appear among the results, spreading over 8,199 images. To represent the correction samples, the proposed system randomly adds 911 images out of these frames to the self-learning dataset. Additionally, the system arbitrarily picks 3,089 samples out of the 40,165 images providing just true positives, to keep the useful information of the source data.

To complete the self-learning dataset, the Botlek-SSD is applied on the temporary set to automatically generate the target-domain adaptation candidate samples. In this step, the system detects the boxes that provide confidence scores higher than 0.1. Although this low threshold value seems to increase the risk of false detections, the subsequent temporal filtering approach automatically verifies the target-domain adaptation samples and removes the irrelevant boxes. However, these exceptional rare cases occur when the illumination of the scene suddenly changes, or the detector recognizes a water region as a vessel. Nevertheless, these cases occur at a negligible rate. Here, the system selected 2,205 samples out of the 5,480 temporary set images and added them to the self-learning dataset.

Finally, the target-domain adapted model is produced by finetuning the Botlek-SSD on the self-learning dataset for 2,000 iterations with the learning rate of 0.0001.

4.2   Validation Results

In this subsection, we compare the self-learned SSD with the PASCAL-SSD and the Botlek-SSD. We also investigate the temporal filtering performance.

Temporal Filtering Performance: The proposed self-learning framework applies a low confidence score to produce a high number of candidate samples. This low score often results in many false detections of irrelevant objects. Since the initial model is already trained on vessels, and vessels intrinsically expose a structure in pixels, these false detections rarely occur on structureless dynamic water pixels. According to our experiments, partly-stationary background areas are the most likely regions that cause this detection noise. Our detector often produces false detections on the bridges and vessel-like buildings. Consequently, the proposed framework uses the temporal information of the frame sequences to identify and ignore the falsely produced candidate labels through the temporal filtering approach. In this subsection, we provide the statistical analysis of the temporal filtering algorithm.

The statistical analysis is as follows. After applying the Botlek-SSD (initial model) to the 5,480 images of the temporary set, the images and their corresponding candidate labels are processed by the temporal filtering block. This filter removes 3,275 images, since each frame has neither a detection, nor one or more produced candidate labels surviving the temporal filtering. In order to provide a statistical analysis on the performance of the proposed temporal filtering method, we investigate the remaining images. Since manual validation of all the labels from 2,205 remaining filtered images is too labor intensive, we explore 250 randomly selected annotated images for an approximate analysis. Prior to the temporal filter, the selected images contain 1,276 candidate labels, including 743 noise labels and 533 vessel labels. The filter correctly removes 680 noise boxes, while falsely keeping 63 noise labels as a vessel, i.e. 91.52% of the noise labels are correctly removed. Moreover, the filter correctly retains 454 vessel labels, which means only 14.82% of the vessels are removed by the filter. Overall, 58.23% of the provided candidates were noise labels prior to filtering and the temporal filter decreased this ratio to 4.94%. Figure 4 illustrates two examples on how the temporal filtering removes the falsely detected candidate labels.

Fig. 4. Two temporal filtering output examples.

Self-learning Framework Performance: Generally in a real-world outdoor monitoring application, items like the object size, distance to the camera, noise, occlusion, truncation, scene illumination and weather conditions, are considered when defining the performance expectations from the system. In order to accurately analyze the efficiency of the proposed target-domain adaptation approach, we select the vessel size, occlusion, and truncation as the criteria to derive the complete dataset into three versions of varying detection difficulty as follows:

- *Easy evaluation dataset*: the bounding-box size is more than 10,000 pixels, no occlusion, and no truncation;
- *Moderate evaluation dataset*: the bounding-box size is between 3,000 and 10,000 pixels, less than 30% of the vessel pixel area is occluded or truncated;
- *Hard evaluation dataset*: the bounding-box size is less than 3,000 pixels, more than 30% of the vessel pixel area is occluded or truncated.

We evaluate the previously introduced three methods on each level of difficulty. Tables 1, 2, and 3, illustrate the results. Each dataset class is tested three times with different Intersection-over-Union (IoU) thresholds. All the methods have performed the detection with the confidence score of 0.5. According to Table 1 (easy case), although the two vessel-adapted networks produce more true positives, the PASCAL-SSD surprisingly outperforms these methods in terms of the Average Precision (AP). However, by increasing the level of difficulty, the vessel-adapted methods produce better results. On the Moderate evaluation dataset, the Botlek-SSD is still outperformed by the PASCAL-SSD in terms of AP by 10%. However, the self-learned SSD produced the same AP as the PASCAL-SSD while showing a 6% higher F1-score, since it provides 235 more correct detections and 88 less object misses.

Table 1. Method comparison on easy evaluation dataset.

IoU	PASCAL-SSD			Botlek-SSD			Self-learned SSD		
	0.3	0.4	0.5	0.3	0.4	0.5	0.3	0.4	0.5
TP	874	843	825	858	843	817	911	898	881
FP	621	625	640	874	889	915	760	773	790
FN	245	249	264	234	249	275	181	194	211
AP	0.58	0.57	0.56	0.50	0.49	0.47	0.55	0.54	0.53
F1	0.66	0.66	0.65	0.61	0.60	0.58	0.66	0.65	0.64

Table 2. Method comparison on moderate evaluation dataset.

IoU	PASCAL-SSD			Botlek-SSD			Self-learned SSD		
	0.3	0.4	0.5	0.3	0.4	0.5	0.3	0.4	0.5
TP	1230	1214	1182	1361	1337	1286	1481	1459	1417
FP	495	511	543	830	854	905	567	589	631
FN	1196	1212	1244	1065	1089	1140	945	967	1009
AP	0.71	0.70	0.69	0.62	0.61	0.59	0.72	0.71	0.69
F1	0.59	0.58	0.57	0.59	0.58	0.56	0.66	0.65	0.63

Table 3. Method comparison on hard evaluation dataset.

IoU	PASCAL-SSD			Botlek-SSD			Self-learned SSD		
	0.3	0.4	0.5	0.3	0.4	0.5	0.3	0.4	0.5
TP	1479	1457	1417	1690	1660	1593	1784	1758	1711
FP	268	290	330	541	571	638	286	312	359
FN	3615	3637	3677	3404	3434	3501	3310	3336	3383
AP	0.85	0.83	0.81	0.76	0.74	0.71	0.86	0.85	0.83
F1	0.43	0.43	0.41	0.46	0.45	0.43	0.50	0.49	0.48

We select the Hard evaluation dataset with IoU $= 0.5$ as the criterion to compare the three methods in detail. For this dataset, the self-learned method outperforms the Botlek-SSD by 12% in terms of the AP. It also produces 279 less false detections, 118 less missed detections and 118 more true positives. Although the PASCAL-SSD is comparable with the proposed method in AP by producing a just 2% lower value, it provides 294 less correct detections, which means that network results in a 5.8% higher miss rate. Additionally, the proposed method outperforms both the PASCAL-SSD and the Botlek-SSD by 7% and 5%, respectively, for the F1-score. Figure 5 provides a comparison of the outputs of the methods on four evaluation frames. It is important to mention here that the initial model used in this paper is produced by finetuning the PASCAL-SSD on the non-public Botlek dataset. In case that an initial model is created only on the PASCAL dataset, e.g. without finetuning on a specific labeled maritime dataset, the performance results of the framework may become lower.

Fig. 5. Comparison of methods. From left to right, columns represent the outputs of the PASCAL-SSD, the Botlek-SSD, and the Self-learned SSD, respectively.

5   Discussions and Conclusions

The traditional object detection methods often fail to detect vessels under severe weather or raging water conditions. Additionally, the false negative probability of the detection of stationary vessels increases. However, a ConvNet-based system can enhance the possibilities of successfully addressing the vessel detection problem in the industry-oriented maritime surveillance applications, since ConvNets search for the desired objects independent of the surroundings.

In order to achieve robust results with ConvNets for a specific application, one needs to finetune a pre-trained model on a comprehensive annotated dataset collected from the desired target domain. However, by changing the location or capturing equipment, a system would need a new training dataset. Nevertheless, manual creation of a labeled training set is costly in terms of time. In order to solve this problem, the state-of-the-art methods are broadly exploiting semi-supervised techniques to design a framework that automatically finetunes a pre-trained ConvNet from the new raw data. Therefore, this paper has proposed a robust ConvNet self-learning framework for maritime vessel detection.

In this work, we first finetune a pre-trained single shot detector on an annotated maritime image set. This provides an initial vessel model, which is affected by the current domain characteristics. Second, we develop a self-learning framework which automatically generates the candidate labels from the target domain data, and performs a temporal filtering approach to verify the labeled samples. Finally, the system finetunes the model on the produced self-learning dataset. When applying this proposed framework to a SSD trained on a vessel-oriented dataset, the resulting network outperforms the initial model with a promising average precision of 83% at a high detection rate. This method also provides a 5% higher F-1 score. We have also presented an annotated evaluation dataset for the vessel detection problem, which contains challenging scenes and scenarios.

Future work will improve the proposed method in producing more verified labels from the target-domain data. Moreover, we plan to improve the detection efficiency on the vessel positioning at a far distance from the camera.

Acknowledgement. This work is supported by the European ITEA APPS project. We thank the company Vinotion for providing the Botlek dataset to us. We also show our gratitude to the company NVIDIA for granting us a "TITAN X PASCAL" GPU.

References

1. Khurana, P., Sharma, A., Singh, S.N., Singh, P.K.: A survey on object recognition and segmentation techniques. In: 3rd International IEEE Conference on Computing for Sustainable Global Development (INDIACom) (2016)
2. Shantaiya, S., Verma, K., Mehta, K.: A survey on approaches of object detection. Int. J. Comput. Appl. (0975–8887), **65**(18) (2013)
3. Bidyalakshmi Devi, R.B., Jina Chanu, Y., Singh, K.M.: A survey on different background subtraction method for moving object detection. Int. J. Res. Emerg. Sci. Technol. **3**(10) (2016)
4. Abdul Malik, A., Khalil, A., Ullah Khan, H.: Object detection and tracking using background subtraction and connected component labeling. Int. J. Comput. Appl. (0975–8887), **75**(13) (2013)

5. Ghahremani, A., Bondarev, E., de With, P.H.N.: Water region extraction in thermal and RGB sequences using spatiotemporally-oriented energy features. IS&T Electronic Imaging - Algorithms and Systems, USA (2017)
6. Druzhkov, P.N., Kustikova, V.D.: A survey of deep learning methods and software tools for image classification and object detection. Pattern Recognit. Image Anal. **26**(1), 9–15 (2016)
7. Cabrera-Vives, G., Reyes, I., Forstert, F., Estevez, P.A., Maureira, J.C.: Supernovae detection by using convolutional neural networks. In: International Joint Conference on Neural Networks, JCNN (2016)
8. Liu, W., et al.: SSD: single shot multibox detector. In: Leibe, B., Matas, J., Sebe, N., Welling, M. (eds.) ECCV 2016. LNCS, vol. 9905, pp. 21–37. Springer, Cham (2016). https://doi.org/10.1007/978-3-319-46448-0_2
9. Maâmatou, H., Chateau, T., Gazzah, S., Goyat, Y., Amara, N.E.B.: Transductive transfer learning to specialize a generic classifier towards a specific scene. In: VISIGRAPP (4: VISAPP) (2016)
10. Mhalla, A., Chateaub, T., Maâmatoua, H., Gazzaha, S., Amara, N.E.B.: SMC faster R-CNN: toward a scene-specialized multi-object detector. Comput. Vis. Image Underst. **164**, 1–13 (2017)
11. All, K., Hasler, D., Fleuret, F.: Flowboost—appearance learning from sparsely annotated video. In: IEEE Conference on Computer Vision and Pattern Recognition (CVPR), pp. 1433–1440 (2011)
12. Wang, M., Li, W., Wang, X.: Transferring a generic pedestrian detector towards specific scenes. In: IEEE Conference on Computer Vision and Pattern Recognition (CVPR), pp. 3274–3281 (2012)
13. Aytar, Y., Zisserman, A., Rasa, T.: Model transfer for object category detection. In: International IEEE Conference on Computer Vision, pp. 2252–2259 (2011)
14. Pan, S.J., Tsang, I.W., Kwok, J.T., Yang, Q.: Domain adaptation via transfer component analysis. IEEE Trans Neural Netw. **22**, 199–210 (2011)
15. Li, X., Ye, M., Fu, M., Xu, P., Li, T.: Domain adaption of vehicle detector based on convolutional neural networks. Int. J. Control. Autom. Syst. **13**(4), 1020–1031 (2015)
16. Wang, X., Hua, G., Han, T.X.: Detection by detections: non-parametric detector adaptation for a video. In: IEEE Conference on Computer Vision and Pattern Recognition (CVPR), pp. 350–357 (2012)
17. Wang, X., Wang, M., Li, W.: Scene-specific pedestrian detection for static video surveillance. IEEE Trans. Pattern Anal. Mach. Intell. **36**(2), 361–374 (2014)
18. Simonyan, K., Zisserman, A.: Very deep convolutional networks for large-scale image recognition. In: NIPS (2015)

2D and 3D Pattern Classification

Rapid Urban 3D Modeling for Drone-Based Situational Awareness Assistance in Emergency Situations

Inge Coudron[✉] and Toon Goedemé[✉]

KU Leuven, EAVISE Research Group,
Jan Pieter De Nayerlaan 5, Sint-Katelijne-Waver, Belgium
{inge.coudron,toon.goedeme}@kuleuven.be

Abstract. Drones are becoming a necessary and invaluable tool in many industries, as well as in emergency response situations. They can assist emergency-services in hazardous situations to get better situational awareness. This may lead to an improved rescue-coordination, increased personal safety for agents in the field and less personal, physical and financial damages as a result of a faster and better intervention. Photo-realistic 3D models generated from the drone video data, for example, can provide situational awareness as it is easier to understand the scene by visualizing it in 3D. The 3D model can be viewed from different perspectives and provides an instant overview of the situation. In contrast to SLAM which is fast but sparse, and SfM-MVS which is dense but slow, we present a pipeline that produces a dense photo-realistic 3D model of the event site in near real time by fusing oblique images with pre-recorded, publicly available LiDAR datasets.

Keywords: Computer vision · 3D model · Large-scale reconstruction · Real time processing · Geo-registration

1 Introduction

As a first step towards supporting emergency response operations with improved situational awareness, this paper investigates a method for rapid 3D modeling of the emergency scene using drone images. The obtained 3D model can serve as the basis for a decision support system through which additional semantic information about the scene can be dynamically added and visualized. These include, for example, the location of other first responders and victims, possible hazards or a temperature texture overlay acquired with a thermal camera.

Two types of techniques have been widely used for the 3D reconstruction of outdoor environments, namely Structure from Motion (SfM) [4] and Simultaneous Localization and Mapping (SLAM) [3]. The former is traditionally performed in an off-line fashion on an unordered set of images potentially taken in different conditions. On the other hand, visual SLAM using only a camera, is supposed to

© Springer Nature Switzerland AG 2019
L. Chen et al. (Eds.): RFMI 2017, CCIS 842, pp. 139–150, 2019.
https://doi.org/10.1007/978-3-030-19816-9_11

work in real-time on an ordered sequence of images acquired from a fixed camera set-up. Both techniques result in a sparse point cloud corresponding to the locations of the estimated feature points. However, the low spatial resolution of this sparse representation limits the desired level of detail required for interpreting the 3D model.

In order to obtain a more visually appealing 3D reconstruction, the sparse point cloud is often first densified using a Multi-view Stereo (MVS) approach such as PMVS [6] or SURE [10]. Next, a surface reconstruction algorithm computes a triangle mesh that can be textured. These last two steps are computationally expensive and can take up to several hours or days even on a modern desktop, depending on the number of images and their resolution. However, since emergency response is a very time-critical application of imaging and 3D reconstruction, these long processing times are not feasible in a (near) real-time environment.

To conclude, the sparse point cloud reconstructed by SfM or SLAM can be computed efficiently in (near) real-time, but it is not visually appealing. On the other hand, performing additional steps to create a textured mesh is computationally too expensive in case of emergency response applications. A lot of research has already been done to produce denser SLAM [3] or faster MVS [8], but none of it is conclusive. These contradicting demands can only be met by adding a priori information. Therefore, instead of using only the images from the drone, we propose to fuse these images with publicly available airborne LiDAR data from which a complete but untextured 3D model can be reconstructed in advance.

The focus in our application is on building emergencies such as fire. When an emergency call comes in, the drone is directed towards the building of interest. During the flight, a virtual 3D model of the emergency scene can already be constructed based on the LiDAR data. The drone flies around the building of interest and captures images at various viewpoints. These images are individually registered with the LiDAR data to infer the camera poses. In combination with the computed camera poses, the images can be used to texture the 3D model.

2   Related Work

The most challenging task in the proposed workflow (Fig. 1) is registering the 2D images with the 3D LiDAR data. There are a number of different issues that make this task very difficult. To start with, there is a dimensionality gap. Furthermore, the datasets are likely captured under different circumstances such as different seasons, different traffic conditions or environmental changes due to rebuildings. The 2D-3D matching can be described as a camera pose estimation problem. The camera parameters, location and orientation, have to be determined from a single perspective image with respect to the 3D coordinates of a real world scene. Different approaches have already been suggested to solve this problem. These can be largely divided into two categories: feature-based or image-based.

The feature-based approaches try to match geometric features such as lines or points. In [13], for example, line segments in both the 2D images and the

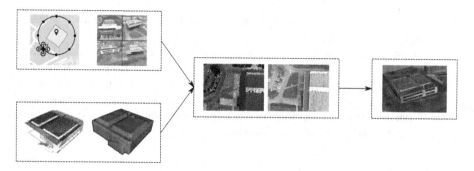

Fig. 1. Urban 3D modeling workflow: (Sect. 3.1) images from the building of interest are captured with a drone flying along a circular path with the camera pointing towards the building, (Sect. 3.2): a complete 3D model is generated in advance from pre-recorded publicly available LiDAR data, (Sect. 3.3) the camera pose for a single view is determined by maximizing the similarity between the captured image and a synthetically generated view from that pose. The registered oblique images can be mapped onto the 3D model using open source software such as *texrecon* [12]

3D LiDAR data are extracted. For a given set of camera parameters, the 3D line segments are projected in 2D. Using a feature called 3 connected segments (3CS), the line segments from the images and LiDAR data can be matched. Two matches are sufficient to compute the homography, but in order to make it more robust a RANSAC approach is used. The method works well on high altitudes where a lot of building contours are visible. However, it is expected to perform less good in our situation, where a single building takes up most part of the image and therefore drastically reduces the number of building contours that can be used for matching.

Another feature-based approach using point correspondences was proposed by [11]. They try to match 2D image features and 3D scene points, reducing it to a perspective-n-point problem. However, this method assumes the point cloud is obtained from an offline Structure-from-Motion reconstruction. As a consequence, every 3D point can be associated with at least two image descriptors such as SIFT or SURF. By extracting local features in the query image and matching them to the database descriptors, correspondences are established between the 2D features and 3D points. From these 2D-3D correspondences the camera pose can be estimated.

Image-based approaches on the other hand generally render the 3D points to generate 2D synthetic views in order to bridge the dimensionality gap. In [2], the camera pose estimation was reduced to a perspective-n-point problem as well. In this case, 2D-2D point correspondences between the query image and synthetic view were established by matching local features. The 3D positions of the synthetically generated can easily be determined by using the depth buffer information from the rendering procedure. Note that in this case terrestrial LiDAR data was used instead of airborne LiDAR data. Using airborne LiDAR data would probably have a negative impact on the algorithm since building facades, which takes up most part in oblique images, are only represented sparsely leading to large gaps in the synthetic views.

The most similar to our approach is [9]. It tries to register the synthetic view with respect to the query image by minimizing a mutual information metric. The downhill simplex optimizer is utilized to infer the camera pose parameters. However, as suggested by [14], the downhill simplex optimizer only works best for small perturbations. Therefore, in our approach a different optimizer is used, that is more robust to coarse initializations.

3   Materials and Methods

3.1   Drone-Based Image Acquisition

For image acquisition a DJI Phantom 3 was used as flying platform. The Phantom 3 is equipped with a 12 megapixel camera with a resolution of 4000×3000 pixels. To ensure the building of interest is seen from all general view angles, the drone flies on a circular path around the building with the optical axis of the camera facing towards the center. The images in our dataset were captured at an altitude of approximately 35 m under an angle of $30°$.

3.2   Surface Reconstruction from Airborne LiDAR Data

The underlying 3D mesh onto which the texture will be mapped, is inferred from pre-recorded and publicly available airborne LiDAR data. The process for generating a triangle mesh from the point cloud data is shown in Fig. 2. First, the 3D point cloud is converted to a 2.5D Digital Elevation Model (DEM). Then, it is extruded into a voxel grid based on the elevation data. The result is again a 3D point cloud, but now the holes in the building facades, which are typical for airborne LiDAR data, are filled. From this 3D point cloud a proper triangle mesh can be computed.

LiDAR   →   DEM   →   Voxels   →   Mesh

Fig. 2. Surface reconstruction from airborne LiDAR data: A Digital Elevation Model (DEM) is generated from the 3D points belonging to the building of interest. The 2.5D grid is extruded back into 3D to fill the holes in the facades. A watertight mesh is computed from the cleaned up point cloud.

Since the LiDAR data is georeferenced, we can use the building footprints from GIS data to extract the points belonging to the building of interest. First, the 3D points are projected onto a 2D grid. The resolution of the grid was chosen with respect to the point density of our LiDAR data. The average point density is 8 points per square meter. Therefore, the grid resolution was set to $\sqrt{(8)} \approx 0.35$. In each grid cell the highest elevation value is retained. Next, an inverse distance weighted square moving window of 7 cells is used to fill cells in the grid that have null values. Then, the 2D grid cells are extruded into a 3D voxel grid depending on the elevation. The actual mesh is generated by computing the concave hull of all occupied voxel centers. The same process can be repeated for other neighboring buildings in order to create a complete virtual urban 3D model as can be seen in Fig. 3.

Fig. 3. Urban 3D model: a complete virtual 3D world is generated by performing the processing steps from the previous figure on all neighboring buildings.

3.3   Registration of LiDAR Data and Images

The basic elements of our image registration framework are described in Fig. 4. A similarity metric is computed to quantify the similarity between the query image and the synthetic view. The optimizer searches the camera pose that maximizes this similarity metric. In each optimization step, the new camera parameters are used to rerender the synthetic view. These three steps are repeated until a stop criterion is met.

Synthetic 2D View Generation. A direct point based rendering approach is applied for the synthetic view generation. To this end, we use OpenGL's GL_POINTS to render the 3D point cloud data. In OpenGL a calibrated camera can be simulated by computing the projection matrix from the intrinsic parameters of the camera according to Eq. 1, where f_x, fy are the focal lengths, c_x, c_y the coordinates of the principal point, w, h the width and height of the

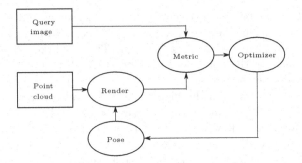

Fig. 4. Interactions among the components of our image registration technique

image and f, n the far and near clipping plane. The modelview matrix represents the coordinate system transformation for the given camera pose. By setting these two matrices, the point cloud can be rendered as if seen from that camera viewpoint.

$$
\begin{bmatrix}
\frac{2 \cdot f_x}{w} & 0 & \frac{2 \cdot c_x}{w} - 1 & 0 \\
0 & \frac{2 \cdot f_y}{h} & \frac{2 \cdot c_y}{h} - 1 & 0 \\
0 & 0 & -\frac{f+n}{f-n} & \frac{-2 \cdot f \cdot n}{f-n} \\
0 & 0 & -1 & 0
\end{bmatrix}
\tag{1}
$$

Since the resolution of the images is very large compared to the spatial resolution of the LiDAR data, rendering the point cloud using the original camera parameters would result in a very sparse image. Therefore, the images were resized to 10% of the original image size. Consequently, the camera parameters were rescaled accordingly. An example of such a synthetic 2D view generated using OpenGL is shown in Fig. 5.

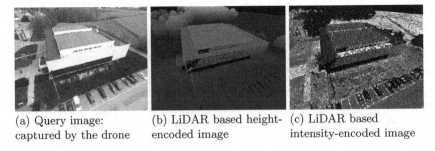

(a) Query image: captured by the drone

(b) LiDAR based height-encoded image

(c) LiDAR based intensity-encoded image

Fig. 5. Synthetic 2D view generation from 3D LiDAR data

Similarity Metric Calculation. An important design choice in image registration is the selection of an appropriate similarity measure. In this work, mutual information was chosen as similarity measure since it has proven to be accurate and robust for multi-modal matching [7]. It measures the mutual dependence between the underlying intensity distributions of the images. The larger this measure the stronger the dependence. The mutual information between an image A and B is calculated as:

$$MI(A, B) = \sum P_{A,B}(a, b) \log \frac{P_{A,B}(a, b)}{P_A(a) \cdot P_B(b)} \tag{2}$$

The joint probability matrix can be computed as the normalized 2D histogram, were the normalization factor equals the number of histogram bins N. The sum of the rows and the columns, respectively, gives the marginal probability distributions of image A and B:

$$P_{A,B}(a, b) = \frac{h(a, b)}{N}$$
$$P_A(a) = \sum_b P_{A,B}(a, b) \tag{3}$$
$$P_B(b) = \sum_a P_{A,B}(a, b)$$

Intensity Based Optimization. In this work, an evolutionary algorithm is used for image registration. Evolutionary algorithms have been proven to be a promising solution, since they are able to perform a robust search in complex search spaces like those arising in image registration [14]. The structure of a classic evolutionary algorithm is as follows:

Algorithm 1. Evolutionary algorithm

INITIALIZE population with random candidate solutions
EVALUATE each candidate solution
while *Termination condition not reached* **do**
   SELECT individuals for the next generation
   RECOMBINE pairs of parents
   MUTATE the resulting offspring
   EVALUATE each candidate solution
end while

The construction of the actual evolutionary algorithm can be divided into three parts: (1) the definition of an appropriate structure to represent the solution; (2) determination of the fitness function; and (3) the design of the genetic operators. In our work a candidate solution encodes the 6-DOF camera pose consisting of the 3-DOF orientation and 3-DOF position. As described earlier, mutual information is used to evaluate the fitness of a candidate. The genetic operators are the core of the evolutionary algorithm. They define how to generate new solutions from the existing ones. First, we reduce the number of individuals by keeping only 40% of the solutions based on their fitness value. This is in fact called a 'rank selection'. Next, two parent solutions are selected based on the closest Euclidean distance of their variables. An offspring of these parents is calculated as the average of the variables of both parents. Finally, each offspring is mutated by adding random perturbations to the original variables.

4   Experimental Results

We show the results of our algorithm with a collection of five images taken from a building on our campus. As no GPS/INS data was available, the initial poses were selected manually. For this a georeferenced orthomosaic image and the corresponding digital elevation model was used. First, matching feature points were selected in the query image and orthomosaic. Using the raster information from the orthomosaic and the digital elevation model, the 3D coordinates of the point correspondences could be computed. Finally, solving the Perspective-n-Points problem yielded an initial camera pose, which also serves as the ground truth pose.

Several experiments were conducted. First, different variations of the similarity measure were compared. To this end, the mutual information is calculated while the camera parameter being evaluated is varied. The other parameters are held constant at their correct values. We experimented with the number of histogram bins N used for calculating the mutual information. As suggested in [7], using Sturges' Rule for calculating the number of histogram bins not only makes the image registration more efficient but also more accurate. The same conclusion can be drawn for our image set as can be seen in Fig. 6 where the similarity measure is plotted for small perturbations from the estimated ground truth pose. As the top graph of Fig. 6 shows, using 256 bins results in a shift of the maximum, which is the optimal point, for certain degrees of freedom. As the LiDAR data also contains intensity values, we also explored the mutual information between the query image and synthetic intensity image. Figure 6 shows that this metric is too noisy for accurate registration. To conclude, the metric using only depth information and 18 histogram bins performed best.

Next, the robustness of our algorithm was tested by artificially perturbing the camera positions. The translation parameters were randomly perturbed by maximally $\pm 5\,$m and the rotation parameters were perturbed by maximally $\pm 3°$. For each of the images 100 coarse initializations were simulated this way. The mean deviation of the optimized camera parameters from the estimated ground truth pose is shown in Fig. 7. It was apparent by visual inspection that the order of magnitude of the deviations is close enough for texture mapping.

Finally, our approach was visually compared with current state-of-the-art open source Structure from Motion approaches, namely Multi-View Environment (MVE) [5] and OpenDroneMap (ODM) [1]. For the texture mapping of the oblique images onto our virtual 3D model, the same library [12] was used as in MVE and ODM. Both approaches produced a 3D model in about half an hour. With our approach, it takes on average 4 s to register a single oblique image to the LiDAR data. In contrast to the Structure from motion approaches, we don't

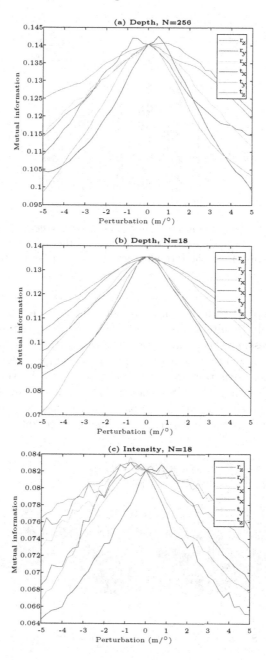

Fig. 6. Plots of the mutual information as each of the camera parameters (r_x: angle of rotation around the x-axis, t_x: translation in the direction of the x-axis, etc.) are perturbed from the estimated ground truth pose. (a) Mutual information between the query image and height-encoded LiDAR image using 256 histogram bins,(b) Mutual information between the query image and height-encoded LiDAR image using 18 histogram bins, (c) Mutual information between the query image and intensity-encoded LiDAR image using 18 histogram bins

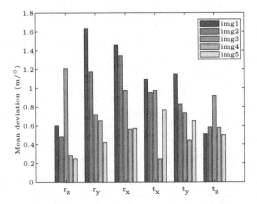

Fig. 7. Plots of the mean deviation of the camera parameters (r_x: angle of rotation around the x-axis, t_x: translation in the direction of the x-axis, etc.) found by the optimization algorithm from the estimated ground truth pose for each image in our image set.

require any overlap between the images, as each image is registered individually. As a result we only require 5 images to texture the complete 3D model, which reduces the processing time significantly. Including the texture mapping, the total reconstruction will take on average 29 s. If we compare the models visually we can see another advantage (see Fig. 8) of our approach over the others. 3D models generated with SfM-MVS typically suffer from holes. As our model is pre-generated from LiDAR data, some parts of the mesh may not be textured, but at least all underlying structures are visible and accurate.

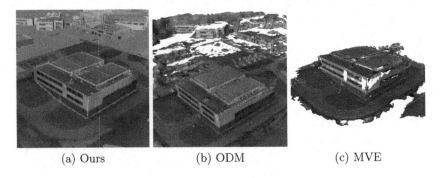

(a) Ours   (b) ODM   (c) MVE

Fig. 8. Comparison of different 3D modeling approaches

5   Conclusions and Future Work

We have presented our custom pipeline for the registration of 3D LiDAR data and 2D oblique images. The registration of multi-modal 2D/3D datasets is inherently difficult due to fundamental different nature of the data. To overcome this problem, the dimensionality gap was first bridged by rendering the 3D point cloud into 2D for the camera poses computed in each optimization step. The similarity between these multi-modal images was measured using mutual information. Our experimental results show that this choice is indeed suitable for multi-modal registration. We further demonstrated the robustness of our approach by randomly perturbing the camera parameters from the ground truth.

Future research plans include reconsidering using the intensity values from the LiDAR data for matching. The results revealed that on our image set this metric did not demonstrate adequate quasi-convexity. This is probably due to the noisy nature of the rendered synthetic 2D view. One possibility is to apply a preprocessing filter on the rendered image, that removes the noise such as anisotropic diffusion filter. Another possibility is to use a variant of the mutual information metric such as Quadratic Mutual Information. We will also explore the applicability of our approach for registering thermal images with the LiDAR data as this is certainly relevant for improving situational awareness for firefighters.

References

1. Fitzsimmons, S., Dakota, B., Toffanin, P.: OpenDroneMap (2017)
2. Bodensteiner, C., Hebel, M., Arens, M.: Accurate single image multi-modal camera pose estimation. In: Kutulakos, K.N. (ed.) ECCV 2010. LNCS, vol. 6554, pp. 296–309. Springer, Heidelberg (2012). https://doi.org/10.1007/978-3-642-35740-4_23
3. Engel, J., Schöps, T., Cremers, D.: LSD-SLAM: large-scale direct monocular SLAM. In: Fleet, D., Pajdla, T., Schiele, B., Tuytelaars, T. (eds.) ECCV 2014. LNCS, vol. 8690, pp. 834–849. Springer, Cham (2014). https://doi.org/10.1007/978-3-319-10605-2_54
4. Forsyth, D., Ponce, J.: Computer Vision: A Modern Approach. Prentice Hall, Upper Saddle River (2011)
5. Fuhrmann, S., Langguth, F., Goesele, M.: MVE: a multi-view reconstruction environment. In: Proceedings of the Eurographics Workshop on Graphics and Cultural Heritage, GCH 2014, Aire-la-Ville, Switzerland, Switzerland, pp. 11–18. Eurographics Association (2014)
6. Furukawa, Y., Ponce, J.: Accurate, dense, and robust multi-view stereopsis. In: 2007 IEEE Conference on Computer Vision and Pattern Recognition, pp. 1–8, June 2007
7. Rosin, P., Marshall, D., Legg, P., Morgan, J.: Improving accuracy and efficiency of registration by mutual information using Sturges' histogram rule. In: Medical Image Understanding and Analysis, pp. 26–30 (2007)
8. Locher, A., Perdoch, M., Gool, L.V.: Progressive prioritized multi-view stereo. In: 2016 IEEE Conference on Computer Vision and Pattern Recognition (CVPR), pp. 3244–3252, June 2016
9. Mastin, A., Kepner, J., Fisher, J.: Automatic registration of LIDAR and optical images of urban scenes. In: 2009 IEEE Conference on Computer Vision and Pattern Recognition, pp. 2639–2646, June 2009
10. Rothermel, M., Wenzel, K., Fritsch, D., Haala, N.: Sure: photogrammetric surface reconstruction from imagery (2013)

11. Sattler, T., Leibe, B., Kobbelt, L.: Improving image-based localization by active correspondence search. In: Fitzgibbon, A., Lazebnik, S., Perona, P., Sato, Y., Schmid, C. (eds.) ECCV 2012. LNCS, vol. 7572, pp. 752–765. Springer, Heidelberg (2012). https://doi.org/10.1007/978-3-642-33718-5_54

12. Waechter, M., Moehrle, N., Goesele, M.: Let there be color! Large-scale texturing of 3D reconstructions. In: Fleet, D., Pajdla, T., Schiele, B., Tuytelaars, T. (eds.) ECCV 2014. LNCS, vol. 8693, pp. 836–850. Springer, Cham (2014). https://doi.org/10.1007/978-3-319-10602-1_54

13. Wang, L., Neumann, U.: A robust approach for automatic registration of aerial images with untextured aerial LIDAR data (2009)

14. Zhang, X., Shen, Y., Li, S.: A hybrid genetic algorithm for medical image registration with downhill simplex method (2009)

Defining Mesh-LBP Variants for 3D Relief Patterns Classification

Claudio Tortorici[1]([✉]) [iD], Naoufel Werghi[1], and Stefano Berretti[2]

[1] Khalifa University, Abu Dhabi, UAE
{Claudio.Tortorici,Naoufel.Werghi}@kustar.ac.ae
[2] University of Florence, Florence, Italy
Stefano.Berretti@unifi.it

Abstract. Extending the concept of texture to the geometry of a mesh manifold surface, opened the way to the idea of classifying 3D relief patterns as an emerging topic in 3D Computer Vision, with several potential applications. In this paper, we propose an original modelling solution to address this novel task. Following the recent introduction of the LBP computation framework on mesh manifolds (mesh-LBP), we first extend this framework to the different variants of 2D LBP by defining mesh-LBP variants. The compliance of these extensions with the original LBP in terms of uniformity is also investigated. Then, we proposed a complete framework for relief patterns classification, which performs mesh preprocessing, multi-scale mesh-LBP extraction and descriptors classification. Experimental results on the SHREC'17 dataset showed competitive performance with respect to state of the art solutions.

1 Introduction

The recent advancements of 3D imaging technologies resulted in a new generation of acquisition devices capable of capturing the geometry of 3D objects. High-resolution 3D static scanners as well as devices with 3D dynamic acquisition capabilities that provide a continuous flow of the 3D geometry of a scene are now available. In addition to this, the geometric and photometric information are often captured in a synchronized way. The geometric information captured by such devices represents the 3D coordinates of a set of samples of the object surface, typically in the form of a point cloud. However, directly processing point clouds is not convenient or even possible so that other representation formats have established. Depth images are one of the most commonly used imaging modality, since they permit a straightforward extension to the depth dimension of many computer vision and pattern recognition solutions developed in the literature for analyzing the photometric information in 2D images. Though the idea of extending 2D techniques is attractive, this modality loses the full 3D geometry by reducing it to a 2.5D projection. Instead, the full 3D shape information of an object can be preserved and encoded in a simple, compact and flexible format by using a triangular mesh manifold. However, passing from a point cloud to a mesh manifold is not an easy problem in itself: reconstructing

© Springer Nature Switzerland AG 2019
L. Chen et al. (Eds.): RFMI 2017, CCIS 842, pp. 151–166, 2019.
https://doi.org/10.1007/978-3-030-19816-9_12

the real structure of the manifold surface is often difficult, especially in the case of objects with complex topology or when multiple scans of the same object must be merged together [28].

Using mesh manifolds as inputs, several studies addressed the problem of retrieving/classifying 3D shapes based on their similarities [28]. In most of the cases, synthetic models generated by ad-hoc softwares have been used, while reconstructed meshes have been considered more rarely. An even less investigated but emerging problem, which is of interest for its potential application in several contexts, is that of classifying 3D relief patterns. A peculiar characteristic of patterns is the fact their style does not depend by the overall structure of the shape, rather it identifies parts and local properties that are independent of the global shape. In particular, relieves of interest are those characterized by some form of regularity and repeatability across the surface so that they can be regarded as the 3D geometric equivalent of textures in 2D images. Examples are knitted fabrics, artworks' patterns, artists' styles or natural structures like tree barks [24], rock types or engravings [40], etc. Automatically assigning a class label to a given, unknown, 3D relief pattern requires to address a number of challenges, witch include: (1) Defining a suitable surface descriptor capturing the relief patterns; (2) Finding an appropriate distance measure between descriptors; (3) Adopt effective classification tools based on the distance between pattern descriptors.

A recent trend, motivated by outstanding results in several challenging contexts, applies deep convolutional neural network architectures to solve a number of detection, recognition and classification problems in 2D still images or videos [14,17,27]. The application of such deep learning tools is facilitated by the grid structure of images and the access to large repositories of training data. Less obvious appears the extension of such framework to geometric contexts, such as graphs, matrix manifolds, or meshes [6]. Though some results in this direction do exist, they are not yet as competitive as 3D "classic" solutions [12] and consolidated as in 2D. The need for large training dataset remains also an obstacle in 3D applications due to the difficulty of acquiring very large repositories of 3D scans [30]. The recent PointNet deep learning solution proposed by Charles et al. [7], while addresses effectively object classification in point cloud format, is suited for volumetric objects rather than shape texture variations on the manifold.

On another side, LBP has been one of the most simple and widely spread local texture descriptor in 2D and 2.5D. LBP has been proposed as texture descriptor for 2D still images for the first time by Ojala et al. [23]. Thanks to its simplicity and discriminative power, LBP has been successfully implemented for Visual Inspection [18], Remote Sensing [9], Motion Analysis [31], Face Recognition [1,2] and Expression Recognition [25] in both 2D and 2.5D supports. However, its application to mesh manifolds could not be achieved till a mesh-version was introduced by Werghi et al. [35–38].

Based on the above considerations, in this paper, we propose a novel solution for 3D relief patterns classification, which relies on the extension of LBP and its variants to mesh manifolds. In doing so, as first contribution of our work, we define the mesh-LBP variants as counterparts of LBP variants on the triangular mesh manifold support, and assess their descriptive capabilities. Then, as second contribution, we propose an original modeling approach that uses mesh-LBP variants in the task of relieves classification. This is obtained by presenting a complete framework that includes a suitable preprocessing of the mesh, multi-scale extraction of mesh-LBP descriptors, and descriptors classification using SVM.

In the rest of the paper, we first discuss, in Sect. 2, previous works that address description and classification of relief patterns. Then, in Sect. 3, an overview of LBP and some of its main variants is exposed. Afterwards, the respective mesh implementations of LBP variants are proposed and analyzed in Sect. 4. The inclusion of mesh-LBP variants into a complete classification solution is defined in Sect. 5. Experimental evaluation of the proposed method in the task of relief pattern classification is presented in Sect. 6. Discussion and conclusions are reported in Sect. 7.

2   Related Work

The problem of relief pattern classification is of quite new definition. Therefore, most of the works that we summarize in the following have been presented and participated to the SHREC'17 contest, track on "Retrieval of surfaces with similar relief patterns" [5].

One of the first work addressing the problem of effectively describing 3D relief patterns is due to Werghi et al. [32,33]. In their work, mesh-LBP was proposed as a extension of LBP to mesh manifolds. They also showed the applicability of this approach for geometric texture retrieval for a small set of prototype meshes.

In order to capture texture features of object surface, Tatsuma and Aono [5] estimated statistics of local features extracted from the depth-buffer image as a shape descriptor. To emphasize the texture of object surface, they converted the depth-buffer image into the LBP image. For feature detection and description from the LBP image (LBPI), the KAZE features [3] was employed.

Limberger and Wilson [5] proposed a curvature-based Laplace Beltrami operator (KLBO) to describe the relief patterns of surfaces. After computing the eigendecomposition of the KLBO, the Improved Wave Kernel signature (IWKS) [16] was computed and encoded using two different encoding schemes: the Fisher Vector (FV) or the Super Vector (SV). Lastly, differences between encodings were computed using Euclidean distance, after reducing feature dimensionality by computing PCA.

Siprian and Bustos [5] applied the Signature Quadratic Form Distance (SQFD) [4] along with intrinsic spectral descriptors for relief retrieval. On the one hand, the SQFD distance is used as a suitable and effective alternative to compare 3D objects represented as a collection of local features [26]. On the other hand, spectral features have proven to be robust against several transformations, while keeping discriminative geometric information. This proposal combined these two methods in order to represent and assess the similarity between relief patterns.

In [5], Velasco-Forero and Fehri, proposed an image covariance descriptor from morphological transformation of local curvature estimation for a given 3D mesh (CMC). Four main components were used to compute this descriptor: (1) The local principal curvatures and the Gaussian curvature were first computed; (2) Curvature values on the 3D surface were projected to a flat 2D surface. Accordingly, the boundary of the mesh, i.e., the set of vertices that are only referenced by a single triangle in the mesh was found. Three curvature images for the boundary were then derived using SVM for solving a regression problem on the boundary points; (3) Morphology operators were then applied to the curvature images, with 32 transformations with a final total of 96 images; (4) The covariance matrix of 96 images was computed, thus producing a descriptor as a square matrix of size 96×96. The similarity between two meshes was calculated via their representation as covariance matrices.

Sun et al. [5] developed on the idea of modelling convex/concave properties and local geometrical features by the interior dihedral angle of each edge of the mesh. In doing so, they proposed a statistical feature called Interior Dihedral Angle Histogram (IDAH). Firstly, they calculated all the interior dihedral angles of the model surface. Then, the distribution histogram was calculated in different intervals. Finally, they adopted the Manhattan distance between histograms to describe the model similarity. Also, the authors converted the model into a "geometry image". The 3D model is parametrized on a spherical domain and then mapped onto an octahedron, which is then cut on its edges obtaining a flat and regular geometry image. HOG features are extracted from the geometry image (GI HOG).

Masoumi et al. [5] used a Geodesic Multi-Resolution (GMR) descriptor [20] by incorporating the vertex area into the definition of spectral graph wavelet [15] in a bid to capture more geometric information and, hence, further improve its discriminative ability. Moreover, Mexican hat wavelet has been utilized as a generating kernel, which considers all frequencies equally-important overall as opposed to the cubic spline kernel [15]. Furthermore, in order to capture the spatial relations between features, the proposed geodesic multiresolution descriptor was weighted by geodesic exponential kernel. While this approach focused primarily on 3D object retrieval, it is fairly general and can be used to address a variety of shape analysis problems, including segmentation and classification [19].

3   Background on LBP and LBP Variants

On its first definition, LBP generates a binary sequence for each image pixel (from now on referred as *central pixel*) analyzing its neighborhood inside a 3×3 window. According to (1), each neighbor pixel value (n_i) is compared with the central one (n_c), assigning 1 if the value is greater or equal, and 0 otherwise:

$$LBP(n_c) = \sum_{i=0}^{N-1} s(n_i - n_c) \cdot 2^i \, , \tag{1}$$

where $s(x)$ is the step function. Then, the binary value is multiplied by the power of two with respect to the given pixel position. Later on, in [22] a multi-scale and rotation invariant LBP version was presented.

One of the firstly proposed LBP variant is the *Median Binary Pattern* (MBP) [10]. Compared to standard LBP that uses n_c as threshold, the simple local median among all the neighbor values is used to reduce the error caused by noise. MBP is, therefore, a 9 bits pattern since it considers the central pixel like its surroundings.

In [41], a combination of binary patterns is used for Face Recognition. *Completed Local Binary Pattern* (CLBP) considers not only the sign of $d_i = n_i - n_c$ (CLBP-S in (1)), but also its magnitude $|d_i|$ (CLBP-M) and central pixel intensity (CLBP-C), adding more discriminant power:

$$\text{CLBP-M}_{N,R}(c) = \sum_{i=0}^{N-1} t(n_i, c) \cdot 2^i \, , \tag{2}$$

$$\text{CLBP-C}(c_I) = t(n_c, c_I), \quad t(x, y) = \begin{cases} 1 \ x \geq y \\ 0 \ x < y \end{cases} \tag{3}$$

CLBP-S/M/C are then combined in different configurations, such as histograms concatenation or multi-dimensional histogram computation.

A new branch of LBP variants expanded after the first presentation of a *Center-Symmetric LBP*. CS-LBP compares center-symmetric pair of pixels ignoring the central pixel value [11]. This technique halves the number of comparisons, leading to faster computation and smaller descriptor size. Without n_c, CS-LBP requires a threshold τ:

$$CS\text{-}LBP_{R,N}(\tau) = \sum_{i=0}^{(N/2)-1} s\left(n_i - n_{i+(N/2)}\right) \cdot 2^i \tag{4}$$

being n_i and $n_{i+(N/2)}$ the pairs of center-symmetric values, while $s(x)$ is the step function.

To overcome the limitation of the threshold, in [39] an *Improved CS-LBP* (ICS-LBP) has been designed. Similarly to (4), ICS-LBP compares center symmetric couples of pixels using the central pixel value as discriminant:

$$ICS\text{-}LBP_{R,N} = \sum_{i=0}^{(N/2)-1} s\left(n_i, n_c, n_{(i+N/2)}\right) \cdot 2^i \, ,$$

$$\text{where } s = \begin{cases} 1 \text{ if } \begin{cases} n_i \geq n_c \geq n_{i+(N/2)} \\ \text{or} \\ n_i < n_c < n_{i+(N/2)} \end{cases} \\ 0 \text{ otherwise} \end{cases} \tag{5}$$

Otherwise, it is possible to replace n_c with the mean $m = \frac{1}{N}\sum_{i=0}^{N-1} n_i$, to reduce noise dependency as discussed in [13].

In [8], *Centralized Binary Pattern* (CBP) takes the advantage of comparing center-symmetric couple of pixels, but it also comprehends the value of the central pixel, applying the largest weight to it. In this way, the effectiveness of the central pixel value is strengthened, and a discriminant power is added to a smaller size descriptor:

$$
\begin{aligned}
CBP_{R,N} = & \sum_{i=0}^{(N/2)-1} s\left(n_i - n_{i+(N/2)}\right) \cdot 2^i + \\
& s\left(n_c - \frac{1}{N+1}\left(\sum_{i=0}^{N-1} n_i + n_c\right)\right) \cdot 2^{\frac{N}{2}}
\end{aligned}
\tag{6}
$$

Another family of LBP variants is characterized by the use of masks on window's values. While conventional LBP encodes the values as a non-directional 1st order operator among local neighbors, in [21] a Sobel operator is applied to generate a first order derivative along x and y directions to characterize the image information: where $*$ is the convolution operator with the original image. Then, the gradient magnitude image $I_{gm} = \sqrt{I_x^2 + I_y^2}$ is obtained. The LBP is finally generated using (1) with I_{gm} values encoding the magnitude of local variations.

4   Mesh-LBP Variants

Mesh-LBP is an LBP-like descriptor employed on mesh manifolds [33], particularly in 3D face recognition [37]. While the potentiality of using a real 3D support has been investigated in [29,38], the possibility to export successfully 2D LBP variants to the mesh manifold has to be addressed yet. While standard LBP compares 8 pixels belonging to a circle of a certain radius around a central pixel, mesh-LBP generates a concentric sequence of ring-like patterns around a central facet, whereby facets are ordered in a circular fashion in each ring. Mesh-LBP computation is shown in (7), whereby r and m are the ring number, and the number of facets per ring, respectively, s is the step function, and h is a scalar function on the mesh. $\alpha(k)$ is a discrete function, where k represents the facet position.

$$
meshLBP_m^r(f_c) = \sum_{k=0}^{m-1} s(t) \cdot \alpha(k) \qquad \text{with } t = h(f_k^r) - h(f_c)
\tag{7}
$$

Two functions were defined in the mesh-LBP, namely, $\alpha_1(k) = 1$ that sums the digits of the pattern; and $\alpha_2(k) = 2^k$ that multiplies single digit by a power of 2, as originally proposed in [23].

So far, seven mesh-LBP variants have been implemented and tested: (a) mesh-MBP, (b) mesh-CSLBP, (c) mesh-ICSLBP, (d) mesh-ICSLBP-M with central facet value replaced by the mean across the ring as threshold, (e) mesh-CBP,

(f) mesh-CLBP and (g) mesh-LBP-Sobel. Considering these seven variants, the original mesh-LBP with the two functions α_1 and α_2, and the three scalar functions on the mesh (*Local Depth* (LD), *Mean Curvature* (H), and *Curvedness* (C)), we have a total of $8 \times 2 \times 3 = 48$ mesh-LBP variants. We can categorize these in α_1 and α_2 variants. Also, since the LBP is a differential operator, we can categorize the variants as first-order and second order differentiation variants, depending on the fact the scalar function on the mesh represents a raw entity (e.g., LD) or a derivative entity (e.g., H and C).

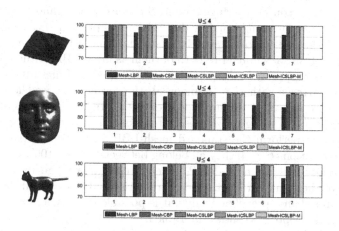

Fig. 1. Uniformity analysis performed on three sample meshes from different datasets. The histograms show the percentage of patterns with a number of 0/1 transitions $U \leq 4$. Reported results have been obtained with the H descriptor.

Table 1. Comparison of pattern size and histogram (Hist) size for $\alpha_1(k)$ and $\alpha_2(k)$, for the different mesh-LBP variants.

Mesh-LBP variant	Pattern size	U	Hist-size α_1	Hist-size α_2
mesh-MBP	12	6	13	2973
mesh-CS variants	6	4	7	63
mesh-CBP	7	4	8	115
mesh-CLBP	25	6	26	380103

In the particular case of mesh-MBP, $\alpha_1(k)$ is meaningless because it uses a median threshold; while for mesh-CLBP, $\alpha_2(k)$ is skipped because of its pattern length (see Table 1). Therefore, the total number of variants investigated is 42.

We compared the mesh-LBP variants to the standard mesh-LBP. First, we focused on the uniformity aspect of the mesh-LBP variants descriptor (see Sect. 4.1); then, we reported results for 3D geometric texture detection (see Sect. 4.2).

4.1   Uniformity

In [22], evaluating the rotation invariant pattern, authors counted the number of 0/1 transitions in the binary pattern, and evaluated their frequency of occurrence. Then, they observed that most of the pattern configurations had a number of transitions (U) less than 2, So, a unique label (defined as "uniform") can be assigned to all the patterns with number of transitions above 2; that grouping method allows reducing the descriptor size, while increasing its accuracy.

The same analysis has been performed for all our mesh-LBP variants considering $R = 1, \ldots, 7$ concentric rings around the central facet, and $N = 12$ points at each ring. Since uniformity mainly depends on the pattern of the specific variant, mesh-LBP-Sobel performs exactly as standard mesh-LBP, so regarding the uniformity analysis we will refer to both of them as mesh-LBP. Although Center-Symmetric based approaches, especially mesh-CSLBP and mesh-ICSLBP, have over 70% of patterns with $U \leq 2$ among all the seven rings, we choose a more conservative value $U \leq 4$. Figure 1 depicts the average percentage of uniform patterns, with $U \leq 4$ using the H descriptor. As shown in the figure, four variants over six outperform the standard mesh-LBP percentage of patterns with number of transitions $U \leq 4$: they all belong between $97\% - -100\%$ even at rings 6 and 7. Mesh-CLBP and mesh-MBP, instead, reach an average above 85% with $U \leq 6$ due to their pattern length and characteristics. Grouping all the patterns with U greater than a predefined value, it is possible to considerably reduce the size of $\alpha_2(k)$ descriptors as shown in Table 1.

4.2   Geometric Texture Detection on Mesh Manifolds

In this section, we report a proof of the suitability of mesh-LBP variants in an applicative task of geometric texture detection. The idea here is to use a patch of a mesh with a particular geometric pattern of the surface (this can be regarded as the surface equivalent of the texture concept used for 2D images) as a probe, and verify the capability of the mesh-LBP variant descriptors of detecting the presence of similar surface patterns in large mesh surfaces. This task is performed using the two surfaces illustrated in Fig. 2. The texture patterns are different from the ten textures classes used in the previous experience. For each mesh, we selected a small texture patch of its surface, and used it as a query (probe) against all the other meshes (gallery). For comparing the probe with the meshes, we used a straightforward solution, where the mesh-LBP descriptor of the probe is compared exhaustively against the gallery using the Bhattacharya distance as a minimum distance criterion. Figure 2 depicts the distance mapped on the two objects across the different variants and the detected textures. The results showed evidence of the mesh variants capacity for detecting texture on the mesh, with a best performance noticed for the CLBP variant. Though some false positive patches are noticed, this is expected due to the naive minimum distance criterion we used here.

5 Relief Patterns Classification

In this Section, we propose to use the mesh-LBP variants for relief pattern classification. These patterns are given by geometric corrugations of the mesh with some regularity and repetition and can be regarded as the surface equivalent of textures in 2D images. Similarly to the 2D case, relief patterns (or geometric texture) are difficult to represent and classify. They may be repetitions of simple textons of any size, or spread on the whole surface (see Fig. 3a, b). To handle such variety, we decided to represent the texture using multi-scale histograms computed on circular regions. The possibility to describe the texture with different scale factors helps to cope with different texture typology.

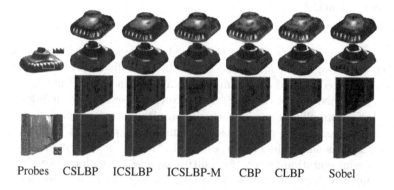

Probes   CSLBP   ICSLBP   ICSLBP-M   CBP   CLBP   Sobel

Fig. 2. Sample probe texture, the Bhattacharya distance maps (first and third row), and the detected texture (second and fourth) obtained for two different object models. All results have been obtained with the α_1-LD configuration.

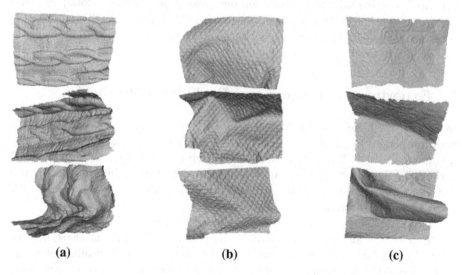

(a)   (b)   (c)

Fig. 3. Example relief patterns from three classes are given in (a), (b) and (c).

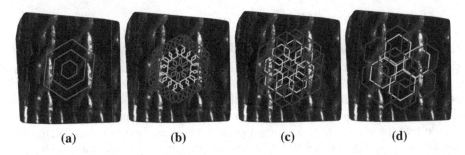

(a)   (b)   (c)   (d)

Fig. 4. The multi-scale regions used to describe a mesh sample are reported: 4a concentric rings, where the sampling points are located; 4b-4d multi-scale region extraction. Regions are highlighted in red, yellow and blue from the inner to the outer rings in 4a (Color figure online).

We used *Ordered Rings of Facet* (ORF) [34] to generate three concentric rings (Fig. 4a). Such rings are sampled according to their diameter. Circular regions are then extracted around each sampled point, and mesh-LBP histogram computation is applied on the covered region. To comprise multi-scale information, the number of sampled points at each ring and the circular region size are varied. While increasing the region size, the number of points at each concentric ring decreases as shown in Fig. 4b, c and d. Finally, in order to augment the histogram representation power, the multi-scale descriptors have been generated at three different locations for each training sample, while only one location is used for the test.

Such descriptors are used to feed an SVM classifier. Here, two types of classification have been used: (1) **One-vs-all** that trains one SVM for each class. In this case, positive examples come from one class, while negative examples come from all the other classes. (2) **One-vs-one** that trains $\frac{n(n-1)}{2}$ SVMs, where n is the number of classes. For each SVM, positive examples come from one class, and negatives from another one.

6   Experimental Results and Evaluation Protocol

In Sect. 4, we have introduced the mesh-LBP variants and investigated their main properties in a set of tests that proved their relevance with respect to the original mesh-LBP. Based on this, in the following we experiment the mesh-LBP variants in the specific task of relief patterns classification. In doing so, we use a dataset introduced for an open competition that allows us to compare with state of the art solutions.

Recently, a new database has been released for the SHREC'17 contest track on *"Retrieval of surfaces with similar relief patterns"* [5]. The database is composed by different patches of various textiles, each acquired in different poses and deformed shape situations (a total of 180 models referred as *original* surfaces). For each scan, three processing operations, designed to alter the mesh connectivity, have been applied to obtain, respectively, meshes with 5K, 10K and 15K vertices. The database has a total of 720 samples (see Fig. 3 for some examples).

The SHREC'17 competition protocol required the participants to submit a 720×720 matrix of mutual distances between all the database samples. Organizers elaborated such matrices and evaluated them using several criteria such as Nearest Neighbor (NN), First Tier (FT), Second Tier (ST) and other distances differentiating between the full dataset (720 samples) and the dataset composed by the 180 original meshes. Also, confusion matrices obtained from the NN classification were presented from the best results of each participant.

6.1 Results and Comparative Evaluation

In our tests, we performed the same experiment of the SHREC'17 competition with our representation based on mesh-LBP variants comparing our results with those obtained by the SHREC participants. We performed the experimentation on all the 7 mesh-LBP variants, plus the original mesh-LBP. Each variant has been computed using Mean curvature (H), Curvedness (C) and Local Depth (LD) in both their variants α_1 and α_2 as described in Sect. 4.

The database is split into 5 folds: 4 used for training, and 1 for testing. The classification is repeated five times in order to use all the 5 folds as test samples.

Globally, the methods presented in [5] perform quite poorly. In Table 2, we compare the best results obtained by SHREC participants on the full database against those resulting with our method and a baseline method proposed by SHREC'17 organizers. The baseline method consist of a 128 bins histogram of the minimal curvature of the surface (CH). SHREC participants used different distances to compare their descriptors in the NN classification. We adopted the Bhattacharyya, Cosine and χ^2 distances obtaining the same score among all the variants tested. All our variants outperform the others, overtaking even the best KLBO-FV-IWKS result.

Since such results have been obtained with NN classification, they can be biased by the inclusion of 4 meshes of the same original sample (i.e., meshes obtained by resampling the original mesh with 5K, 10K and 15K vertices). Therefore, organizers performed the same evaluation on the 180 original samples to get a better understanding of the classification capabilities of the different approaches when considering only the different samples of the same class, avoiding comparison with resampled meshes. In this evaluation, all presented methods drastically decreased their performance, getting a maximum of 63.3% (CMC-2), while KLBO-FV-IWKS scored only 52.2% at its best value. The aim of such experiment is to judge the method performance on practical applications, evaluating their ability in pattern retrieval: KLBO-FV-IWKS, in fact, seems to include global shape information in its classification producing such accuracy decay (from 98.6% to 52.2% on its best result).

Table 2. Comparison with the results of the SHREC'17 competition as reported in [5]. Scores refer to the full dataset using Nearest Neighbor (NN) classification. We report generically "Mesh-LBP Variants" since they all score the same.

Classification method		NN
[5]	CH	19.60%
	LBPI	82.80%
	IDAH-1	39.00%
	IDAH-2	30.60%
	GI HOG	68.60%
	SQFD-SIHKS	16.80%
	SQFD-HKS	53.60%
	SQFD-WKS	51.00%
	CMC-1	71.80%
	CMC-2	76.30%
	CMC-3	64.70%
	KLBO-FV-IWKS	**98.60%**
	KLBO-SV-IWKS	97.80%
	GMR	7.90%
Mesh-LBP Variants		**99.77%**

We designed a method capable of measuring the class discrimination using SVM as described in Sect. 5. To design a fair comparison, we need to specify that the protocol implemented is not exactly the same as for the SHREC'17 competition. Indeed, it considers all the database samples, however the contribution of resampled meshes during the training phase is minimal, and does not substantially affect the class discrimination. In the hypothetic best case, three samples of the same patch would be on the training set, while one used as test; with 48 samples per class, and our 5-folds classification method, the three meshes would be less than 7.8% of the training sample, while 5.2% and 2.6% if the samples in the training are two or one, respectively. As shown in Table 3, our mesh representation based on mesh-LBP variants clearly outperforms results presented in [5]. The LD descriptor scores the best among all the mesh-LBP variants except for mesh-CSLBP. Moreover, the ability to shrink the histogram size of some mesh-LBP variants (see Table 1), allowed us to gain on the SVM training performances. In fact, α_2 descriptors show remarkable scores all between 93.60% and 98.53%.

Table 3. Average classification using SVM and 5-folds cross validation. All the mesh variants/descriptors combination for α_1 are reported, while only the Center-Symmetric based variants for α_2 are reported for efficiency reasons.

Descriptor combination	α_1		α_2	
	One-vs-All	One-vs-One	One-vs-All	One-vs-One
Mesh-LBP-H	74.67%	89.20%		
Mesh-LBP-C	79.73%	89.47%		
Mesh-LBP-LD	84.40%	96.00%		
Mesh-CSLBP-H	55.07%	71.73%	97.73%	97.60%
Mesh-CSLBP-C	50.53%	72.27%	97.07%	97.07%
Mesh-CSLBP-LD	44.27%	71.73%	94.93%	95.20%
Mesh-ICSLBP-H	70.27%	85.73%	93.60%	93.73%
Mesh-ICSLBP-C	69.47%	84.13%	95.20%	94.93%
Mesh-ICSLBP-LD	75.20%	91.73%	98.00%	97.87%
Mesh-ICSLBP-M-H	69.07%	82.80%	95.47%	95.47%
Mesh-ICSLBP-M-C	69.07%	80.93%	96.40%	96.53%
Mesh-ICSLBP-M-LD	72.80%	88.40%	96.80%	97.07%
Mesh-CLBP-H	82.93%	91.73%		
Mesh-CLBP-C	84.53%	92.93%		
Mesh-CLBP-LD	87.07%	96.27%		
Mesh-CBP-H	53.60%	70.67%	97.20%	96.93%
Mesh-CBP-C	47.87%	72.80%	96.67%	96.93%
Mesh-CBP-LD	50.13%	80.00%	**98.53%**	**98.53%**
Mesh-LBPSobel-H	61.87%	71.60%		
Mesh-LBPSobel-C	58.40%	74.00%		
Mesh-LBPSobel-LD ·	75.33%	88.80%		

7   Discussion and Conclusion

In this paper, we extended different varieties of LBP variants to the mesh manifold, whereby we derived a total of 48 variants on the mesh by combination of different scalar functions on the mesh and binary digits weights.

Our study reveals that the mesh variants preserve the original behavior of their 2D counterparts with regard to the uniformity aspect. Also, a comparative study for geometric texture detection, has shown mesh-LBP variants capabilities to enhance further analysis tasks on mesh manifold. Referring to Table 1, four new mesh-LBP variants substantially reduced the computational cost by bringing down the histogram size to 63 and 155, as compared to the original size of 1125 in the original mesh-LBP. Our experiments reveal that such small size mesh-LBP boost the SVM training efficiency without compromising the accuracy. Comparing with the most recent state of the art works proposed for relief patterns classification, tested on the SHREC'17 data set, SVM results showed a clear improvement brought by our mesh-LBP extension approach.

References

1. Ahonen, T., Hadid, A., Pietikäinen, M.: Face recognition with local binary patterns. In: Pajdla, T., Matas, J. (eds.) ECCV 2004. LNCS, vol. 3021, pp. 469–481. Springer, Heidelberg (2004). https://doi.org/10.1007/978-3-540-24670-1_36
2. Ahonen, T., Hadid, A., Pietikainen, M.: Face description with local binary patterns: application to face recognition. IEEE Trans. Pattern Anal. Mach. Intell. **28**(12), 2037–2041 (2006)
3. Alcantarilla, P.F., Bartoli, A., Davison, A.J.: KAZE features. In: Fitzgibbon, A., Lazebnik, S., Perona, P., Sato, Y., Schmid, C. (eds.) ECCV 2012. LNCS, vol. 7577, pp. 214–227. Springer, Heidelberg (2012). https://doi.org/10.1007/978-3-642-33783-3_16
4. Beecks, C., Uysal, M.S., Seidl, T.: Signature quadratic form distances for content-based similarity. In: ACM International Conference on Multimedia, pp. 697–700 (2009). https://doi.org/10.1145/1631272.1631391
5. Biasotti, S., et al.: Shrec'17 Track: Retrieval of surfaces with similar relief patterns (2017). https://hal.archives-ouvertes.fr/hal-01500436~diglib.eg.org/handle/10.2312/3dor20171058
6. Bronstein, M.M., Bruna, J., LeCun, Y., Szlam, A., Vandergheynst, P.: Geometric deep learning: going beyond euclidean data. IEEE Signal Process. Mag. **34**(4), 18–42 (2017)
7. Charles, R.Q., Hao, S., amd J.G. Leonidas, M.K.: Pointnet: deep learning on point sets for 3D classification and segmentation. In: IEEE International Conference on Computer Vision and Pattern Recognition. IEEE (2017)
8. Fu, X., Wei, W.: Centralized binary patterns embedded with image euclidean distance for facial expression recognition. In: 2008 Fourth International Conference on Natural Computation. vol. 4, pp. 115–119. IEEE (2008). http://ieeexplore.ieee.org/document/4667260/
9. Guo, D., Atluri, V., Adam, N.: Texture-based remote-sensing image segmentation. In: 2005 IEEE International Conference on Multimedia and Expo, pp. 1472–1475 (2005)
10. Hafiane, A., Seetharaman, G., Palaniappan, K., Zavidovique, B.: Rotationally invariant hashing of median binary patterns for texture classification. In: Campilho, A., Kamel, M. (eds.) ICIAR 2008. LNCS, vol. 5112, pp. 619–629. Springer, Heidelberg (2008). https://doi.org/10.1007/978-3-540-69812-8_61
11. Heikkilä, M., Pietikäinen, M., Schmid, C.: Description of interest regions with local binary patterns. Pattern Recognit. **42**(3), 425–436 (2009). http://linkinghub.elsevier.com/retrieve/pii/S0031320308003282
12. Ioannidou, A., Chatzilari, E., Nikolopoulos, S., Kompatsiaris, I.: Deep learning advances in computer vision with 3D data: a survey. ACM Comput. Surv. **50**(2), 20:1–20:38 (2017). https://doi.org/10.1145/3042064
13. Junding, S., Shisong, Z., Xiaosheng, W.: Image retrieval based on an improved CS-LBP descriptor. In: 2010 2nd IEEE International Conference on Information Management and Engineering, pp. 115–117 (2010). http://ieeexplore.ieee.org/lpdocs/epic03/wrapper.htm?arnumber=5477432
14. LeCun, Y., Bengio, Y., Hinton, G.: Deep learning. Nature **521**, 436–444 (2015)

15. Li, C., Ben Hamza, A.: A multiresolution descriptor for deformable 3D shape retrieval. Vis. Comput. **29**(6), 513–524 (2013). https://doi.org/10.1007/s00371-013-0815-3
16. Limberger, F.A., Wilson, R.C.: Feature encoding of spectral signatures for 3D non-rigid shape retrieval. In: British Machine Vision Conference, pp. 1–13
17. Litjens, G.J.S., et al.: A survey on deep learning in medical image analysis. CoRR abs/1702.05747 (2017). http://arxiv.org/abs/1702.05747
18. Mäenpää, T., Viertola, J., Pietikäinen, M.: Optimising colour and texture features for real-time visual inspection. Pattern Anal. Appl. **6**(3), 169–175 (2003). https://doi.org/10.1007/s10044-002-0179-1
19. Masoumi, M., Hamza, A.B.: Spectral shape classification: a deep learning approach. J. Vis. Commun. Image Represent. **43**, 198–211 (2017). http://www.sciencedirect.com/science/article/pii/S1047320317300019
20. Masoumi, M., Li, C., Hamza, A.B.: A spectral graph wavelet approach for non-rigid 3D shape retrieval. Pattern Recognit. Lett. **83**, 339–348 (2016). http://www.sciencedirect.com/science/article/pii/S0167865516300617
21. Moore, S., Bowden, R.: Local binary patterns for multi-view facial expression recognition. Comput. Vis. Image Underst. **115**, 541–558 (2011)
22. Ojala, T., Pietikainen, M., Maenpaa, T.: Multiresolution gray-scale and rotation invariant texture classification with local binary patterns. IEEE Trans. Pattern Anal. Mach. Intell. **24**(7), 971–987 (2002). http://ieeexplore.ieee.org/document/1017623/
23. Ojala, T., Pietikäinen, M., Harwood, D.: A comparative study of texture measures with classification based on featured distributions. Pattern Recognit. **29**(1), 51–59 (1996). http://linkinghub.elsevier.com/retrieve/pii/0031320395000674
24. Othmani, A., Voon, L.F.L.Y., Stolz, C., Piboule, A.: Single tree species classification from terrestrial laser scanning data for forest inventory. Pattern Recognit. Lett. **34**(16), 2144–2150 (2013). http://www.sciencedirect.com/science/article/pii/S0167865513002997
25. Shan, C., Gong, S., McOwan, P.: Facial expression recognition based on local binary patterns: a comprehensive study. Image Vis. Comput. **27**(6), 803–816 (2009). http://www.sciencedirect.com/science/article/pii/S0262885608001844
26. Sipiran, I., Lokoc, J., Bustos, B., Skopal, T.: Scalable 3D shape retrieval using local features and the signature quadratic form distance. Vis. Comput. (2016). https://doi.org/10.1007/s00371-016-1301-5
27. Sze, V., Chen, Y., Yang, T., Emer, J.S.: Efficient processing of deep neural networks: a tutorial and survey. CoRR abs/1703.09039 (2017). http://arxiv.org/abs/1703.09039
28. Tangelder, J.W., Veltkamp, R.C.: A survey of content based 3D shape retrieval methods. Multimedia Tools Appl. **39**(3), 441–471 (2008). https://doi.org/10.1007/s11042-007-0181-0
29. Tortorici, C., Werghi, N., Berretti, S.: Boosting 3D LBP-based face recognition by fusing shape and texture descriptors on the mesh. In: 2015 IEEE International Conference on Image Processing (ICIP), pp. 2670–2674. IEEE (2015). http://ieeexplore.ieee.org/document/7351287/
30. Wang, P., Li, W., Ogunbona, P.O., Wan, J., Escalera, S.: RGB-D-based motion recognition with deep learning: a survey. Int. J. Comput. Vis. (2017, to appear)
31. Wang, X., Mirmehdi, M.: Archive film restoration based on spatiotemporal random walks. In: Daniilidis, K., Maragos, P., Paragios, N. (eds.) ECCV 2010. LNCS, vol. 6315, pp. 478–491. Springer, Heidelberg (2010). https://doi.org/10.1007/978-3-642-15555-0_35

32. Werghi, N., Berretti, S., Bimbo, A., Pala, P.: The mesh-LBP: computing local binary patterns on discrete manifolds. In: Proceedings of the IEEE International Conference on Computer Vision Workshops, pp. 562–569 (2013)

33. Werghi, N., Berretti, S., Del Bimbo, A.: The mesh-LBP: a framework for extracting local binary patterns from discrete manifolds. IEEE Trans. Image Process. **24**(1), 220–235 (2015)

34. Werghi, N., Rahayem, M., Kjellander, J.: An ordered topological representation of 3D triangular mesh facial surface: concept and applications. EURASIP J. Adv. Signal Process. **2012**(1), 144 (2012)

35. Werghi, N., Tortorici, C., Berretti, S., del Bimbo, A.: Local binary patterns on triangular meshes: concept and applications. Comput. Vis. Image Underst. **139**, 161–177 (2015). http://linkinghub.elsevier.com/retrieve/pii/S1077314215000843

36. Werghi, N., Tortorici, C., Berretti, S., Del Bimbo, A.: Computing local binary patterns on mesh manifolds for 3D texture retrieval. In: Proceedings of the 2015 Eurographics Workshop on 3D Object Retrieval, pp. 91–94 (2015)

37. Werghi, N., Tortorici, C., Berretti, S., Del Bimbo, A.: Representing 3D texture on mesh manifolds for retrieval and recognition applications. In: 2015 IEEE Conference on Computer Vision and Pattern Recognition (CVPR), 07–12 June, pp. 2521–2530. IEEE (2015). http://ieeexplore.ieee.org/document/7298867/

38. Werghi, N., Tortorici, C., Berretti, S., Del Bimbo, A.: Boosting 3D LBP-based face recognition by fusing shape and texture descriptors on the mesh. IEEE Trans. Inf. Forensics Secur. **11**(5), 964–979 (2016). http://ieeexplore.ieee.org/document/7373633/

39. Wu, X., Sun, J.: An effective texture spectrum descriptor. In: 2009 Fifth International Conference on Information Assurance and Security. vol. 2, pp. 361–364. IEEE (2009). http://ieeexplore.ieee.org/document/5283492/

40. Zeppelzauer, M., et al.: Interactive 3D segmentation of rock-art by enhanced depth maps and gradient preserving regularization. J. Comput. Cult. Herit. **9**(4), 19 (2016). https://doi.org/10.1145/2950062

41. Guo, Z., Zhang, L., Zhang, D.: A completed modeling of local binary pattern operator for texture classification. IEEE Trans. Image Process. **19**(6), 1657–1663 (2010). http://ieeexplore.ieee.org/document/5427137/

A Normalized Generalized Curvature Scale Space for 2D Contour Representation

Ameni Benkhlifa[✉] and Faouzi Ghorbel

Grift Group, Cristal Laboratory, National School of Computer Sciences,
Université de la Manouba, 2010 Manouba, Tunisia
`ameni.benkhlifa@ensi-uma.tn, faouzi.ghorbel@ensi.rnu.tn`
`http://www.ensi.rnu.tn/`

Abstract. Here, we intend to propose a discrete normalization of the Generalized Curvature Scale Space (GCSS). The GCSS is an Euclidean invariant planar contour descriptor. It consists on the convolution of the contour by Gaussian functions with different scales. The points having the same curvature values as the selected extremums are the considered key points. This representation implies different number of descriptors from a shape to another. Thus, a step of redistribution of the key points is requested. Therefore, a discrete normalization approach is proceeded. The descriptor is composed by the curvature variation of the key points at the smoothed curve. Several datasets were used to carry on the experiments and to verify the accuracy, the stability and the robustness of the novel description. The Dynamic Time Warping distance is the similarity metric used. Experimental results show that considerable rates of image retrieval are reached comparing to the state of the art.

Keywords: 2D shape description · Curvature Scale Space ·
Iso-curvature · Shape classification

1 Introduction

The wide range of applications in computer vision demonstrates the importance of its associated algorithms in many disciplines such as digital medicine, biology, multimedia, remote sensing, robotics. Thus, many benchmarks, created by expert groups of standardization to test and verify these algorithms, witness the importance of the considered problem. Hence, the interest of the classification of shapes is no longer to be proved. However, it is well-known that the problem of 2D shape description is difficult. The shape is a subject to many nonlinear deformations like noise and occlusion, or Euclidean or affine geometric transformations caused by different poses. Such description have often to verify at least the following properties: the efficiency, the stability, the complementeness and the invariance with respect to any transformation belongs to planar Euclidean transformations group $E(2)$.

© Springer Nature Switzerland AG 2019
L. Chen et al. (Eds.): RFMI 2017, CCIS 842, pp. 167–177, 2019.
https://doi.org/10.1007/978-3-030-19816-9_13

In this context, many approaches were proposed. These methods could be classified into two major classes: region-based and contour-based ones.

In the first category, we find methods that characterize the shape content. They exploit the information that contain its pixels. Such kind of methods consider the details of the image. Hence, they are reliable for the description of complex shapes like logos, trademarks as mentioned in the work of Kim et al. [1]. Many works were proposed in this context, such as the 2D Zernike moments based methods as complex moments [1,2]. These methods are very sensitive to local changes such as occlusion or overlapping objects. There are also the 2D Fourier descriptors based methods such as the generic Fourier descriptor of Zang et al. [3] which applied 2-D Fourier transform on polar raster sampled shape image. They also proposed the Enhanced generic Fourier descriptor in [4] which derived the generic Fourier descriptor from the rotation and scale normalized shape. The multi-scale Fourier-based descriptor proposed by Direkoglu et al. [5] represented the shape using its boundary and its content using the Gaussian filter in many scales. It is $E(2)$-invariant and robust to noise. Ghorbel et al. [6] proposed the analytical Fourier Mellin transform which gave also an invariant description for region. In the same context, we find the approach presented by Hong et al. [7] which is based on a kernel descriptor that characterizes local shape.

The second class contains the boundary based methods. There are the Fourier descriptors applied in [8–11]. They extracted the global features of the contour.

However other methods treat local features. We find the descriptor of Hoffman et al. [12] who partitioned the curve into parts at negative curvature minima which enhanced the object recognition. Xu et al. [14] proposed another method called contour flexibility which represents the deformable potential at each point of the contour. Klassen et al. [16] presented a differential geometric curve representation using its direction and curvature functions. Shu et al. [17] proposed a descriptor named contour points distribution histogram which is based on the distribution of points on object contour under polar coordinates. In the work of Sebastian et al. [18], the contour was characterized by two intrinsic properties: its length and the curvature variations and use them for registration and matching. Their method is called Curve Edit. There is also the descriptor of Belongie et al. [19]. It consists of an algorithm called the Shape Context. At each reference point of the contour, they captured the distribution of the remain points. For two similar contours, the corresponding points had similar shape contexts. This correspondence gives an optimal registration. A new distance called the Inner-Distance was suggested by Ling et al. [20]. It is defined as the length of the shortest path between feature points. This distance can replace the Euclidean distance for complex shapes. It was combined with several methods such as the Shape context [19]. There is also the work of Laiche et al. [21] which is a part-based approach for contour description called Curve Normalization. They represented the shape boundary by an ordered sequence of parts. Then, they associated each part with the cubic polynomial curve using the Least Squared method. A multiscale approaches also were developed. The Angle Scale Descriptor was proposed by Fotopoulou et al. [15]. It consisted of computing the angles between points of the contour in different scales. Another multiscale method of Mokhtarian et al. [22]. It is the curvature scale space which is based on the computation of the maxima of the curvature of the smoothed shape by Gaussian functions in different scales.

In this paper, we intend to propose a discrete normalization of the Generalized Curvature Scale Space proposed in [23]. It is a contour-based descriptor, that we nominate Normalized Generalized Curvature Scale Space (N-GCSS). Our approach is based on the iso-curvature parameterization [24] which is invariant to Euclidean transformations $E(2)$ and CSS [22] method that extracts the extremums of the shape in different scales. In a chosen set of scales, we extract the local extremums of the curvature. We select only those superior to a given threshold. Our descriptor is formed by the points of the contour having the selected curvature levels. Besides, the number of interest point obtained is not the same to all the shapes. Therefore, a novel discrete normalization is proceeded. N-GCSS gives an $E(2)$-invariant non uniform parameterization of the contour since it is constructed by the curvature values of the selected points.

The following paper is organized as follows: we describe the steps of our approach in the second section. In the third section, we expose and discuss the results of the application of our approach using the MPEG7 Set A Part-A1, MPEG7 CE SHAPE-1 Part-B [26] and HMM GPD datasets.

2   Normalized-Generalized Curvature Scale Space

In this section, a detailed description of the GCSS [23] and the discrete normalization will be presented.

2.1   Generalized Curvature Scale Space

The Generalized Curvature Scale Space of [23] corresponds to a set of finite and $E(2)$ invariant points. This representation gives a set of points in the strong variation regions. The GCSS deals with an injective closed contour denoted by C. For a given set of scales $\sigma \in \Sigma$, they applied the Curvature Scale Space proposed by [22]. For each σ the smoothed contour C_σ is given as follows:

$$
\begin{aligned}
C_\sigma : [0,1] &\to \mathbb{R}^2 \\
t &\mapsto [x(t,\sigma), y(t,\sigma)]^t
\end{aligned}
\tag{1}
$$

In order to extract the key points, the curvature $\kappa(t,\sigma)$ at each point of the smoothed contour C_σ is computed as follows 2:

$$
\kappa(t,\sigma) = \frac{x_t(t,\sigma)y_{tt}(t,\sigma) - y_t(t,\sigma)x_{tt}(t,\sigma)}{(x_t^2(t,\sigma) + y_t^2(t,\sigma))^{3/2}}
\tag{2}
$$

$x_t(t,\sigma)$, $y_t(t,\sigma)$, $x_{tt}(t,\sigma)$ and $y_{tt}(t,\sigma)$ are respectively the first and the second derivatives of $x(t,\sigma)$ and $y(t,\sigma)$. The extremums of $\kappa(t,\sigma)$ are stored in ℓ_σ.

A chosen threshold τ was fixed in order to remove the low curvature extremums.

$$\ell_\sigma(\tau) = \{\ell_\sigma \quad ; \ell_\sigma > \tau\} \tag{3}$$

Since the curvature κ_σ is not a bijective function, the selected points consists of the reciprocal image of $\kappa_\sigma^{-1}(\{\ell_\sigma^j(\tau)\})$.

$$\kappa_\sigma^{-1}(\{\ell_\sigma^j(\tau)\}) = \{t_i^j \quad /\kappa_\sigma(t_i^j) = \ell_\sigma^j(\tau)\} \tag{4}$$

where i is the index of the point on C_σ and j is the index of the level. The selected points at each scale σ are saved in a $F_c(\sigma)$. They can be described as follows.

$$F_c(\sigma) = \{C(t_i^j, \sigma) \quad ; t_i^j = \kappa_\sigma^{-1}\{\ell_\sigma^j(\tau)\}\} \tag{5}$$

The obtained descriptors constitute the following F_c.

$$F_c = \bigcup_{\sigma \in \Sigma} F_c(\sigma) \tag{6}$$

Therefore, our descriptor is composed by the curvature values of these key points in the selected scales:

$$F = \bigcup_{\sigma \in \Sigma} F(\sigma) \quad ; F(\sigma) = \kappa_\sigma(F_c(\sigma)) \tag{7}$$

The steps of the GCSS are described in Fig. 1.

2.2   Discrete Normalization of the Key Points

GCSS could be seen also as a new parameterization of the contour. Such parameterization is $E(2)$-invariant as the curvature. However, in the discrete case, F_c is a set of unordered points of C because it is a resampling procedure of the points. In the last step, the obtained set of points is ordered. Such set is distributed non-uniformly and we have more points in strong curvature areas. In order to make the number of points in F_c the same for all contours in the dataset, a discrete normalization step is proceeded.

We denote by N the number of key points from GCSS of a given curve ie $N = card(F_c)$. However, the wished number of points is N_w. Let F_c^* be the normalized set. In order to obtain N_w interest points from the total N, we start by computing the cumulative distance between the starting point P_1 and P_i where i the ith point. This procedure is equivalent to define a finite function from $1..N$ to an interval $[0, a]$ from $\mathbb{R}$. We consider $S(P_i)$ defined as follows:

$$S(P_i) = \int_{\widehat{P_1, P_i}} ||C'(t)|| dt \tag{8}$$

Hence, we resample regularly the abscissa vector $[P_1..P_N]$ into $[P_1^*..P_{N_w}^*]$. We compute $S(P_i^*)$ and we search the nearest points $S(P_j)$.

$$\underset{j}{\mathrm{argmin}} \, ||S(P_i^*) - S(P_j)|| \tag{9}$$

Figure 2 gives an illustration of the proposed normalization procedure for $N = 28$ and $N_w = 10$.

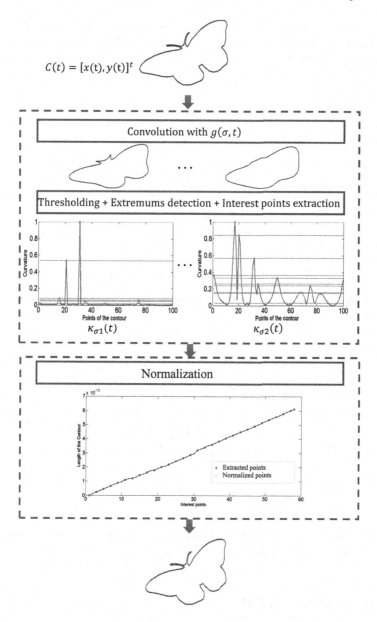

Fig. 1. The block diagram of the normalized Generalized Curvature Scale Space.

2.3   The Invariance to $E(2)$

The Normalized Generalized Scale Space descriptor is based on the computation of the curvature of the smoothed contour in given scales. As the curvature behavior is the same whatever is the transformation applied to the contour:

rotation, translation or scale, the obtained set of points of C and $g(C)$ is the same. Where g is an $E(2)$ transformation. The problem of the starting point is resolved by the use of the Dynamic Time Warping [28] as similarity metric. Figure 3 demonstrates well the distribution of the key points and their invariance under $E(2)$.

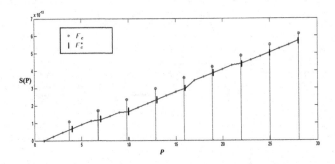

Fig. 2. A discrete normalization example from $N = 28$ to $N_w = 10$

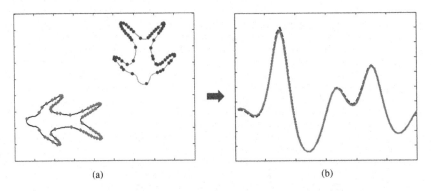

Fig. 3. The invariance under $E(2)$ transformation (a) point of interest on the original curves (b) the curvature variation of the two signatures.

3   Experiments and Results

The performance of the N-GCSS is tested on three datasets and evaluated in terms of shape retrieval efficiency and precision-recall curves. The datasets used for the experimentations are: HMM GPD and MPEG7 CE Shape-1 Part-B [26] and MPEG7 Part-A1. For the recognition, each object is compared to all the shapes in the dataset using the Dynamic Time Warping [28] algorithm and matched to the closest one.

3.1   The Datasets

The HMM GPD is composed of four sub datasets as shows the following Table 1:
bicego-data [25], plane-data, mpeg-data and car-data [27]. We form an other set
of shapes using the four sub datasets (bicego, plane, car and mpeg) by picking
up the 20 first elements of each class. The MPEG7 CE Shape-1 Part-B dataset
[26] is a well-known dataset. It is composed of 1400 elements that are grouped
in 70 classes. Each class contains 20 images.

The MPEG7 Part-A1 is composed of 420 objects grouped in 70 classes. It is
used to test the performance of the descriptor under scale transformations.

Table 1. HMM GPD sub-datasets

Sub-dataset	Number of objects
Bicego	140
Plane	210
Car	120
Mpeg	120
HMM	480

3.2   Results

In this paragraph, the experiments on the above datasets are carried on. The
parameters of N-GCSS are chosen empirically: $\sigma \in 5, 6$ and $\tau = 10^{-3}$ in order to
eliminate the local extremums having very low curvature. We choose $N_w = 100$
the number of key points for each contour.

We proceeded the k nearest neighbors (k-NN) algorithm in order to compute
the pairwise shape matching scores in the recognition step. For each shape, the
distance (Dynamic time warping) is computed from all the other shapes in the
dataset and the knearest neighbors are selected.

To evaluate the performance of our representation and to compare it with
other techniques from the state of the art. Table 2 lists the retrieval results of
our descriptor N-GCSS on HMM GPD dataset using 1NN algorithm. We reach
very high score for Mpeg (100%) and Plane (98.57%) datasets. Although the
Car sub-dataset contains bad quality contours, N-GCSS outperforms the CSS
descriptor [22] and reaches 73.33%. This demonstrates well the robustness of our
descriptor to numerical approximation. This robustness is due to the use of the
multiscale approach in the construction of the proposed approach.

We used also the MPEG7 Part-A1 set in order to test the accuracy of the proposed descriptor under scale transformation. N-GCSS outperforms the Fourier
Descriptor (FD) [11] and Curvature Scale Space (CSS) [22]. The precision-recall
curves are illustrated in Fig. 5. The results prove the accuracy, stability and
invariance to $E(2)$ properties of the proposed representation.

Table 2. Retrieval results on HMM dataset using 1NN algorithm for: N-GCSS and CSS [22]

	Rate N-GCSS (%)	Rate CSS (%)
Bicego	94.29	90.00
Plane	98.57	79.52
Car	73.33	55.00
Mpeg	100	95.83
HMM	85.42	75.62

Table 3. Bull's eye MPEG7 CE SHAPE-1 Part-B [26]

IDSC [20]	85.40%
N-GCSS	77.20%
CPDH [17]	76.56%
SC [19]	76.51%
CSS [22]	75.44%
ASD [15]	70.51%
Curve normalization [21]	50.76%

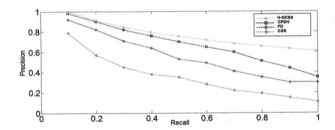

Fig. 4. Retrieval rate for MPEG7 CE Shape-1 Part-B dataset for: N-GCSS, CPDH, FD and CSS

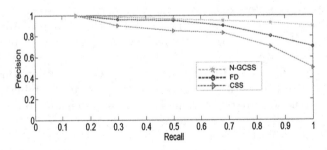

Fig. 5. Precision recall for MPEG7 Part-A1 dataset for: N-GCSS, FD and CSS

Our descriptor was compared also to the Contour Points Distribution Histogram (CPDH) [17], Fourier Descriptor (FD) [11] and Curvature Scale Space (CSS) [22] for MPEG7 CE Shape-1 Part-B [26]. Figure 4 shows the precision-recall curves of the mentioned descriptors on the MPEG7 CE Shape-1 Part-B [26]. The proposed representation gives higher precision rates than the above-mentioned descriptors. By computing the retrieval rate using the 1NN algorithm for this dataset [26], we reached 91.27%.

The performance of the proposed descriptor is compared also with other approaches in the literature. The retrieval rates are measured with the Bull's eyes algorithm. Each shape is considered as a query and we count how many objects within the 40 most similar objects belong to the class of the query. Table 3 lists the Bull's eye scores of some algorithms. We remark that our method gives a competitive score comparing to the state of the art.

4 Conclusion

In this work, we introduced a 2D contour description. It is based on the Generalized Curvature Scale Space of [23]. The GCSS is constructed by a $E(2)$ invariant set of points. This set corresponds to the high curvature zones of a contour. The contribution of this paper lies on the discrete normalization of the obtained key points. This normalization makes comparison between the contours easier. The problem of starting point is overcome by the use of the Dynamic Time Warping [28]. The performance of the normalized GCSS is tested by carrying out many experiments on two well know datasets which are: HMM GPD, MPEG7 CE SHAPE-1 Part-B [26] and MPEG7 Part-A1 and comparing to several descriptors. Results show well the accuracy of our $E(2)$-invariant descriptor and its stability and robustness to numerical approximation.

Many perspectives could be cited to this work. We intend to present a method of choosing the set of scales while considering the complexity of the shape to be analyzed. We look also for a combination of this novel parameterization with other descriptors from the state of the art since the set of key points found can be considered as a non-uniform parameterization of the contour. They are located at strong-curvature zones only. However, the arc-length reparameterization gives a uniform distribution of points which can be a waste of energy. An immigration to the 3D dimension also is among our future work.

References

1. Kim, W.Y., Kim, Y.S.: A region-based shape descriptor using Zernike moments. Signal Process.: Image Commun. **16**, 95–102 (2000)
2. Khotanzad, A., Hong, Y.H.: Invariant image recognition by Zernike moments. IEEE Trans. Pattern Anal. Mach. Intell. **12**, 489–497 (1990)
3. Zhang, D., Lu, G.: Generic Fourier descriptor for shape based image retrieval. In: 2002 IEEE International Conference on Multimedia and Expo, ICME 2002, Proceedings, pp. 425–428. IEEE (2002)

4. Zhang, D., Lu, G.: Enhanced generic Fourier descriptors for object-based image retrieval. In: 2002 IEEE International Conference on Acoustics, Speech, and Signal Processing (ICASSP), pp. IV–3668. IEEE (2002)
5. Direkoglu, C., Nixon, M.S.: Shape classification using multiscale Fourier-based description in 2-D space. In: 2008 9th International Conference on Signal Processing, ICSP 2008, pp. 820–823. IEEE (2008)
6. Ghorbel, F.: Towards a unitary formulation for invariant image description: application to image coding. Ann. Telecommun. **53**, 242–260 (1998)
7. Hong, B.W., Prados, E., Soatto, S., Vese, L.: Shape representation based on integral kernels: application to image matching and segmentation. In: 2006 IEEE Computer Society Conference on Computer Vision and Pattern Recognition, pp. 833–840. IEEE (2006)
8. Ghorbel, F.: Stability of invariant Fourier descriptors and its inference in the shape classification. In: 11th IAPR International Conference on Pattern Recognition, vol. III. Conference C: Image, Speech and Signal Analysis, Proceedings, pp. 130–133. IEEE (1992)
9. Persoon, E., Fu, K.S.: Shape discrimination using Fourier descriptors. IEEE Trans. Pattern Anal. Mach. Intell. 388-397 (1986)
10. Wallace, T.P., Wintz, P.A.: An efficient three-dimensional aircraft recognition algorithm using normalized Fourier descriptors. Comput. Graph. Image Process. **13**, 99–126 (1980)
11. Rui, Y., She, A.C., Huang, T.S.: A modified Fourier descriptor for shape matching in MARS. Image Databases Multimed. Search **8**(1998), 165–180 (1997)
12. Hoffman, D.D., Richards, W.A.: Parts of recognition. Cognition **18**, 65–96 (1984)
13. Siddiqi, K., Kimia, B.B.: Parts of visual form: computational aspects. IEEE Trans. Pattern Anal. Mach. Intell. **17**, 239–251 (1995)
14. Xu, C., Liu, J., Tang, X.: 2D shape matching by contour flexibility. IEEE Trans. Pattern Anal. Mach. Intell. **31**, 180–186 (2009)
15. Fotopoulou, F., Economou, G.: Multivariate angle scale descriptor of shape retrieval. Proc. Signal Process Appl. Math. Electron. Commun. 105–108 (2011)
16. Klassen, E., Srivastava, A., Mio, M., Joshi, S.H.: Analysis of planar shapes using geodesic paths on shape spaces. IEEE Trans. Pattern Anal. Mach. Intell. **26**, 372–383 (2004)
17. Shu, X., Wu, X.J.: A novel contour descriptor for 2D shape matching and its application to image retrieval. Image Vis. Comput. **29**(4), 286–294 (2011)
18. Sebastian, T.B., Klein, P.N., Kimia, B.B.: On aligning curves. IEEE Trans. Pattern Anal. Mach. Intell. **25**(1), 116–125 (2003)
19. Belongie, S., Malik, J., Puzicha, J.: Shape matching and object recognition using shape contexts. IEEE Trans. Pattern Anal. Mach. Intell. **24**(4), 509–522 (2002)
20. Ling, H., Jacobs, D.W.: Shape classification using the inner-distance. IEEE Trans. Pattern Anal. Mach. Intell. **29**(2), 286–299 (2007)
21. Laiche, N., Larabi, S., Ladraa, F., Khadraoui, A.: Curve normalization for shape retrieval. Signal Process.: Image Commun. **29**(4), 556–571 (2014)
22. Mokhtarian, F., Abbasi, S., Kittler, J.: Robust and efficient shape indexing through curvature scale space. In: Proceedings of the 1996 British Machine and Vision Conference BMVC. Citseer (1996)
23. Benkhlifa, A., Ghorbel, F.: A novel 2D contour description generalized curvature scale space. In: Ben Amor, B., Chaieb, F., Ghorbel, F. (eds.) RFMI 2016. CCIS, vol. 684, pp. 129–140. Springer, Cham (2017). https://doi.org/10.1007/978-3-319-60654-5_11

24. Bannour, M., Ghorbel, F.: Isotropie de la representation des surfaces; application a la description et la visualisation d' objets 3D. In: Conference on Proceedings of RFIA, pp. 275-282 (2000)
25. Bicego, M., Murino, V., Figueiredo, M.A.: Similarity-based classification of sequences using hidden Markov models. Pattern Recogn. **37**, 2281–2291 (2004)
26. Latecki, L.J., Lakamper, R., Eckhardt, T.: Shape descriptors for non-rigid shapes with a single closed contour. In: IEEE Conference on Computer Vision and Pattern Recognition, Proceedings, pp. 424–429. IEEE (2000)
27. Thakoor, N., Gao, J., Jung, S.: Hidden Markov model-based weighted likelihood discriminant for 2-D shape classification. IEEE Trans. Image Process. **16**, 2707–2719 (2007)
28. Sankoff, D., Kruskal, J.B. (eds.): Time Warps, String Edits, and Macromolecules: The Theory and Practice of Sequence Comparison. Addison-Wesley Publication, Reading (1983)

Watermarking, Segmentation and Deformations

A New Watermarking Method Based on Analytical Clifford Fourier Mellin Transform

Maroua Affes[(✉)], Malek Sellami Meziou[(✉)], and Faouzi Ghorbel[(✉)]

CRISTAL Laboratory, GRIFT Research Group, Manouba, Tunisia
maroua.affes@ensi-uma.tn, malek.meziou@gmail.com,
Faouzi.ghorbel@ensi.run.tn

Abstract. Here, we intend to introduce a new Fourier Transform. The well-known Analytical Fourier Mellin Transform (AFMT) will be defined on Clifford Algebra in order to process colored images. The proposed Fourier Transform is called Clifford Analytical Fourier Mellin Transform (CAFMT). Its magnitude, same as AFMT modulus, is invariant against planar similarities, not only on gray level images but also on colored images. Using ACFMT magnitude, we propose a robust watermarking technique in the frequency domain.

Keywords: Analytical Fourier Mellin Transform · Clifford Transform · Robust watermarking method

1 Introduction

Nowadays, many techniques are proposed to protect the intellectual property rights of multimedia data such as digital watermarking. It consists of embedding a mark into an input signal or its Fourier transform. Often, watermarking methods are categorized by processing domain and watermark signal type. In all cases, the following constraints must be considered: good visual fidelity and robustness of the watermark against common image processing geometric attacks are essential.

Digital image watermarking can be applied in either spatial domain or frequency domain or both of them. With the spatial watermarking methods, the image is directly manipulated to embed the mark in some pixels. However, the frequency watermarked methods decompose initially the image into frequencies coefficients and the embedding is done by changing the transform coefficients. Generally, the embedding process and extraction process have common steps and a same frequency transform. Applying spatial domain watermarking method is easier than the transform domain watermarking method [1]. But, the mark is simpler to detach from cover image by pixel-wise forgery attack. That's why, the frequency domain watermarking is mostly used than to spatial domain. Since, they give the mark higher robustness and offer resistance to image manipulations [2]. Also, they have a high level of imperceptibility. The transforms currently used are: Discrete Cosine Transform (DCT), Discrete Fourier Transform (DFT), Discrete Wavelet Transform, etc.

© Springer Nature Switzerland AG 2019
L. Chen et al. (Eds.): RFMI 2017, CCIS 842, pp. 181–191, 2019.
https://doi.org/10.1007/978-3-030-19816-9_14

Authors in [3] present efficient method of watermarking using the DCT (Discrete Cosinus Transform) magnitude. Ruanaidh et al. [4] suggest a robust watermarking technique based on the DFT (Discret Fourier Transform) phase. Pereira and Pun in [5] propose a robust watermarking algorithm using a new template integrated in image able to estimate the geometrical attacks and inverse it before extraction processes. The wavelet transform was usually used in image watermarking [6]. First, the original image is decomposed into multi subbands which present low and high frequency components. after that, the mark is embedded into some subbands.

In this article, we focus on the frequency watermarking techniques which is based on the Fourier transform. This transform allows researchers to extract features that are invariant to geometric transformations as rotation, translation and scaling. Several invariant descriptors have been proposed in the literature, we can cite, for example, the Generic Fourier Descriptors [7] and the Generalized Fourier Descriptors [8]. These descriptors are based on the discrete Fourier transform (DFT) which ensures the invariance of amplitude to translation. Also, other descriptors called the Mellin Analytic Fourier Descriptors have been introduced. They ensure the invariant to rotation and scale transformations by converting the image to polar or log-polar domain [9]. These descriptors form a complete family of invariants and have been used usually for grayscale images or in marginal treatment that consider each colorimetric plane separately.

To avoid this marginal treatment, Sangwine et al. [10] in 2000 proposed the "Quaternionic Color Fourier Transform". Based on this transform, Guo and Zhu [11] introduced the Quaternionic Fourier-Mellin Descriptors. In 2010, Batard et al. [12] proposed a more rigorous mathematical formulation of color transform, called the "Fourier Transform Clifford" and applicable directly to the color images. By analogy with the work done by Batard et al. [12], Mennesson [13] defined the "Fourier-Mellin Clifford Descriptors" that are based both on the Fourier transform Mellin and Clifford algebra. These descriptors appeared as a promising tool in the processing of color images only for shape recognition. Given the important proprieties of these descriptors, we propose to integrate them into a color watermarking system.

In this paper, we give an overview of some Fourier transforms used in watermarking technology. Then we will present our new method which is based on Analytical Clifford Fourier Mellin Transform. Experimental results will be presented in the Sect. 4. We will eventually conclude and suggest some possible perspectives for future work.

2   New Watermarking Method Based on ACFMT

In this section, we will introduce the Analytical Clifford Fourier Mellin transform. This transform will be used later to propose a robust watermarking algorithm against geometric attacks.

Let f denote a function of a grayscale image, represented with polar coordinates (r and θ) defined over a compact set of $\mathbb{R}_+^* \times S^1$ [14, 15]. The Fourier Mellin Transform of f is given by:

$$M_f(k, v) = \frac{1}{2} \int_0^\infty \int_0^{2\pi} f(r, \theta).r^{iv}.e^{-ik\theta}.\frac{dr}{r}.d\theta, \forall (k, v) \in Z \times R \tag{1}$$

f is assumed to be assumable over $\mathbb{R}_+^* \times S^1$ under the measure i.e. $\frac{dr}{r}.d\theta$

$$\int_0^\infty \int_0^{2\pi} \left| f(r, \theta).r^{-iv}.e^{-ik\theta} \right|.\frac{dr}{r}.d\theta = \int_0^\infty \int_0^{2\pi} f(r, \theta).dr.d\theta < \infty \tag{2}$$

This hypothesis is not justified over $\mathbb{R}_+^* \times S^1$. Indeed, the integral diverges near the origin as $f(0, \theta)$ is generally non-zero. A rigorous approach has been introduced to tackle the divergence problem, Ghorbel in [16] suggested computing the FMT of $f_\sigma = r^\sigma f(r, \theta)$ instead of $f(r, \theta)$ where σ is a fixed and strictly positive real number. The Analytical Fourier Mellin transform has the following expression:

$$M_{f\sigma}(k, v) = \frac{1}{2} \int_0^\infty \int_0^{2\pi} f(r, \theta).r^{\sigma-iv}.e^{-ik\theta}.\frac{dr}{r}.d\theta, \forall (k, v) \in Z \times R \tag{3}$$

The AFMT presents enormous benefits but it can be computed only on gray level images. Quaternion transform and Clifford transform have been proposed to overcome this problem. First, the QFT is defined by replacing the imaginary complex i in the exponential of the Fourier transform by a pure and unitary quaternion μ belongs to $\mathbb{H}_1$. A color image is then considered as a function $\mathbb{R}^2$ on $\mathbb{R}_{4,0}$:

$$f(x) = r(x)i + v(x)j + b(x)k \tag{4}$$

After that, a pixel of a color image f can be extended as follows:

$$f(x) = r(x)e_1 + v(x)e_2 + b(x)e_3 + 0e_4 \tag{5}$$

Where $x = (x_1, x_2)$ and r, v and b are respectively the red, green and blue channels pixel with coordinates (x_1, x_2).

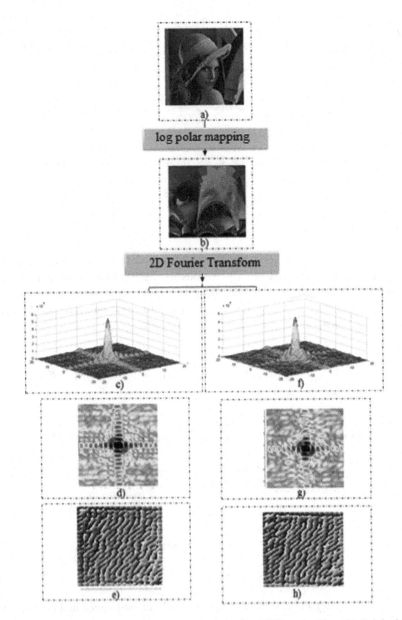

Fig. 1. The visualization of the Analytic Clifford Fourier Mellin transform: (a) Original image with size of 512×512 (b) Log-polar mapping of (a) image (c) 3D spectrum representation of the CFT (parallel part) (d) 2D spectrum representation of the CFT (parallel part) (e) Phase representation of the CFT (parallel part) (f) 3D spectrum representation of the CFT (orthogonal part) (g) 2D spectrum representation of the CFT (orthogonal part) (h) Phase representation of the CFT (orthogonal part)

The CFT generalizes the Color QFT [11]. The CFT is parameterized by a unit vector B whose expression is as follows:

$$\hat{f}_B(u) = \int_{R_2} e^{\frac{1}{2}<u,x>B} e^{\frac{1}{2}<u,x>I_4B} f(x) e^{-\frac{1}{2}<u,x>B} e^{-\frac{1}{2}<u,x>I_4B} dx \qquad (6)$$

Where $\diamond$ represents the scalar product, I_4 is the scalar pseudo of $\mathbb{R}_{4,0}$ and B is its unit bi-vector. Within the Clifford algebras, a vector can be decomposed into a parallel part and an orthogonal part relative to a bivector B. The above equation can be rewritten as follows by this decomposition [13]:

$$\hat{f}_B(u) = \hat{f}_{\|B}(u) + \hat{f}_{\perp B}(u) \qquad (7)$$

Where $\hat{f}_{\|B}(u) = \int_{R_2} f_{\|B}(x) e^{-<u,x>B} dx$ and $\hat{f}_{\perp B}(u) = \int_{R_2} f_{\perp B}(x) e^{-<u,x>I_4B} dx$

In order to combine the CFT with MFT, Mennesson in [13] proposed the Clifford Fourier Mellin transform.

$$\hat{f}_B(m,n) = \int_0^\infty \int_0^{2\pi} r^{m-1} e^{\frac{1}{2}n\theta(B+I_4B)} f(r,\theta) e^{-\frac{1}{2}n\theta(B+I_4B)} dr.d\theta \qquad (8)$$

This transform is divergent near the origin. We propose to compute the Analytical CFMT with the log-polar sampling $(q = ln(r))$. The Analytical CFMT that we note ACFMT is defined by the following expression:

$$\hat{f}_B(m,n) = \int_0^\infty \int_0^{2\pi} e^{q\sigma+m-1} e^{\frac{1}{2}n\theta(B+I_4B)} f(e^q,\theta) e^{-\frac{1}{2}n\theta(B+I_4B)} dq.d\theta \qquad (9)$$

Where I_4 is the scalar pseudo of $\mathbb{R}_{4,0}$ and B is its unit bi-vector. And $f(e^q, \theta)$ represents the log-polar transform of the image f. To simplify the computational complexity, we use the fast approximation [14]. Figure 1 shows the steps to estimate the Fourier Transform Mellin Clifford Analytics and display the results of each step.

3   The Proposed Algorithm

In this section, we will present our proposed method which done in frequency domain. We use the CFT as a Fourier transform applicable directly on color image. With the CFT, we avoid a marginal treatment and we ensure that there is not appearance of false color. Besides, the mark will be more robust.

We will use the decomposition of the CFT in order to embed the mark. In [17], we set up a small experiment to choose the embedding plane; we embed the mark *W* in three different locations: the parallel part, in the orthogonal part and in both of them. The results demonstrate that the emending in the parallel part deteriorate less the perceptual image quality.

Also, to make our method more robust, we used the local Harris features which can synchronize the embedded regions and the extracted regions. They provide a potential solution for watermarking to improve the robustness [18]. In fact, the interest points present a center of circular regions which contains the mark. These same regions may be identified in extraction process even after geometric distortions.

3.1   Embedding Process

In Fig. 2, we present the general diagram of our watermarking method. The embedding process has the following steps:

- Transform the image to gray scale image to detect the interest points.
- Generate some non-overlapped interest regions.
- Generate a bitmap, denoted ξ, which contains "1" if the block $B(i)$ of $\widehat{f}_{\|B}$ is valid i.e the block has a bit of the watermark. The validity condition is compute by the next steps:
  - ACFMT is applied to each selected block
  - Two mid-frequency coefficients are selected, $|Q(k_i, l_j)|$ and $|Q(k_n, l_m)|$:

    If $|Q(k_i, l_j)| > Q(k_n, l_m)|+p$,
      So $\xi(i) \leftarrow 1$; the Block B(i) is valid.
    Else
        $\xi(i) \leftarrow 0$.
    End if

  Where p is a marginal noise, in the experiment $p = 0.5$.
- Generate the mark W, $\{W_i, i = 0...N\}$. Its size is the number of "1" in the map. In order to overcome the corruption of the mark due to attacks, we use the Hamming code as an error correcting codes. So, the watermark is divided into some words, each word contains 4 bits. The Hamming code is then applied to each word to generate (7-4) single bit error correcting code. The use of error-correction codes ensures a better-quality signal at the receiver [19].

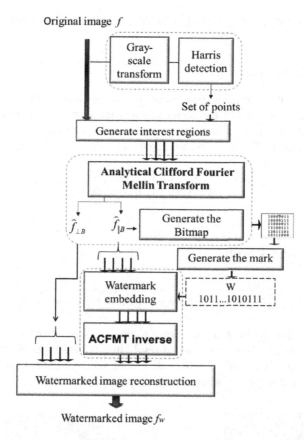

Fig. 2. Embedding process

- Embed the mark in valid regions, each region will contain one bit. To do that, we modified $|Q(k_i, l_j)|$ and $|Q(k_n, l_m)|$ and denoted the watermarked coefficients by $|Q'(k_i, l_j)|$ and $|Q'(k_n, l_m)|$, we apply the fellow steps:

If $\xi(i) = 1$

Apply the ACFMT;

If $W_i = 1$ So

$|Q'(k_i, l_j)| = |Q(k_n, l_m)|$ and $|Q'(k_n, l_m)| = |Q(k_1, l_1)|$; (we permute $|Q(k_i, l_j)|$ and $|Q(k_n, l_m)|$)

Else $|Q'(k_i, l_j)| = |Q(k_i, l_j)|$ and $|Q'(k_n, l_m)| = |Q(k_n, l_m)|$;

Endif

Apply the Inverse of ACFMT on each block.

Else Pass to the next region;

Endif

- The watermarked image f_w is then obtained by combining the watermarked blocks with the others blocks.

3.2 Extraction Process

The first steps of the extraction process are the same steps to those in embedding process. With the presence of the secret key and the map ξ, we can specify which blocks are watermarked. So, when $\xi(i) = 1$, we transform B(i) to ACFM domain. The watermark is extracted by the following equation:

$$W'_i = \begin{cases} 1, & Q'(k_n, l_m)| > |Q'(k_i, l_j)| \\ 0, & Q'(k_n, l_m)| < |Q'(k_i, l_j)| \end{cases} \tag{10}$$

4 Experimental Results

For all tests, we chose $|Q(k_i = 3, l_j = 2)|$ and $|Q(k_n = 1, l_m = 4)|$ as two mi-frequency coefficients of ACFMT. They have been modified to carry one-bit watermark in each region.

We used the PSNR (Peak Signal Noise Ratio) to measure imperceptibility of the mark. Figures 3 and 4 show the obtained result after the insertion of the mark in the parallel plane. The value of the PSNR is depending on the number of interest regions modified. In fact, it decreases when the size of the mark increases.

(a)   (b)

Fig. 3. Visual quality experiment (a) originale image, (b) watermarked image where PSNR = 38.44 dB

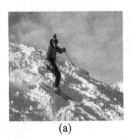   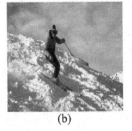

(a)   (b)

Fig. 4. Visual quality experiment (a) originale image (reference 6106), (b) watermarked image where PSNR = 47.55 dB

To evaluate the robustness of the proposed algorithm, we compute the Bit Error Rate. It presents the ratio between the numbers of incorrect bits transmitted to the total number of bits. The following table describes the error rate of mark estimation after some attacks on the image "Lena" and some images taken from the BSD300 set (The Berkeley Segmentation Dataset) (Table 1).

Table 1. Error rate after some geometric attacks applied on "Lena" image.

Image reference/attacks	Lena	61060	46076	78004	22090	8068	10081	15011	28083	35049
Rotation 1°	0,3	0	0	0,1	0,1	0	0,1	0,1	0	0
Rotation 5°	0.2	0.2	0	0.3	0.2	0	0	0	0.2	0
Rotation 10°	0.3	0.3	0	0.1	0.1	0.1	0	0	0	0.2
Translation 1 (5, 5)	0	0	0	0	0	0	0	0.2	0	0
Translation 2 (1, 3)	0	0	0	0	0	0.1	0	0	0.1	0
Scaling 0, 7	0.3	0	0.1	0.2	0.1	0.1	0.2	0	0	0.1
Scaling 0, 9	0.2	0	0.1	0.2	0	0	0	0.3	0	0
Scaling 1, 1	0	0	0	0.2	0.1	1	0	0	0	0.2

The proposed method is robust since the amplitude of the Fourier transform is invariant against translation and scaling. Also, it is robust against rotation since the insertion takes place after log-polar mapping.

The zero value of BER indicates that the mark extracted correctly. However, the higher value of BER is 0.3 which indicates that there is a fail in detection process. This fail comes from the fact that the set of points changes after geometric attacks.

5   Conclusion and Perspectives

In this paper, we introduced a new method of invisible watermarking based on ACFMT. The proposed algorithm is robust against geometric attacks because we synchronize the mark with the image content by embedding the mark in interest regions. The mark is imperceptible as it is inserted into the parallel part $\hat{f}_{\|B}$ of the Clifford Transform. The BER values showed that our scheme is effective in watermark recovering. But, its payload depends on the number of valid interest regions.

Future work will aim to extend it to enhance the robustness and to ensure that the mark can be extracted fairly accurately. Also, we will study the robustness against compression attacks.

References

1. Mishra, A., Jain, A., Narwaria, M., Agarwal, C.: An experimental study into objective quality assessment of watermarked images. Int. J. Image Process. (IJIP) 5(2), 199 (2011)
2. Potdar, V.M., Han, S., Chang, E.: A survey of digital image watermarking techniques. In: 2005 3rd IEEE International Conference on Industrial Informatics, INDIN 2005, pp. 709–716. IEEE, August 2005
3. Burgett, S., Koch, E., Zhao, J.: Copyright labeling of digitized image data. IEEE Commun. Mag. 36(3), 94–100 (1998)
4. Ruanaidh, J.J.K.O., Dowling, W.J., Boland, F.M.: Phase watermarking of digital images. In: 1996 International Conference on Image Processing, Proceedings, vol. 3, pp. 239–242. IEEE, September 1996
5. Pereira, S., Pun, T.: Robust template matching for affine resistant image watermarks. IEEE Trans. Image Process. 9(6), 1123–1129 (2000)
6. Kundur, D., Hatzinakos, D.: A robust digital image watermarking method using wavelet-based fusion. In: 1997 International Conference on Image Processing, Proceedings, vol. 1, pp. 544–547. IEEE, October 1997
7. Zhang, D., Lu, G.: Shape-based image retrieval using generic Fourier descriptor. Signal Process.: Image Commun. 17(10), 825–848 (2002)
8. Smach, F., Lemaître, C., Gauthier, J.P., Miteran, J., Atri, M.: Generalized Fourier descriptors with applications to objects recognition in SVM context. J. Math. Imaging Vis. 30(1), 43–71 (2008)
9. Derrode, S., Ghorbel, F.: Robust and efficient Fourier-Mellin transform approximations for gray-level image reconstruction and complete invariant description. Comput. Vis. Image Underst. 83(1), 57–78 (2001)
10. Sangwine, S.J., Ell, T.A., Blackledge, J.M., Turner, M.J.: The discrete Fourier transform of a colour image. Image Process. II Math. Methods Algorithms Appl. 430–441 (2000)
11. Guo, L.Q., Zhu, M.: Quaternion Fourier-Mellin moments for color images. Pattern Recogn. 44(2), 187–195 (2011)
12. Batard, T., Berthier, M., Saint-Jean, C.: Clifford Fourier transform for color image processing. In: Bayro-Corrochano, E., Scheuermann, G. (eds.) Geometric Algebra Computing, pp. 135–161. Springer, London (2010). https://doi.org/10.1007/978-1-84996-108-0_8. 5, 11, 12, 17, 18, 49, 51, 61, 63, 87, 108, 123, 124
13. Mennesson, J., Saint-Jean, C., Mascarilla, L.: Color Fourier-Mellin descriptors for image recognition. Pattern Recognit. Lett. 40, 27–35 (2014)
14. Derrode, S.: Représentation de formes planes à niveaux de gris par différentes approximations de Fourier-Mellin analytique en vue d'indexation de bases d'images, Doctoral dissertation, Rennes 1 (1999)
15. Ghorbel, F.: Application de la transformée de Fourier généralisée au problème de l'invariance en reconnaissance de formes a niveaux de gris. In: 14° Colloque sur le traitement du signal et des images, FRA. GRETSI, Groupe d'Etudes du Traitement du Signal et des Images (1993)
16. Ghorbel, F.: A complete invariant description for gray-level images by the harmonic analysis approach. Pattern Recognit. Lett. 15(10), 1043–1051 (1994)
17. Affes, M., Meziou, M.S., Ghorbel, F.: Robust color watermarking method based on Clifford transform. In: Blanc-Talon, J., Distante, C., Philips, W., Popescu, D., Scheunders, P. (eds.) ACIVS 2016. LNCS, vol. 10016, pp. 453–464. Springer, Cham (2016). https://doi.org/10.1007/978-3-319-48680-2_40

18. Papakostas, G.A., Tsougenis, E.D., Koulouriotis, D.E., Tourassis, V.D.: On the robustness of Harris detector in image watermarking attacks. Opt. Commun. **284**(19), 4394–4407 (2011)
19. MacWilliams, F.J., Sloane, N.J.A.: The Theory of Error-Correcting Codes. Elsevier (1977)

Simultaneous Semi-supervised Segmentation of Category-Independent Objects from a Collection of Images

Hager Merdassi[1(✉)], Walid Barhoumi[1,2(✉)],
and Ezzeddine Zagrouba[1(✉)]

[1] Institut Supérieur d'Informatique, Research Team on Intelligent Systems
in Imaging and Artificial Vision (SIIVA), LR16ES06 Laboratoire de recherche
en Informatique, Modélisation et Traitement de l'Information
et de la Connaissance (LIMTIC), Université de Tunis El Manar,
2 Rue Abou Raihane Bayrouni, 2080 Ariana, Tunisia
hager.merdassi@hotmail.fr,
walid.barhoumi@enicarthage.rnu.tn,
ezzeddine.zagrouba@fsm.rnu.tn
[2] Ecole Nationale d'Ingénieurs de Carthage, Université de Carthage,
45 Rue des Entrepreneurs, Charguia II, 2035 Tunis-Carthage, Tunisia

Abstract. This work is about simultaneous segmentation of different foreground objects from a collection of images with heterogeneous contents. Our idea is to propagate the segmentation information between images in order to detect foreground objects in all these images simultaneously, under the hypothesis of using categorized or uncategorized images, rather than resorting to image co-segmentation that forces the use of similar categorized images. In fact, given an input image, the objective is to integrate seamlessly other images in the general foreground model, in order to benefit the segmentation of the foreground objects in this image. Indeed, the proposed method aggregates general information, on foregrounds as well as on backgrounds, from a collection of images. To this end, the method is based on an energy minimization function. The linear dependence of the foreground histograms is firstly estimated to optimize the proposed energy function. Then, an iterative optimization of each image permits to remarkably optimize the final segmentation result for all images composing the input collection. Extensive experiments demonstrate that the suggested method allows full-object segmentation of the foreground from a collection of images composed of different classes of objects. Indeed, the validation of the accuracy on four challenging datasets (iCoseg, Oxford Flowers, Caltech101 and Berkeley) shows that the proposed method compares favorably with the state-of-the-art of foreground object segmentation from a collection of images. Besides, it has the challenging ability to deal accurately with uncategorized objects.

Keywords: Category-independent objects · Foreground segmentation · Linear dependence · Co-segmentation

L. Chen et al. (Eds.): RFMI 2017, CCIS 842, pp. 192–203, 2019.
https://doi.org/10.1007/978-3-030-19816-9_15

1 Introduction

The current explosion in digital images led to the emergence of methods and algorithms that proposed to exploit these images, resulting in better applications for users to interact with these data. Nevertheless, seen the diversity of the used environments, these datasets are often noisy even for categorized objects' collections. In addition, these datasets are typically heterogeneous and very large. Thus, there is an urgent need for standard methods to efficiently segment objects of interest in large image collections with heterogeneous contents. In fact, object segmentation from a collection of images forms an essential step for many computer vision applications [1, 2], such as content-based image structuration, indexing and retrieval, interactive image editing, scene understanding, action recognition [3, 4], image annotation, human pose estimation [5, 6], object recognition [7, 8] and facial detection [9, 10].

Most existing relevant methods, for this purpose, mainly those based on co-segmentation, aim to extract the shared object from a set of images, having varying sizes and characteristics but related to the shared object. Recently, co-segmentation methods perform well if the appearance of the shared objects in a set of images has different degrees of variability. Nevertheless, since even a single object is often comprised of heterogeneous textures and colors, the accurate co-segmentation of foreground objects is still an open research problem. To deal with this problem, we propose in this work simultaneous segmentation method of salient objects by analyzing image collections consisting of heterogeneous images from various sources.

The main idea of the proposed method is that the visual appearances are often shared between objects of the same category, and even over disparate categories [11]. Thus, we propose a method that leads to extract foreground objects in a set of images, whether this collection of images contains similar images (*i.e.* belonging to the same semantic class) or heterogeneous ones (*i.e.* images belonging to different semantic classes). The core objective of this method is to orient the problem of salient object detection to a much easier problem of co-segmentation. Moreover, we explore the linear dependence of the foreground histograms, in order to segment accurately objects independently of their classes.

The remaining part of this paper is organized as follows. In Sect. 2, we briefly discuss the related work on the foreground object extraction. In Sect. 3, we describe the proposed method for segmenting foreground objects in a set of images with heterogeneous contents. Extensive experiments, on various challenging datasets, are summarized in Sect. 4. Finally, we produce a conclusion with some directions for future works in Sect. 5.

2 Related Work

In this section, we review related work on the general framework of foreground object extraction in digital images. In fact, many methods have been recently proposed for extracting salient objects from a clean collection of categorized images, where categorized objects are referred to objects in the same category [12]. These methods address the problem of joint segmentation of different instances of a single category of

194 H. Merdassi et al.

object across a collection of images [13], in order to exploit a large amount of contextual information from the image collection to optimize the separation between the foreground objects and the background. Such an issue is referred to as the co-segmentation of categorized objects, a closely related task to co-detection [14, 15], and has been actively studied in recent papers [16, 17]. In fact, co-detection and co-segmentation methods were introduced to exploit the collective power of a collection of images. In particular, most co-segmentation methods [18–20] are based on low-level image appearance information and they formulated the problem of co-segmentation as an energy minimization problem. Image co-segmentation methods started by segmenting the common objects in two images of an object [20], multiple images with the same single object [21], multiple classes in each image [22] or multiple images with more than one object in an image [23].

More recently, other methods focused on the co-segmentation of multiple image groups with different characteristics but related to the same general object [17]. Indeed, various methods [13] have focused on simultaneous segmentation of categorized objects, through either supervised learning (given user interactions) [23–25] or unsupervised learning [26, 27], from all images. Most of these methods model the appearance cues [23, 24], the object shape [27] and/or subspace structure [23] across the image collection. In fact, there exist two main families of methods. On the one hand, to benefit object segmentation, co-segmentation methods rely on shared appearance of the object of interest between views, high variability between backgrounds across views, and discrimination between foreground and background appearance distributions [28]. On the other hand, silhouette-coherent extraction methods approaches rely on geometric consistency of the segmentations, usually building some form of dense shape representation of the foreground object [28].

Since silhouette-coherent extraction methods are complex and computationally involved due to the updates of dense shape representations [28], co-segmentation methods are much more used. In general, most existing methods of segmentation of categorized objects were built on the assumption that all images in the input collection contain the target object. Thus, they may not work well when there are some noisy images (i.e. images that do not involve the target category of object) in the given collection, what is the case for collections gathered by a text query from image search engines [13]. To overcome this limitation, we propose in this work a method for the joint co-segmentation of foreground objects from all images in a heterogeneous collection.

The suggested work goes one step further to directly segment uncategorized object from a noisy image collection, while previous works all assumed that images from the input collection all contain the same target categorized object. There are few co-segmentation methods [22, 29] that further conduct the co-segmentation of multiple objects of multiple categories. These methods assume that each image should contain at least one object among multiple known categories. In contrast, we co-segment simultaneously a collection of uncategorized images with different object instances of unlimited number of unknown categories.

3 Proposed Method

Our intuition is to obviously profit of foreground information as well as of background information, notably the spatial context, across a collection of uncategorized images in order to provide valuable information for object segmentation. In fact, the proposed method is based on linear dependence of the generated foreground histograms. This leads to an interesting optimization model and effective solutions for tandem objects segmentation of a high number of images. In fact, solving the co-segmentation problem usually returns to the minimization of an energy function that can be generally represented by:

$$\Xi(I_1, I_2, \ldots, I_n) = \sum_{i=1}^{n} \sum_{p} D_{i,p} x_p + \sum_{i=1}^{n} \sum_{p \sim q} S_{i,pq} |x_p - x_q| + \alpha \cdot G(F_1, F_2, \ldots, F_n), \tag{1}$$

where, $\zeta = \{I_1, I_2, \ldots, I_n\}$ is the input collection of n images. The first two terms are the Markov random field (MRF) energy terms for each image, where D and S are a data term and a smoothness term, respectively. The variables x_p and x_q denote the pixel label, such that $x = 0$ for background and $x = 1$ for foreground. The last term G is a global term that penalizes the difference, or maximizes the similarity, between the foreground histograms F_i, where $i \in \{1, \ldots, n\}$, relatively to the n input images. The coefficient α expresses the relative weights of the global term. Several methods [18–20, 22, 30–36] have been recently introduced to evaluate the global term. They are based on the general model of (1). Nevertheless, they only focus on similar images, where simultaneous segmentation of different images has not been explored. In this work, we tackle the above problem, in order to segment the foreground objects from a set of images with homogeneous or heterogeneous contents.

The first step of the proposed method looks to generate histograms of the input images. It consists in providing a binary segmentation of each image in order to separate the foreground from the background. In fact, given the number of bins K, each pixel of each image is associated to one of the K bins of the corresponding histogram. Then, a binary segmentation of each image partitions the set of pixels into foreground and background pixels, using the decision variable for segmentation x, and we define a K-dimensional vector $\overrightarrow{H_i}$ for each image I_i, where $\vec{H}_i(k)$ is the number of pixels in the image I_i that were associated to the kth histogram bin. Then, we derive a matrix H of size $K \times n$ that includes all the generated histograms $\vec{H}_i(k)$, each as a column. This matrix can be expressed by the sum of the two matrices F and B [19]:

$$H = F + B, \tag{2}$$

where, $F = [F_1, \ldots, F_n]$ and $B = [B_1, \ldots, B_n]$ are the foreground and background histograms.

The purpose of the second step is to make the columns of F similar for foreground objects of the same class and dissimilar for different foreground objects, while segmenting simultaneously objects from all input images. Note that the matrix F of size $K \times n$ gathers all generated histograms of the foregrounds, such that each column of the produced matrix F corresponds to the foreground histogram of an input image. To do that, we made use of linear dependence of the foreground histograms' vectors and this task returns to search the rank of F. In fact, for similar objects, foreground vectors F_i must be similar or linearly dependent in the general case to assume invariance against scale variation. Thus, the rank r of F must be equal to one. Otherwise, for heterogeneous images, foreground vectors F_i must be dissimilar or linearly independent and the rank r of F should be equal to the number of foreground objects in the input collection. In cases where a precise matrix F of rank r cannot be found, a "slack" in the form of a small (sparse) residual [21] P, may be permitted, where $F = R + P$. Once we defined the matrix R, the object segmentation model also includes the MRF segmentation terms for each image. Thus, the object segmentation energy is expressed by the following minimization problem:

$$\min_x \sum_{i=1}^{n} \left(\sum_{p=1}^{L} D_{i,p} x_{i,p} + \sum_{p=q=1,p \sim q}^{L} S_{i,pq} y_{i,pq} + \alpha |F_i - R_i|_2^2 \right), \qquad (3)$$

where, $x_{i,p} \in \{0,1\}, y_{i,pq} \in \{0,1\}$, D and S are the data and smoothness terms of the random Markov field, $F_i = \vec{H}_i x_i$ and $y_{i,pq} = |x_{i,p} - x_{i,q}|$. The variables $x_{i,p}$ and $x_{i,q}$ denote the labeling x of two neighboring pixels p and q of the ith image, and $rank(R)$ is the number of the foreground objects in the studied collection. Then, the objective model penalizes P to minimize the proposed energy function and to make a small variation within the matrix R. Thus, the proposed objective model is expressed as follows:

$$\min_x \sum_{i=1}^{n} \left(\sum_{p=1}^{L} D_{i,p} x_{i,p} + \sum_{p=q=1,p \sim q}^{L} S_{i,pq} y_{i,pq} + \alpha |P_i|_2^2 \right), \qquad (4)$$

where, P_i is the residual matrix of the ith image. In addition, we assume that Gaussian mixture model (GMM) weight is generated and already available for each image. This is used to construct a Markov random field data term and the smoothness term that will be used for the object segmentation.

4 Results

In this section, we present the experimental results of the proposed method (PM) on various standard datasets. In fact, Fig. 1a presents a sample of object segmentation outputs for the image classes "skating", "airshows_plane" and "pandas" from the iCoseg dataset, and Fig. 1b illustrates the obtained results for a sample of 18 flower images, covering many species, from the Oxford Flowers dataset. In our experiments for both datasets, we used different groups of similar images, with varied number of images in each group, as well as varied foreground positions, shapes, locations, colors and sizes in each image. We conclude that the proposed method allows a precise segmentation of the objects of interest in all the images simultaneously. Note that in accordance with existing works [20, 21, 30], generation of histograms is based on the use of a combination of color, texture features, and SIFT. The number of bins for each color channel was between 10–20.

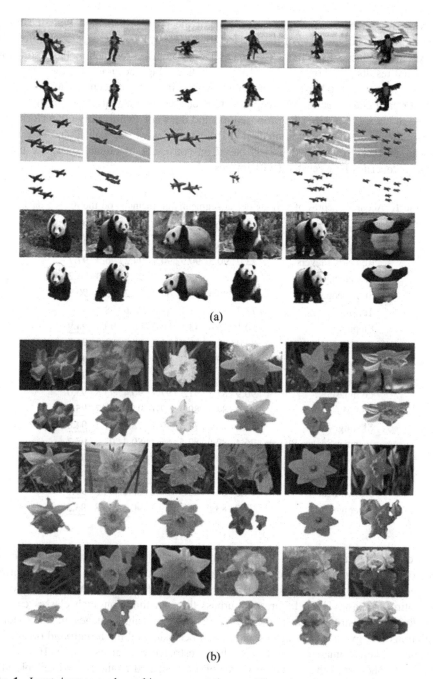

(a)

(b)

Fig. 1. Input images and resulting segmentations, while using the proposed method, for categorized objects from the iCoseg dataset (a) and the Oxford Flowers dataset (b).

198   H. Merdassi et al.

Moreover, Table 1 shows a comparison of the proposed method with the most relevant methods of the state-of-the-art [16, 30–32, 35, 37]. In fact, accuracy scores, on sixteen image classes from the iCoseg dataset, are computed for each method (some of the visual results are shown in Fig. 1a). We notice a high accuracy for the proposed method compared to other co-segmentation works, in terms of accuracy average, and even for each class separately, except for three classes ("taj mahal", "gymnastics" and "statue of liberty"). Indeed, the proposed method does not significantly outperform the state-of-the-art cosegmentation method [32] for two classes "taj mahal" and "statue of liberty". In fact, this method [32] is based on consistent functional maps for transporting properties between the RGB images.

Table 1. Accuracy scores of various object segmentation methods on the iCoseg dataset.

iCoseg datasets	[30]	[31]	[35]	[37]	[32]	[16]	PM
Alaskan Brown Bear	74.8	86.4	90.0	90.0	90.4	93.5	**96.1**
Red Sox Players	73.0	90.5	90.9	90.9	94.2	96.5	**97.7**
Stonehenge1	56.6	87.3	63.3	91.3	92.5	93.0	**96.2**
Stonehenge2	86.0	88.4	88.8	84.2	87.2	83.5	**90.9**
Taj mahal	73.7	88.7	91.1	81.7	**92.6**	88.7	88.1
Elephant	70.1	75.0	43.1	86.2	86.7	90.4	**96.9**
Panda	84.0	60.0	92.7	92.2	88.6	81.2	**96.7**
Kite	87.0	89.8	90.3	94.9	93.9	96.6	**98.3**
Kite Pandas	73.2	78.3	90.2	90.9	93.1	83.8	**97.3**
Gymnastics	90.9	87.1	91.7	**97.7**	90.4	95.8	93.0
Ferrari	85.0	84.3	89.9	92.7	95.6	91.7	**95.5**
Skating	82.1	76.8	77.5	79.9	78.7	81.7	**94.8**
Women Soccer Players	76.4	82.6	87.5	86.7	89.4	93.0	**95.7**
Balloon	85.2	89.0	90.1	92.7	90.4	96.5	**99.3**
Statue of Liberty	90.6	91.6	93.8	91.1	**96.8**	92.7	91.0
Brown bear	74.0	80.4	95.3	86.2	88.1	94.8	**97.7**
Average	78.9	83.5	85.4	89.3	90.5	90.8	**95.3**

Besides, the state-of-the-art cosegmentation method [37] outperforms the proposed method for the "gymnastics" class. This method [37] uses a dense correspondences between images to capture the sparsity and visual variability of the common object over the entire database. These failures to surpass these methods on such classes can be explained by the strong edges in the background for "taj mahal" images, the view-point variations for "gymnastics" images and partial occlusions of the foreground object for "statue of liberty" images. Note that we have restricted our selves to only 16 classes, among 38 ones, seen that accuracy scores of all compared methods are available just for the classes presented in the Table 1. Moreover the code of some methods has not been made available, thus, we directly report the accuracy scores provided in their papers.

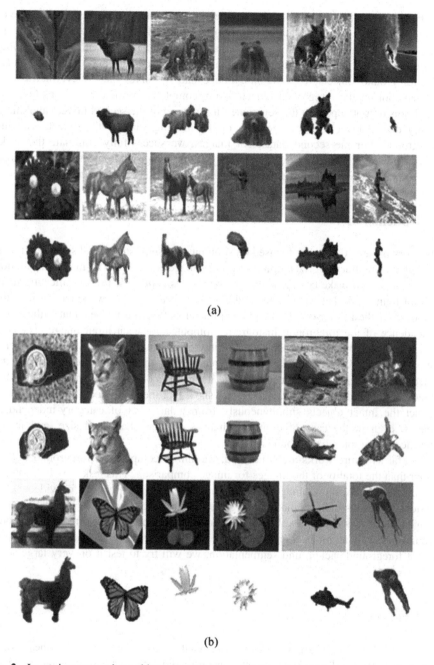

Fig. 2. Input images and resulting segmentations, while using the proposed method, for uncategorized objects from the Berkeley dataset (a) and the Caltech101 dataset (b).

Furthermore, Fig. 2 shows object segmentation results on a challenging sample of images form the Berkeley dataset (Fig. 2a) and the Caltech101 dataset (Fig. 2b). In fact, for the first image dataset, we selected some complex images with high variability of the foreground and background. The obtained results are very encouraging, even for tiny foreground objects (e.g. the first image and the sixth one). Nevertheless, the segmentation of the foreground objects is not complete for some rare cases (e.g. the deer horns do not appear in the segmented foreground of the second image) and this is mainly due to the close homogeneity, of the missing parts of the object, with the background. For the second dataset of images, we successfully eliminate the background, however, we do not extract perfectly all the foreground objects. The challenge of this image dataset lies in the extreme changes in lighting of the foreground objects.

5   Conclusion

The work presented here has focused on simultaneous semi-supervised segmentation of categorized and uncategorized objects from an image collection. The main contribution of this work is to make co-segmentation approaches applicable to a significantly more general framework that has not been addressed before, as far as we know. In fact, the proposed method is based on energy minimization function that evaluates the linear dependence of the foreground histograms computed for each input image. The proposed method, which is applicable to a variety of object categories, will be beneficial, for segmenting foreground objects independently of their classes, especially if the object of interest is not in the center of the image or is of size different from the other objects' sizes. Indeed, experimental results show that the suggested method is able to extract the intact objects simultaneously from a large set of category-independent images, even in the case of dramatic changes of their shape and size, and in the presence of complex backgrounds.

As far as future works are concerned, we aim to compare the foreground objects rather than the totality of the images for image comparison. This task may be explored for image classification, image retrieval and key frame extraction for videos [38]. Besides, as results indicate that the suggested method scales easily to large number of images, since it is able to exploit a large amount of contextual information (on foregrounds as well as on backgrounds) from the image collection what permits more robust foreground/background segmentation, we will try to test it on very large-scale datasets.

References

1. Li, Y., Hou, X., Koch, C., Rehg, J.M., Yuille, A.L.: The secrets of salient object segmentation. In: IEEE Conference on Computer Vision and Pattern Recognition, pp. 4321–4328 (2014). https://doi.org/10.1109/cvpr.2014.43
2. Xiao, J., Ehinger, K.A., Hays, J., Torralba, A., Oliva, A.: SUN database: exploring a large collection of scene categories. Int. J. Comput. Vision 119(1), 3–22 (2016). https://doi.org/10.1007/s11263-014-0748-y

3. Zhang, H., Zhou, W., Reardon, C., Parker, L.E.: Simplex-based 3D spatio-temporal feature description for action recognition. In: Proceedings of the IEEE Computer Society Conference on Computer Vision and Pattern Recognition, pp. 2067–2074 (2014). https://doi.org/10.1109/cvpr.2014.265

4. Tian, Y., Luo, P., Wang, X., Tang, X.: Pedestrian detection aided by deep learning semantic tasks. In: Proceedings of the IEEE Computer Society Conference on Computer Vision and Pattern Recognition, pp. 5079–5087 (2015). https://doi.org/10.1109/cvpr.2015.7299143

5. Cherian, A., Mairal, J., Alahari, K., Schmid, C.: Mixing body-part sequences for human pose estimation. In: IEEE Conference on Computer Vision and Pattern Recognition (CVPR 2014), pp. 2361–2368 (2014). https://doi.org/10.1109/cvpr.2014.302

6. Dantone, M., Gall, J., Leistner, C.: Human pose estimation using body parts dependent joint regressors. In: IEEE Conference on Computer Vision and Pattern Recognition (CVPR 2013), pp. 3041–3048 (2013). https://doi.org/10.1109/cvpr.2013.391

7. Zhu, F., Jiang, Z., Shao, L.: Submodular object recognition. In: Proceedings of the IEEE Computer Society Conference on Computer Vision and Pattern Recognition, pp. 2457–2464 (2014). https://doi.org/10.1109/cvpr.2014.315

8. Lo Presti, L., La Cascia, M.: 3D skeleton-based human action classification: a survey. Pattern Recogn. **53**, 130–147 (2016). https://doi.org/10.1016/j.patcog.2015.11.019

9. Ding, L., Martinez, A.M.: Precise detailed detection of faces and facial features. In: 26th IEEE Conference on Computer Vision and Pattern Recognition, pp. 1–7 (2008). https://doi.org/10.1109/cvpr.2008.4587812

10. Haoxiang, L., Zhe, L., Xiaohui, S., Brandt, J., Gang, H.: A convolutional neural network cascade for face detection. In: IEEE Conference on Computer Vision and Pattern Recognition, pp. 5325–5334 (2015). https://doi.org/10.1109/cvpr.2015.7299170

11. Kim, J., Grauman, K.: Shape sharing for object segmentation. In: Fitzgibbon, A., Lazebnik, S., Perona, P., Sato, Y., Schmid, C. (eds.) ECCV 2012. LNCS, vol. 7578, pp. 444–458. Springer, Heidelberg (2012). https://doi.org/10.1007/978-3-642-33786-4_33

12. Li, K., Zhang, J., Tao, W.: Unsupervised co-segmentation for indefinite number of common foreground objects. IEEE Trans. Image Process. (2016). https://doi.org/10.1109/tip.2016.2526900

13. Wang, L., Hua, G., Xue, J., Gao, Z., Zheng, N.: Joint segmentation and recognition of categorized objects from noisy web image collection. IEEE Trans. Image Process. **23**(9), 4070–4086 (2014). https://doi.org/10.1109/TIP.2014.2339196

14. Bao, S.Y., Xiang, Y., Savarese, S.: Object co-detection. In: Fitzgibbon, A., Lazebnik, S., Perona, P., Sato, Y., Schmid, C. (eds.) ECCV 2012. LNCS, vol. 7572, pp. 86–101. Springer, Heidelberg (2012). https://doi.org/10.1007/978-3-642-33718-5_7

15. Shi, J., Liao, R., Jia, J.: CoDeL: a human co-detection and labeling framework. In: Proceedings of the IEEE International Conference on Computer Vision, pp. 2096–2103 (2013). https://doi.org/10.1109/iccv.2013.262

16. Fu, H., Xu, D., Lin, S., Liu, J.: Object-based RGBD image co-segmentation with mutex constraint. In: Proceedings of the IEEE Computer Society Conference on Computer Vision and Pattern Recognition, pp. 4428–4436 (2015). https://doi.org/10.1109/cvpr.2015.7299072

17. Meng, F., Cai, J., Li, H.: Cosegmentation of multiple image groups. In: Computer Vision and Image Understanding, vol. 146, pp. 67–76 (2016). https://doi.org/10.1016/j.cviu.2016.02.004

18. Rother, C., Kolmogorov, V., Minka, T., Blake, A.: Cosegmentation of image pairs by histogram matching - incorporating a global constraint into MRFs. In: Proceedings of the IEEE Computer Society Conference on Computer Vision and Pattern Recognition, vol. 1, pp. 994–1000 (2006). https://doi.org/10.1109/cvpr.2006.91

19. Mukherjee, L., Singh, V., Dyer, C.R.: Half-integrality based algorithms for cosegmentation of images. In: IEEE Computer Society Conference on Computer Vision and Pattern Recognition Workshops, pp. 2028–2035 (2009). https://doi.org/10.1109/cvprw.2009.5206652

20. Hochbaum, D.S., Singh, V.: An efficient algorithm for co-segmentation. In: Proceedings of the IEEE International Conference on Computer Vision, pp. 269–276 (2009). https://doi.org/10.1109/iccv.2009.5459261

21. Mukherjee, L., Singh, V., Peng, J.: Scale invariant cosegmentation for image groups. In: Proceedings of the IEEE Computer Society Conference on Computer Vision and Pattern Recognition, pp. 1881–1888 (2011). https://doi.org/10.1109/cvpr.2011.5995420

22. Joulin, A., Bach, F., Ponce, J.: Multi-class cosegmentation. In: Proceedings of the IEEE Computer Society Conference on Computer Vision and Pattern Recognition, pp. 542–549 (2012). https://doi.org/10.1109/cvpr.2012.6247719

23. Mukherjee, L., Singh, V., Xu, J., Collins, M.D.: Analyzing the subspace structure of related images: concurrent segmentation of image sets. In: Fitzgibbon, A., Lazebnik, S., Perona, P., Sato, Y., Schmid, C. (eds.) ECCV 2012. LNCS, vol. 7575, pp. 128–142. Springer, Heidelberg (2012). https://doi.org/10.1007/978-3-642-33765-9_10

24. Cui, J., et al.: Transductive object cutout. In: 26th IEEE Conference on Computer Vision and Pattern Recognition, CVPR 2008 (2008). https://doi.org/10.1109/cvpr.2008.4587589

25. Law, Y.N., Lee, H.K., Ng, M.K., Yip, A.M.: A semisupervised segmentation model for collections of images. IEEE Trans. Image Process. **21**(6), 2955–2968 (2012). https://doi.org/10.1109/TIP.2012.2187670

26. Lee, Y.J., Grauman, K.: Collect-cut: segmentation with top-down cues discovered in multi-object images. In: Proceedings of the IEEE Computer Society Conference on Computer Vision and Pattern Recognition, pp. 3185–3192 (2010). https://doi.org/10.1109/cvpr.2010.5539772

27. Alexe, B., Deselaers, T., Ferrari, V.: ClassCut for unsupervised class segmentation. In: Daniilidis, K., Maragos, P., Paragios, N. (eds.) ECCV 2010. LNCS, vol. 6315, pp. 380–393. Springer, Heidelberg (2010). https://doi.org/10.1007/978-3-642-15555-0_28

28. Djelouah, A., Franco, J.-S., Boyer, E., Le Clerc, F., Perez, P.: Sparse multi-view consistency for object segmentation. IEEE Trans. Pattern Anal. Mach. Intell. **37**(9), 890–903 (2015). https://doi.org/10.1109/TPAMI.2014.2385704

29. Kim, G., Xing, E.P.: On multiple foreground cosegmentation. In: Proceedings of the IEEE Computer Society Conference on Computer Vision and Pattern Recognition, pp. 837–844 (2012). https://doi.org/10.1109/cvpr.2012.6247756

30. Joulin, A., Bach, F., Ponce, J.: Discriminative clustering for image co-segmentation. In: Proceedings of the IEEE Computer Society Conference on Computer Vision and Pattern Recognition, pp. 1943–1950 (2010). https://doi.org/10.1109/cvpr.2010.5539868

31. Rubio, J.C., Serrat, J., Lopez, A., Paragios, N.: Unsupervised co-segmentation through region matching. In: Proceedings of the IEEE Computer Society Conference on Computer Vision and Pattern Recognition, pp. 749–756 (2012). https://doi.org/10.1109/cvpr.2012.6247745

32. Wang, F., Huang, Q., Guibas, L.J.: Image co-segmentation via consistent functional maps. In: Proceedings of the IEEE International Conference on Computer Vision, pp. 849–856 (2013). https://doi.org/10.1109/iccv.2013.110

33. Vicente, S., Kolmogorov, V., Rother, C.: Cosegmentation revisited: models and optimization. In: Daniilidis, K., Maragos, P., Paragios, N. (eds.) ECCV 2010. LNCS, vol. 6312, pp. 465–479. Springer, Heidelberg (2010). https://doi.org/10.1007/978-3-642-15552-9_34

34. Kim, G., Xing, E.P., Fei-Fei, L., Kanade, T.: Distributed cosegmentation via submodular optimization on anisotropic diffusion. In: Proceedings of the IEEE International Conference on Computer Vision, pp. 169–176 (2011). https://doi.org/10.1109/iccv.2011.6126239
35. Vicente, S., Rother, C., Kolmogorov, V.: Object cosegmentation. In: Proceedings of the IEEE Computer Society Conference on Computer Vision and Pattern Recognition, pp. 2217–2224 (2011). https://doi.org/10.1109/cvpr.2011.5995530
36. Ma, T., Latecki, L.J.: Graph transduction learning with connectivity constraints with application to multiple foreground cosegmentation. In: Proceedings of the IEEE Computer Society Conference on Computer Vision and Pattern Recognition, pp. 1955–1962 (2013). https://doi.org/10.1109/cvpr.2013.255
37. Rubinstein, M., Joulin, A., Kopf, J., Liu, C.: Unsupervised joint object discovery and segmentation in internet images. In: Proceedings of the IEEE Computer Society Conference on Computer Vision and Pattern Recognition, pp. 1939–1946 (2013). https://doi.org/10.1109/cvpr.2013.253
38. Barhoumi, W., Zagrouba, E.: On-the-fly extraction of key frames for efficient video summarization. In: AASRI Conference on Intelligent Systems and Control, pp. 78–84 (2013). https://doi.org/10.1016/j.aasri.2013

Brenier Approach for Optimal Transportation Between a Quasi-discrete Measure and a Discrete Measure

Ying Lu[1(✉)], Liming Chen[1], Alexandre Saidi[1], and Xianfeng Gu[2]

[1] Ecole Centrale de Lyon, Écully, France
ying.lu@ec-lyon.fr
[2] Stony Brook University, Stony Brook, USA

Abstract. Correctly estimating the discrepancy between two data distributions has always been an important task in Machine Learning. Recently, Cuturi proposed the Sinkhorn distance [1] which makes use of an approximate Optimal Transport cost between two distributions as a distance to describe distribution discrepancy. Although it has been successfully adopted in various machine learning applications (*e.g.* in Natural Language Processing and Computer Vision) since then, the Sinkhorn distance also suffers from two unnegligible limitations. The first one is that the Sinkhorn distance only gives an approximation of the real Wasserstein distance, the second one is the 'divide by zero' problem which often occurs during matrix scaling when setting the entropy regularization coefficient to a small value. In this paper, we introduce a new Brenier approach for calculating a more accurate Wasserstein distance between two discrete distributions, this approach successfully avoids the two limitations shown above for Sinkhorn distance and gives an alternative way for estimating distribution discrepancy.

1 Introduction

In Machine Learning and Pattern Recognition, the data we always work with are samples. For example in image classification, a sample is an image. Given a fixed type of representation for images, we can consider a space of images in which each dimension represents a feature (*e.g.* a pixel) of image. In this way, we can consider a certain set of images (*e.g.* a set of images correspond to a semantic concept like 'cat') as a distribution (or a measure) over the space of images.

In this situation, it is not easy to estimate this kind of distributions as a continuous probability distribution. Firstly because we usually only have access to a finite number of training samples for a certain set (or a category), compared to the large number of dimensions in the image space, these training samples are always not enough for estimating a continuous probability function[1]. Secondly,

---

[1] https://en.wikipedia.org/wiki/Curse_of_dimensionality.

© Springer Nature Switzerland AG 2019
L. Chen et al. (Eds.): RFMI 2017, CCIS 842, pp. 204–212, 2019.
https://doi.org/10.1007/978-3-030-19816-9_16

when the categories are defined as semantic concepts which are highly abstract, we cannot ensure that they are continuous distributions by nature. For example, if we do interpolation in the space of images between two images of cat, we are not guaranteed to get a new image which can be seen as an image of cat in human eyes (when the two input images are very different, usually what we can get is a image of 'noise').

Therefore, in Machine Learning society, the commonly adopted methods for measuring distance between two distributions are usually sample based methods (*e.g.* two-sample test methods as MMD [2]) or consider distributions as discrete measures (*e.g.* Sinkhorn distance [1]).

In this paper we discuss the application of the Brenier approach [3] for calculating the optimal transportation between a quasi-discrete measure and a discrete measures (a discrete measure can be represented with a finite number of points, each point corresponds to a Dirac measure). The approach introduced in [3] assumes that the target measure is discrete while the source measure is continuous. To estimate the Brenier function and the gradient of objective energy, we need to estimate the Graph of Brenier potential and calculate integration in the source distribution. This could be done for one dimensional or two dimensional spaces in a reasonable time of calculation, while becomes hard for spaces with more than two dimensions.

Therefore, by considering the source measure as a quasi-discrete distribution, we wish to find a way to solve the discrete problems in machine learning and at the same time to avoid the problem of calculation cost for higher dimensional spaces. However the side effect is that when the quasi-discrete measure gets close to a discrete measure, we are not always guaranteed to converge to a solution that preserves the measures.

In the following part of this paper, we firstly introduce the Brenier approach for optimal transportation between a quasi-discrete measure and a discrete measure, and the Gradient Descent algorithm for solving this problem. We then compare the Brenier approach with Sinkhorn approach [1], discuss their advantages and disadvantages. We also show a possible application of Brenier approach for clustering.

2   Brenier Approach for OMT Between a Quasi-discrete and a Discrete Measure

Assume μ and ν two discrete measures represented by two sample sets: $\{\mathbf{x}_1^s, \ldots, \mathbf{x}_{n_s}^s\}$ (source sample set) and $\{\mathbf{x}_1^t, \ldots, \mathbf{x}_{n_t}^t\}$ (target sample set), in the n-dimensional Euclidean space $\mathbb{R}^n$:

$$\mu = \sum_{i=1}^{n_s} p_i^s \delta(\mathbf{x} - \mathbf{x}_i^s), \quad \nu = \sum_{i=1}^{n_t} p_i^t \delta(\mathbf{x} - \mathbf{x}_i^t) \tag{1}$$

where $\delta(\mathbf{x} - \mathbf{x}_i)$ is the Dirac function at location $\mathbf{x}_i$, p_i^s and p_i^t are probability masses associated to the i-th sample in source set and target set respectively, and $\sum_{i=1}^{n_s} p_i^s = \sum_{i=1}^{n_t} p_i^t$.

Given a cost function $c : \mathbb{R}^n \times \mathbb{R}^n \to \mathbb{R}$, the Monge's optimal transport problem is to find the unique measure preserving map $T : \mathbb{R}^n \to \mathbb{R}^n$ (from μ to ν) that minimizes the total transportation cost:

$$\mathcal{C}(T) := \int_{\mathbb{R}^n} c(\mathbf{x}, T(\mathbf{x})) \mathrm{d}\mu(\mathbf{x}) \tag{2}$$

The theorem of Brenier and the variational approach in [3] assumes that the source measure is absolutely continuous (with respect to Lebesgue measure) and the support of source measure is a convex set in $\mathbb{R}^n$, while this is not true for μ. Therefore we introduce a piecewise uniform measure μ' with a compact support set Ω, which could be seen as an approximation to μ. The probability density function of μ' is defined as:

$$f_{\mu'}(\mathbf{x}) = \begin{cases} \frac{p_i^s - p_0/n_s}{\varepsilon^n} & \text{for } \mathbf{x} \in [(\mathbf{x}_i^s)_1 - \frac{\varepsilon}{2}, (\mathbf{x}_i^s)_1 + \frac{\varepsilon}{2}] \times \ldots \\ & \times [(\mathbf{x}_i^s)_n - \frac{\varepsilon}{2}, (\mathbf{x}_i^s)_n + \frac{\varepsilon}{2}], \forall \, i \in \{1, \ldots, n_s\} \\ \\ \frac{p_0}{vol(\Omega) - n_s \varepsilon^n} & \text{for } \mathbf{x} \in \Omega \text{ elsewhere.} \end{cases} \tag{3}$$

where ε and p_0 are very small values. The probability density is uniformly distributed in a small hypercube of volume ε^n around each source sample, and the total probability mass in a small hypercube is defined as the probability mass associated to the center sample minus a small value p_0/n_s. Apart from the small hypercubes around source samples, probability is uniformly distributed in Ω, and the total mass in the rest volume is p_0. Ω could be defined as the smallest hypercube area which contains all source samples.

With this measure μ', we can now apply the theorem of Brenier (Theorem 9.4 in [4]): Let $c(\mathbf{x}, \mathbf{x}') = |\mathbf{x} - \mathbf{x}'|^2$ in $\mathbb{R}^n$, There exists a convex function $f : \mathbb{R}^n \to \mathbb{R}$, its gradient map ∇f gives the solution to the Monge's problem (from μ' to ν), and this map is unique. This convex function is called the Brenier potential, and it should be a solution to the Monge-Ampère equation. In [3] the authors give a variational approach to solve this equation with the equivalent Alexandrov Theorem. We now introduce this approach:

Define a vector $\mathbf{h} = (h_1, \ldots, h_{n_t}) \in \mathbb{R}^{n_t}$. For each target sample $\mathbf{x}_i^t$, we define a hyperplane $\pi_i : \langle \mathbf{x}, \mathbf{x}_i^t \rangle + h_i = 0$ in $\mathbb{R}^n$, the upper envelope of all the hyperplanes forms a piecewise linear convex function:

$$u_{\mathbf{h}}(\mathbf{x}) = \max_{i=1}^{n_t} \{\langle \mathbf{x}, \mathbf{x}_i^t \rangle + h_i\} \tag{4}$$

Denote its graph by $G(\mathbf{h})$, which is an infinite convex polyhedron with supporting planes $\pi_i(\mathbf{h})$. The projection of $G(\mathbf{h})$ induces a polygonal partition of Ω, where each cell $W_i(\mathbf{h})$ is the projection of a facet of $G(\mathbf{h})$ onto Ω. The area of each cell is defined as:

$$w_i(\mathbf{h}) = \int_{W_i(\mathbf{h}) \cap \Omega} f_{\mu'}(\mathbf{x}) \mathrm{d}\mathbf{x} \tag{5}$$

The convex function $u_\mathbf{h}$ on each cell $W_i(\mathbf{h})$ is a linear function $\pi_i(\mathbf{h})$, therefore, the gradient map:

$$grad\ u_\mathbf{h}:\quad W_i \to \mathbf{x}_i^t,\quad \forall i \in \{1,\dots,n_t\} \tag{6}$$

maps each area $W_i(\mathbf{h})$ to a single point $\mathbf{x}_i^t$. The problem is to find a vector $\mathbf{h}$ such that the polygonal partition $\{W_i\}_{i=1}^{n_t}$ of the source support Ω induced by the projection of $G(\mathbf{h})$ on $\mathbb{R}^n$ is measure preserving. In [3] the authors prove that the solutions of this problem are the critical points of the following energy function:

$$E(\mathbf{h}) = \int^{\mathbf{h}} \sum_{i=1}^{n_t} w_i(\mathbf{h})dh_i - \sum_{i=1}^{n_t} p_i^t h_i \tag{7}$$

The first part of this energy function is the volume of the area bounded by the graph $G(\mathbf{h})$, the horizontal plane $\{y = 0\}$, and the cylinder consisting of vertical lines through $\partial\Omega$.

The gradient of this energy function with respect to $\mathbf{h}$ is:

$$\frac{\partial E(\mathbf{h})}{\partial h_i} = w_i(\mathbf{h}) - p_i^t,\quad \forall i \in \{1,\dots,n_t\} \tag{8}$$

In [3] the authors prove that *when Ω is convex, the admissible space H_0 for $\mathbf{h}$ is convex, so is the energy in Eq. (7). Moreover, the unique global minimum $\mathbf{h}_0$ is an interior point of H_0. And the gradient map Eq. (6) induced by the minimum $\mathbf{h}_0$ is the unique optimal mass transport map, which minimizes the total transportation cost Eq. (2) with $c(\mathbf{x}, \mathbf{x}') = |\mathbf{x} - \mathbf{x}'|^2$.*

Since Eq. (7) is convex, we can therefore use a gradient descent approach to solve this problem.

Furthermore, since for source measure μ' the probability masses are concentrated in small areas around the source samples, we wish to simplify the calculation by estimating $G(\mathbf{h})$ with only the source samples instead of all possible points in Ω. Therefore, we can define the approximation of $u_\mathbf{h}$ in Eq. (4) as follows:

$$\hat{u}_\mathbf{h}(\mathbf{x}_i^s) = \max_{j=1}^{n_t}\{\langle \mathbf{x}_i^s, \mathbf{x}_j^t \rangle + h_j\},\quad \forall i \in \{1,\dots,n_s\} \tag{9}$$

A possible problem of Eq. (9) is that there might be some source sample, for example $\mathbf{x}_k^s$, for which the corresponding point $[\mathbf{x}_k^s, \hat{u}_\mathbf{h}(\mathbf{x}_k^s)]$ is situated on the intersection of multiple hyperplanes. In other words, the size of the following set (which is a subset of target sample set) is larger than 1.

$$t(\mathbf{x}_k^s) = \{\mathbf{x}_j^t \mid \langle \mathbf{x}_k^s, \mathbf{x}_j^t \rangle + h_j = \hat{u}_\mathbf{h}(\mathbf{x}_k^s)\} \tag{10}$$

This will make it difficult to calculate cell areas. To solve this problem, currently we use a brute force method by simply uniformly distribute the mass correspond to this source sample $\mathbf{x}_k^s$ onto all cell areas correspond to the target samples in $t(\mathbf{x}_k^s)$.

With the brute force method described above, we can therefore approximately calculate the area of each projected cell $W_j(\mathbf{h})$ as follows instead of using Eq. (5):

$$\hat{w}_j = \sum_{\mathbf{x}_i^s \in W_j(\mathbf{h})} \frac{1}{|t(\mathbf{x}_i^s)|} p_i^s \tag{11}$$

where $|t(\mathbf{x}_i^s)|$ is the size of set $t(\mathbf{x}_i^s)$. The transportation map induced by this approximation of Brenier potential can be expressed as a matrix $\mathbf{T}$ of size $n_s \times n_t$ with each element defined as follows:

$$T_{ij} = \begin{cases} \frac{1}{|t(\mathbf{x}_i^s)|} p_i^s & \text{if } \mathbf{x}_i^s \in W_j(\mathbf{h}) \\ 0 & \text{otherwise} \end{cases} \tag{12}$$

The energy function can also be approximately calculated instead of Eq. (7):

$$\hat{E}(\mathbf{h}) = \sum_{j=1}^{n_t} \sum_{\mathbf{x}_i^s \in W_j(\mathbf{h})} \frac{1}{|t(\mathbf{x}_i^s)|} p_i^s \hat{u}_{\mathbf{h}}(\mathbf{x}_i^s) - \sum_{j=1}^{n_t} p_j^t h_j \tag{13}$$

The gradient descent algorithm to solve this problem can then be defined as follows:

Algorithm 1. Gradient Descent Algorithm for approximately solving OMT

Input: Source sample set: $\{\mathbf{x}_1^s, \ldots, \mathbf{x}_{n_s}^s\}$; Target sample set: $\{\mathbf{x}_1^t, \ldots, \mathbf{x}_{n_t}^t\}$; Number of steps N; Step size λ.

1: Initialize: Vector $\mathbf{p}^s$ of size n_s, where $p_i^s = \frac{1}{n_s}$; Vector $\mathbf{p}^t$ of size n_t, where $p_i^t = \frac{1}{n_t}$;
   Vector $\mathbf{h}$ of size n_t, where $h_i = 0$;
   Inner product matrix $\mathbf{M}$ of size $n_s \times n_t$, where $Mij = \langle \mathbf{x}_i^s, \mathbf{x}_j^t \rangle$;
   Gradient vector $\mathbf{g}$ of size n_t where $g_i = 0$;
   Counter $n_{step} = 0$

2: **while** ($\mathbf{h}$ not converged) and ($n_{step} < N$) **do**

3:    Gradient Descent: $\mathbf{h} = \mathbf{h} - \lambda \mathbf{g}$.

4:    (This step could be done with a series of matrix calculation with $\mathbf{M}$.)
      Update $\hat{u}_{\mathbf{h}}(\mathbf{x}_i^s)$ with Eq. (9) for all source samples.
      Update: Cell areas $\{\hat{w}_j\}_{j=1}^{n_t}$ with Eq. (11).

5:    Update: gradient vector $\mathbf{g}$ where $g_j = \hat{w}_j - p_j^t$.

6:    Update counter: $n_{step} = n_{step} + 1$.

7: **end while**

8: Calculate transportation map $\mathbf{T}$ with Eq. (12).

Output: Transportation map $\mathbf{T}$.

With the resulting transportation plan $\mathbf{T}$, we can further calculate the transportation cost (*i.e.* the Wasserstein distance) as follows:

$$W(\mu', \nu) = \sum_{i=1}^{n_s} \sum_{j=1}^{n_t} T_{ij} |\mathbf{x}_i^s - \mathbf{x}_j^t|^2 \tag{14}$$

3 Brenier v.s. Sinkhorn

In the previous section, we have introduced an approximate approach to find the Brenier potential in order to solve the Optimal Transportation problem. This approximate Brenier approach solves the same kind of problems as considered in [1]. Therefore in this section we compare the proposed approximate Brenier approach with the Sinkhorn approach. The differences are listed as follows:

1. The two methods approach the optimal solution in different ways.
   In each step of the approximate Brenier method, the condition $\mathbf{T}\mathbf{1}_{n_t} = \mu$ always holds[2], while $\hat{\nu} = \mathbf{T}^\top \mathbf{1}_{n_s}$ is approaching the real ν when the number of iteration grows.
   On the other hand, the Sinkhorn method is a matrix balancing method, the two conditions $\mathbf{T}\mathbf{1}_{n_t} = \mu$ and $\mathbf{T}^\top \mathbf{1}_{n_s} = \nu$ hold alternatively during iterations (*i.e.* the first condition holds after updating the vector v, and the second condition holds after updating the vector u), and they tend to both hold when the algorithm converges.

2. In each iteration step of the approximate Brenier method, the current transportation map is always an optimal transportation from μ' to $\hat{\nu} = \mathbf{T}^\top \mathbf{1}_{n_s}$.

3. The Sinkhorn method solves a entropy regularized version of the OT problem. Therefore we can only get the optimal solution of the original OT problem when the coefficient λ of the regularization term tends to zero. However this is hard to achieve because when λ tends to zeros, the matrix balancing becomes instable and we are more easily to face a zero denominator error. In other words, the entropy regularized OT problem demands the transportation plan $\mathbf{T}$ to be not sparse (with no zeros in it), since to use matrix balancing we need the matrix to be with all positive entries.
   Fortunately, we don't have this problem with the approximate Brenier method.

4. The transportation map learned by Brenier method tend to transport each source sample as a whole to some target sample (the situation mentioned in Sect. 2 where a source sample is situated on the intersection of two cells is actually rare in practice.)
   On the other hand, the transportation map learned by Sinkhorn method tend to split a source sample into parts and transport it to a group of target samples.

5. One thing in common about the two methods is that they both can handle abstract distributions, *i.e.* we don't need to know the number of dimensions of the sample space.
   For Sinkhorn all we need to prepare are two vectors of sample weights and a distance matrix (the cost matrix).
   For approximate Brenier all we need to prepare are two vectors of sample weights and a inner-product matrix (the matrix $\mathbf{M}$ defined in Algorithm 1, step 1).

---

[2] Here $\mathbf{1}_d$ is a d-dimensional column vector of ones.

This characteristic makes the two methods flexible for different kinds of applications.

6. The Sinkhorn method is much faster than the Brenier method.
7. The approximate Brenier method is very hard to converge (sometimes impossible to converge) unless the number of source samples is much larger than the number of target samples.
No such problem for Sinkhorn method.
8. The Sinkhorn method has no constraints on the choice of cost metric, while currently the Brenier method only works for quadratic Euclidean distances.
9. A simple experimentation to compare the two methods: the source sample set has 150 samples from a Gaussian mixture distribution, the target sample set has only 2 samples. We set the Sinkhorn regularization coefficient $\lambda = 0.05$, and we use quadratic Euclidean distance as cost metric for both methods, then the resulting Sinkhorn distance is 2053.47, and the calculation time is 0.00335 s; the Brenier distance is 2015.08, and the calculation time is 5.927 s. We can see that the Brenier distance is smaller than the Sinkhorn distance, meaning that the transportation map learned by Brenier method is better than that learned by Sinkhorn method. We also performed a simple linear programming method to solve this problem, the resulting distance is 2015.08 (the same as that with Brenier method), and the calculation time is 0.094 s. We perform a even smaller experiment to show the maps learned by different methods: consider a source set of 10 samples from a Gaussian mixture distribution, and a target set with only 2 samples. Use quadratic Euclidean distance as cost metric. Set $\lambda = 0.05$ for Sinkhorn method. The results are shown in the following, where W means the resulting Wasserstein distance, $\mathbf{T}$ is the transportation map, 'B' represents Brenier, 'S' represents Sinkhorn and 'LP' represents linear programming. We can see from the results that only the Brenier method learns the simple and elegant optimal transportation map.

$$W_B = 2065.694 \qquad W_S = 2116.271 \qquad W_{LP} = 2065.694$$

$$\mathbf{T}_B = \begin{bmatrix} 0.1 & 0. \\ 0.1 & 0. \\ 0.1 & 0. \\ 0.1 & 0. \\ 0.1 & 0. \\ 0. & 0.1 \\ 0. & 0.1 \\ 0. & 0.1 \\ 0. & 0.1 \\ 0. & 0.1 \end{bmatrix} \quad \mathbf{T}_S = \begin{bmatrix} 0.6641 & 0.3359 \\ 0.667 & 0.333 \\ 0.6986 & 0.3014 \\ 0.7877 & 0.2123 \\ 0.7262 & 0.2738 \\ 0.3099 & 0.6901 \\ 0.3352 & 0.6648 \\ 0.2264 & 0.7736 \\ 0.2723 & 0.7277 \\ 0.3127 & 0.6873 \end{bmatrix} \quad \mathbf{T}_{LP} = \begin{bmatrix} 0.1 & 1.35 \times 10^{-8} \\ 0.1 & 1.32 \times 10^{-8} \\ 0.1 & 7.35 \times 10^{-9} \\ 0.1 & 5.25 \times 10^{-9} \\ 0.1 & 1.58 \times 10^{-9} \\ 1.01 \times 10^{-8} & 0.1 \\ 1.26 \times 10^{-8} & 0.1 \\ 4.32 \times 10^{-9} & 0.1 \\ 3.45 \times 10^{-9} & 0.1 \\ 1.05 \times 10^{-8} & 0.1 \end{bmatrix}$$

4   Brenier Approach for Clustering

Inspired by the comparisons shown in the previous section, I think a good way to apply this approximate Brenier approach is to apply it for clustering (because in this case the source samples will be much more than the target samples and the Brenier method is much easier to converge).

For a clustering task, we are given an unlabeled sample set and we are demanded to divide this sample set into clusters, where the samples in a same cluster should be close to each other while samples from different clusters should be far from each other. We can assume the given sample set as the source set $\{\mathbf{x}_i^s\}$, and assume the set of cluster centers, which we need to learn, as the target set $\{\mathbf{x}_j^t\}$. In this case, both the transportation map and the target distribution are unknown variables. We can therefore use an iterative approach (like EM algorithm) where we firstly initialize the target samples $\{\mathbf{x}_j^t\}$ randomly, then we learn the intercepts $\mathbf{h}$ and the target samples $\{\mathbf{x}_j^t\}$ alternatively.

The objective for learning cluster centers $\{\mathbf{x}_j^t\}$ is to minimize the Wasserstein distance between the given samples and the cluster centers, i.e. to minimize Eq. (14). Since $\mathbf{T}$ is a matrix with positive elements, the Eq. (14) is convex with respect to input set $\{\mathbf{x}_j^t\}$. And its gradients with respect to $\{\mathbf{x}_j^t\}$ are:

$$\frac{\partial W}{\partial \mathbf{x}_j^t} = \sum_{i=1}^{n_s} 2T_{ij}(\mathbf{x}_j^t - \mathbf{x}_i^s) \qquad (15)$$

We can therefore use a simple gradient descent algorithm to learn $\{\mathbf{x}_j^t\}$.

We show a simple experiment in the following: given a set of 250 samples (2D points) from a Gaussian mixture distribution (5 Gaussians), we firstly initialize 5 cluster centers randomly, and assume the distribution mass associated to each cluster center is 0.2, then we perform 10 steps of gradient descent for updating cluster centers, where in each step we perform the approximate Brenier method to learn the current optimal transportation map. In each step, the samples which are transported to a same cluster center are considered as a cluster. In Fig. 1 left side we show the initialized clusters (src_1 - src_5) and cluster centers (tar_1 - tar_5). In Fig. 1 right side and in Fig. 2 we illustrate the resulting clusters and corresponding centers in step 1, step 2, step 4, step 6 and step 8. We can see that in only 8 steps the learned cluster centers are nicely located in the center of each Gaussian distribution.

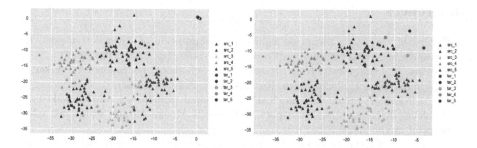

Fig. 1. Approximate Brenier method for clustering: initialization (left) and step 1 (right)

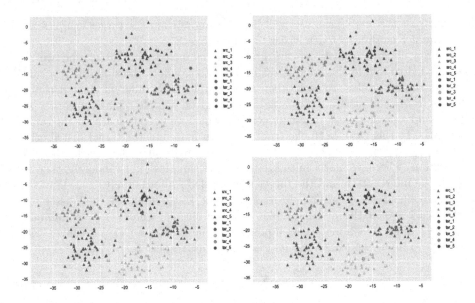

Fig. 2. Approximate Brenier method for clustering: step 2 (top left), step 4 (top right), step 6 (bottom left) and step 8 (bottom right)

5   Conclusion

In this paper we show a simple application of the Brenier approach for approximately solving discrete learning problems. This method is not as time consuming as continues Brenier approach, but is still slower than other methods like Sinkhorn or even linear programming. Although currently it is not perfect, we can still find some shining points in it (as we have discussed in Sect. 3). Therefore we hope to further improve this method and find more applications in machine learning and computer vision.

References

1. Cuturi, M.: Sinkhorn distances: lightspeed computation of optimal transport. In: Advances in Neural Information Processing Systems, pp. 2292–2300 (2013)
2. Gretton, A., Borgwardt, K.M., Rasch, M.J., Schölkopf, B., Smola, A.: A kernel two-sample test. J. Mach. Learn. Res. **13**(Mar), 723–773 (2012)
3. Gu, X., Luo, F., Sun, J., Yau, S.-T.: Variational principles for Minkowski type problems, discrete optimal transport, and discrete Monge-Ampere equations. arXiv preprint arXiv:1302.5472 (2013)
4. Villani, C.: Optimal Transport: Old and New, vol. 338. Springer, Heidelberg (2008). https://doi.org/10.1007/978-3-540-71050-9

Global and Regional Deformation Analysis of the Myocardium: MRI Data Application

Rim Ayari Abid[✉], Asma Ben Abdallah, and Mohamed Hédi Bedoui

Biophysics Laboratory-TIM, UR 08-27 Faculty of Medicine of Monastir,
Monastir, Tunisia
rim.ayari@gmail.com

Abstract. One of the major concerns in cardiac imaging is finding an efficient method for the deformation analysis in the left ventricle of the heart (LV). This paper deals with the results of using a regional analysis of left ventricular of the heart applied on MRI data. Our analysis consists of segmenting 3D objects modeling the myocardium of the LV into 17 regions according to the AHA (American Heart Association) standard. Curvature variation was calculated using the Hotelling MT2 two samples difference metric for the global objects and their different 17 regions during 25 instants of the cardiac cycle. It has been validated with real MRI data. Experimental results demonstrate the great robustness and efficiency of our method to detect pathological regions of myocardium.

Keywords: Heart left ventricle (LV) · 3D object · AHA standard · Surface curvature · MRI data · Modified Hotelling MT2 metric · Regional analysis

1 Introduction

Coronary Artery Disease (CAD) involves the narrowing of the coronary arteries that supply the heart tissue with oxygen and nutrients due to plaque built up along the inner walls of the arteries of the heart. It is the most common cause of heart attacks. The diagnosis of CAD is based on the determination of the site, the extent and the severity of the pathology. In this context, there have been several contributions to determine precisely the location and the extent of stenosis in case of CAD. Among these methods we cite superquadric model [9,13], baseline surface [10], regional volumes evolution [11], quadric fitting methods [1], three-dimensional active mesh models [12] and regional curvature analysis [19]. We note that using curvature values to analyse the LV deformation is one of the most used methods for 2D and 3D images. Several methods used curvatures, we cite Friboulet et al. [20], were they have calculated the curvature distribution on the left ventricle surface using an iterative relaxation scheme. Curvature distribution values is displayed by voxel. From this visualization they

© Springer Nature Switzerland AG 2019
L. Chen et al. (Eds.): RFMI 2017, CCIS 842, pp. 213–220, 2019.
https://doi.org/10.1007/978-3-030-19816-9_17

have evaluated the structural stability of the curvature characteristics with the left ventricle deformation. Clarysse et al. [21] have used regional approach based on curvature values in order to analyze specific areas of the endocardium. They have combined geometrical and spacial information in order to reach spatiotemporal analysis and automatic recognition of deformable surfaces. In a previous work [3,4], we used curvature values to detect pathology extent in data obtained from myocardial scintigraphy imaging techniques. The work presented in this paper consists of using curvature values and the modified Hotelling T2 metric (MT2) to accurately localize and quantify deformations in LV for data obtained from MRI techniques. Our approach was tested on six patients. Each patient had 25 3D object showing its evolution of the different instants between diastole and systole. The paper is organized as follows. First the proposed method and its different steps are detailed. Then, the database which used to validate our approach are presented. After that, the obtained results are discussed. Finally the main conclusions and suggests directions for future works are proposed.

2   Method

The aim of this work is to study the myocardium movement during the cardiac cycle. More precisely, we want to detect regions with pathological behavior. The first step is to study the global variation of the myocardium to know its status: whether it is pathological or not. The second step is to divide the 3D object that modeling the myocardium. We adopt the AHA standard because it allows an adequate sampling.

2.1   Partitioning of *LV* Surfaces into 17 Regional Segments

AHA standard recommends a division into 17 regions as described in Fig. 1. The myocardium is divided into four sections in the long axis, namely the basal, middle cavity, apical and apex regions. The apical part is then geometrically divided into four regions. Each part of the basal and middle cavity is also geometrically divided into six regions.

2.2   Triangular Mesh Generation

Since the curvature computing requires the use of polygonal surface mesh, a triangulating surface process is applied for every resulted region after applying the AHA division. For the triangulation, we adopt the Delaunay triangulation method. According to the Delaunay definition, the triangle circumcircle formed by three points from the original set is empty if it contains no other vertices than its own. Replacing the circles circumscribed by spheres, it is possible to extend the definition to three dimensions.

2.3   Curvature Computation and Modified Hotelling MT2 Metric

In this work, we use the MT2 two-sample group difference metric for the myocardium global and regional analysis. The MT2 metric provides an extent for differences between SPHARM descriptors values at stress and rest. It is very effective for the computation of two group differences. In [6] authors have used the MT2 metric for statistical shape analysis using spherical wavelet shape representation. Given a group i with n_i samples, we designate by μ_i the mean and by Σ_i the covariance of a 3D feature. The MT2 for two groups 1 and 2 is given by Eq. 1.

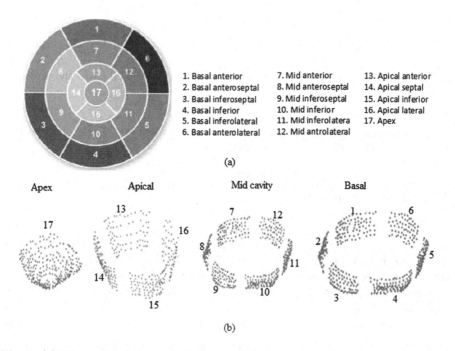

Fig. 1. (a) Standardized international nomenclature for the LV and correspondence on the mesh, (b) LV regions of interest.

$$T2 = (\mu_1 - \mu_2)^T (\Sigma_1 \frac{1}{n1} - \Sigma_2 \frac{1}{n2})^{-1} (\mu_1 - \mu_2) \qquad (1)$$

As descriptors, we use Gaussian and Mean curvature values. Curvature provides information to describe how a surface changes its shape locally. Given a point P on a surface M, we call Vp, the normal vector and W the tangent vector belonging to TpM which is the tangent space (Fig. 2). The curve can be defined as the intersection of M with the plan spanned by the normal vector and W [22]. This plane is given by:

$$(t, s) \mapsto p + tv_p + sw$$

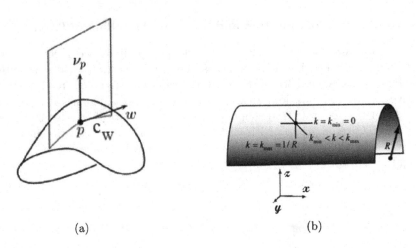

(a)   (b)

Fig. 2. (a) Normal curvature of a point on a surface, (b) directions of the principal curvatures of cylinder (radius R).

The curvature of such a curve C_w is the normal curvature K_w of M in the direction W. Then C_w is given implicitly by:

$$f(p + tv_p + sw) = 0 \ \forall t, s$$

With f is the regular map.

$$K_w = <W, T_p v \cdot W> \tag{2}$$

where $<.,.>$ denotes the standard inner product and $T_p v$ is the Weingarten map [22]. The principal curvatures K_{min} and K_{max} (see Fig. 2) are the extreme normal curvature K_w relative to the principal curvature directions W_{min} and W_{max}. The gaussian curvature K_G is defined as the product of principal curvature as described in Eq. 3.

$$K_G = K_{min} * K_{max} \tag{3}$$

The mean curvature K_M is the arithmetic mean of principal curvatures (Eq. 4).

$$K_M = \frac{K_{min} + K_{max}}{2} \tag{4}$$

3   Experimental Results

3.1   Database Structure

Our database is composed of 150 3D objects outcome of cardiac MRI imaging techniques of six patients. These objects are obtained after a delineation of a set of 2D image sequences. Such a set is used to construct a 3D triangular meshes. Each patient has 25 objects for different 25 instants of cardiac cycle. Figure 3 shows an example of these objects at instants T1, T7 and T25. We note that T1 is the beginning of diastole, T7 is the end of diastole and the beginning of systole and T25 is the instant of end systole.

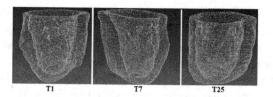

Fig. 3. Rendered surfaces of the myocardium at T1: beginning of diastole, T7: end of diastole and the beginning of systole and T25: end systole.

3.2   Results and Discussion

Firstly, we compute the curvature values of every point in the 25 objects of each patient. The Hotelling MT2 values is then calculated between each two successive instants: we calculate the curvature values variation between T1 and T2, then between T2 and T3 up to T24 and T25. Values are then presented in six curves as shown in Fig. 4.

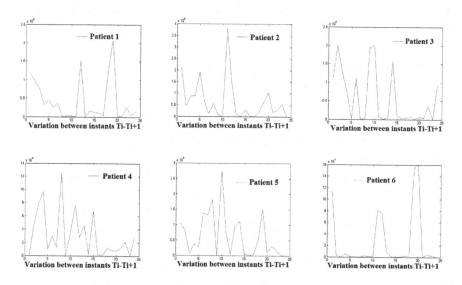

Fig. 4. Global variation of curvature values at 25 instants

This different curves are used to specify the pathological state of the different patients. We noticed that, for patient 1, 2 and 6, the variation of curvature values is lower than other patients. During several instants the myocardium of these patients has not moved well and it had a reduced kinetic. Thus, our approach may be an efficient way for characterizing the myocardium disease severity. We will see later that the regional analysis can provide more significant information about the disease extent of these patients.

Afterwards, we proceeded to the analysis of regional LV deformation. First, each 25 object modeling myocardium of every six patient are divided into 17 regions according to AHA standards. For each region, we proceed by calculating separately its curvatures values after applying the triangulation process. After that, we compute for every region the Hotelling measure between different curvature values. The obtained results are reported in Fig. 5. We are interested in patients 1, 2 and 6. As shown, the regional curves of these patients show a lot of regions with low curvature values variation. This proves that these regions have not a good kinetic. Contractility of regions are low when its MT2 values are not high. More precisely, these regions indicates the poorly irrigated territories of the heart and allows to have a precise location of the ischemia. These results may refine the diagnosis, experts may revise their initial diagnosis based on simple visualization by providing objective arguments. Indeed, our measurements could qualify the site as well as the disease extent.

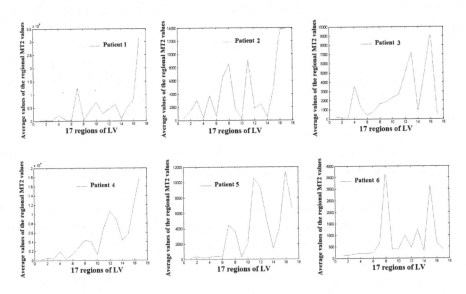

Fig. 5. Average of regional variation of curvature values

4   Conclusion

The present work is aimed at offering a global and regional analysis of the LV in order to refine the diagnosis and specify the ischemic territory. Our approach was tested on 150 3D objects outcome of cardiac MRI imaging techniques of six patients. We used the Hotelling metric MT2 computation for curvature values variation at the vertices of the triangulation of 3D objects modeling the myocardium. In order to progress to a regional analysis, we carried out, a division into 17 regions according to the AHA standard. This method provides a good agreement between the global and regional analysis. These results need to be well oriented by enriching the database and getting supplementing information about the studied patients.

References

1. Su, Y., Zhong, L., Lim, C.W., Ghista, D., Chua, T., Tan, R.S.: A geometrical approach for evaluating left ventricular remodelling in myocardial infarct patients. Comput. Methods Programs Biomed. **108**(2), 1–11 (2012)
2. BenAbdallah, A., Ghorbel, F., Chattia, K., Essabbaha, H., Bedoui, M.H.: A new uniform parameterization and invariant 3D SPHARM shape descriptors for shape analysis of the hearts left ventricle A pilot study. Pattern Recogn. Lett. **13**, 1981–1990 (2010)
3. Ayari, R., BenAbdallah, A., Ghorbel, F., Bedoui, M.H.: Analysis of regional deformation of the heart's left ventricle using curvature values with Hotelling T2 metric. In: IEEE 13th International Conference on Computer Graphics, Imaging and Visualization (CGiV), pp. 115–118 (2016)
4. Ayari, R., Ben Abdallah, A., Ghorbel, F., Bedoui, M.H.: Analysis of regional deformation of the heart left ventricle. Med. Imaging IRBM - Elsevier Innov. Res. BioMed. Eng. **38**, 90–97 (2017)
5. Huang, H., Shen, L., Zhang, R., Makedon, F., Hettleman, B., Pearlman, J.: Surface alignment of 3D spherical harmonic models: application to cardiac MRI analysis. In: Duncan, J.S., Gerig, G. (eds.) MICCAI 2005. LNCS, vol. 3749, pp. 67–74. Springer, Heidelberg (2005). https://doi.org/10.1007/11566465_9
6. Levitt, J.J., Shenton, M.E., Gerig, G., Tannenbaum, A.: Statistical shape analysis of brain structures using spherical wavelets. In: IEEE International Symposium on Biomedical Imaging: From Nano to Macro, pp. 209–212 (2007)
7. Goldberg-Zimring, D., Talos, I.F., Bhagwat, J.G., Haker, S.J., Black, P.M., Zou, K.: H: Statistical validation of brain tumor shape approximation via spherical harmonics for image-guided neurosurgery. Acad. Radiol. **12**(4), 459–466 (2005)
8. Styner, M., Oguz, I., Xu, S., Pantazis, D., Gerig, G.: Statistical group differences in anatomical shape analysis using Hotelling T2 metric. In: Medical Imaging, p. 65123 (2007)
9. Bardinet, E., Cohen, L., Ayache, N.: Tracking and motion analysis of the left ventricle with deformable superquadrics. Med. Image Anal. **1**, 129–149 (1996)
10. Hubka, M., McDonald, J.A., Wong, S., Bolson, E.L., Sheehan, F.H.: Monitoring change in the three-dimensional shape of the human left ventricle. JAm Soc Echocardiogr, v **17**, 404–410 (2004)
11. Bernis, F., Léger, C., Eder, V.: Regional analysis of left ventricle of the heart. Comput. Med. Imaging Graph. **30**, 153–161 (2006)
12. Kermani, S., Moradi, M.H., AbrishamiMoghaddam, H., Saneei, H., Marashi, M.J., ShahbaziGahrouei, D.: Quantitative analysis of left ventricular performance from sequences of cardiac magnetic resonance imaging using active mesh model. Comput. Med. Imaging Graph. **33**, 222–234 (2009)
13. Solina, F., Bajcsy, R.: Recovery of parametric models from range images, the case for superquadrics with global deformation, **12**, 549–553 (1990). IEEE Computer Society Press
14. Young, G.O.: Synthetic structure of industrial plastics (Book style with paper title and editor). In: Peters, J. (ed.) Plastics, vol. 3, 2nd edn, pp. 15–64. McGraw-Hill, New York (1964)

15. Brechbühler, C.H., Gerig, G., Kübler, O.: Parametrisation of closed surfaces for 3D shape description. Comput. Image Vis. Understand. **61**, 154–170 (1995)
16. Kelemen, A., Szekely, G., Gerig, G.: Elastic model-based segmentation of 3D neuroradiological data sets. IEEE Trans. Med. Imaging **18**(10), 828–839 (1999)
17. Styner, M., Lieberman, J.A., Pantazis, D., Gerig, G.: Boundary and medial shape analysis of the hippocampus in schizophrenia. Med. Image Anal. **8**(3), 197–203 (2004)
18. Gerig, G., Styner, M., Jones, D., Weinberger, D., Lieberman, J.: Shape analysis of brain ventricles using SPHARM. In: MMBIA, pp. 171–178 (2001)
19. Mancini, G., DeBoe, S.F., McGillem, M.J., Bates, E.R.: Quantitative regional curvature analysis: a prospective evaluation of ventricular shape and wall motion measurements. Am. Heart J. **116**(6), 1616–1621 (1988)
20. Friboulet, D., Magnin, I.E., Mathieu, C., Pommert, A., Hoehne, K.H.: Assessment and visualization of the curvature of the left ventricle from 3D medical images. Comput. Med. Imaging Graph. **17**, 257–262 (1993)
21. Clarysse, P., Friboulet, D., Magnin, I.E.: Tracking geometrical descriptors on 3D deformable surfaces: application to the left-ventricular surface of the heart. IEEE Trans. Med. Imaging **16**, 392–404 (1997)
22. Kunzinger, M.: Differential Geometry 1. Summer Term (2008)

Author Index

Printed in the United States
By Bookmasters